On *HAPPINESS*

"The readers of this book will find themselves in the presence of an extraordinary human being, one who is equally at home in the culture and science of the West and in the poetry and wisdom of Tibetan Buddhism, and who has made a clear choice. Ricard's compelling personal story beautifully illustrates his message that happiness is to be found in controlling the mind, not circumstances."   — Daniel Kahneman, Princeton University, winner of a Nobel Prize in Economics, 2002

"You may not find happiness in a book, but if reading a book can precipitate a tectonic shift in your life and mind toward robust, genuine, deeply rooted happiness, this would be the book."
                    — Jon Kabat-Zinn, author of *Coming to Our Senses*

"In this highly readable and enlightening volume, Matthieu Ricard offers us the keys to opening up the chambers of the mind where serenity resides. His elegant descriptions show us how the preoccupation with the self leads to the detrimental urges, thoughts, and feelings that present barriers to genuine liberation."
                                               — Aaron Beck, MD, author of *Cognitive Therapy and the Emotional Disorders*

"Writing with grace and clarity, Ricard offers exciting ideas and practical tools for increasing our understanding of ourselves and our relationship to the world."   — Paul Ekman, PhD, author of *Emotions Revealed*

"In his new book *Happiness* Matthieu Ricard combines the talents of philosopher and scientist to produce a rigorous and compelling analysis of his subject. He reminds us that to change the individual is also, ultimately, to change the world."   — George Soros

Happiness

ALSO BY MATTHIEU RICARD

The Monk and the Philosopher (with Jean-François Revel)
The Quantum and the Lotus (with Trinh Xuan Thuan)
Buddhist Himalayas (with Olivier and Danielle Föllmi)
Journey to Enlightenment
Monk Dancers of Tibet
Tibet: A Compassionate Eye

Happiness

*A Guide to Developing Life's
Most Important Skill*

Matthieu Ricard

TRANSLATED BY JESSE BROWNER

LITTLE, BROWN AND COMPANY
New York   Boston

Little, Brown and Company
1271 Avenue of the Americas, New York, NY 10020
Visit our Web site at www.twbookmark.com

First English Language Edition: April 2006

First published in France by NiL éditions, part of Les Éditions Robert Laffont,
as *Plaidoyer pour le bonheur*, 2003

Copyright acknowledgments appear on page 283.

Library of Congress Cataloging-in-Publication Data

Ricard, Matthieu.
[Plaidoyer pour le bonheur. English]
Happiness: a guide to developing life's most important skill / Matthieu Ricard;
translated by Jesse Browner — 1st English ed.
p.   cm.
Includes bibliographical references (p.   ).
ISBN-10: 0-316-05783-5 (hardcover)
ISBN-13: 978-0-316-05783-7 (hardcover)
1. Religious life — Buddhism.   2. Happiness — Religious aspects — Buddhism.
I. Title.
BQ4304.R5313   2006
294.3'444 — dc22   2005028480

10 9 8 7 6 5 4 3 2 1

Q-MB
Book design by Renato Stanisic
Printed in the United States of America

To Jigme Khyentse Rinpoche

Contents

Happiness does not come automatically. It is not a gift that good fortune bestows upon us and a reversal of fortune takes back. It depends on us alone. One does not become happy overnight, but with patient labor, day after day. Happiness is constructed, and that requires effort and time. In order to become happy, we have to learn how to change ourselves.

LUCA AND FRANCESCO CAVALLI-SFORZA

FOREWORD

The first time I met Matthieu Ricard he was huddled over a computer monitor in a back room of Shechen Monastery in Kathmandu, Nepal. Matthieu was overseeing a group of monks who were laboriously copying texts word by word from the traditional long rectangles of woodblock-printed pages, typing them into a computer program with a specially designed Tibetan font.

What had been tall stacks of yellowing handmade paper between hand-carved covers was now stored digitally, in an electronic space the size of the palm of a hand. The digital age had entered the monastery. Now anyone with computer access could tap into texts that for centuries had only been found stored away in hermitages and monasteries in the high, hidden valleys of Tibet. Matthieu was helping to preserve for the modern world wisdom from the ancient.

Matthieu seems the perfect candidate for that task. His background includes one of the finest educations the modern world can offer. He holds a doctorate in biology from the prestigious Pasteur Institute, where his main adviser was a Nobel laureate. And yet he has spent more than a quarter century as a

Buddhist monk in the Himalayas, learning from some of the most fully realized Tibetan teachers of our day.

More recently I've worked with Matthieu as part of the Mind and Life Institute, which brings scientists together in dialogue with Buddhist scholars. That ongoing conversation has resulted in remarkable findings that show how meditation can reshape the brain, strengthening the centers that undergird good feelings and compassion.

Here Matthieu speaks with unparalleled authority. I witnessed him work in collaboration with Professor Richard J. Davidson, head of the Laboratory for Affective Neuroscience at the University of Wisconsin–Madison, as they prepared to pilot a series of brain tests that would be used with advanced meditators. Matthieu was both a key collaborator in considering what measures would make the most sense, and the first experimental subject.

For the first tests, Matthieu lay within the noisy maws of a magnetic resonance imager (MRI), the diagnostic imaging device that uses huge magnets that whirl around a person's body as he or she lies within the machine. The MRI offers a precise image of a person's brain (or other internal tissues), but it is also an ordeal for many people, some of whom panic at being trapped inside the monstrous machine. Matthieu endured his captivity for more than three hours while going through the paces of several kinds of meditation: concentration, visualization, and compassion.

At the end of that grueling session, we rushed into the room to see how Matthieu had held up, slightly apprehensive about the effects of his ordeal. But Matthieu emerged from the machine smiling. His comment: "That was like a miniretreat!"

That reaction to what most people would find overwhelming bespeaks a special state of mind, a capacity for confronting life's ups and downs with equanimity, even joy. And Matthieu, I realize, has that joie de vivre in full measure.

The psychoanalyst C. G. Jung once described the role of a "Gnostic intermediary" as someone who himself plunges into spiritual depths and emerges to bring the vision of that inner possibility to the rest of us. Matthieu fills that role.

Beyond his well-cultivated temperament, Matthieu brings a quiet brilliance and always quick mind. I've witnessed him in sessions of the Mind and Life meetings, where the Dalai Lama explores in depth a scientific topic with a panel of scientific experts. Matthieu often represents the Buddhist perspective, speaking with a fluid intelligence that easily weaves together spiritual and scientific paradigms.

In *Happiness* he draws on both his ease in the world of scientific studies and philosophy and his intimate familiarity with the wisdom traditions of Buddhism, bringing these streams together in a seamless offering. The resulting insights are both inspiring and pragmatic. The vision of happiness conjured here challenges our everyday notions of joy, making a convincing argument for contentment over collecting "good times," for altruism over self-centered satiation. And beyond that, Matthieu suggests how we can all cultivate the very capacity for such happiness.

On the other hand, Matthieu offers no quick fixes, for he knows well that training the mind takes effort and time. Instead he goes to the root of the mechanisms that underlie suffering and happiness, offering refreshing insights into how the mind functions and strategies for dealing with our most difficult emotions. The result is a sound road map, one based on cultivating the conditions for genuine well-being.

A few days after my wife and I first met Matthieu, we happened to share some hours together in the Kathmandu airport, waiting for endlessly delayed flights. Those hours sped by in minutes due to the sheer pleasure of being in Matthieu's orbit. He is without doubt one of the happiest people I know — and happiness is contagious. I wish the reader a similar contagion, enjoying the pleasures to be found in these pages.

Daniel Goleman
Mendocino, California
October 2005

Happiness

INTRODUCTION

When, in the early morning, I sit in the meadow in front of my hermitage, my eyes take in hundreds of miles of lofty Himalayan peaks glowing in the rising sun. The serenity of the scenery blends naturally and seamlessly with the peace within. It is a long way indeed from the Pasteur Institute, where, thirty-five years ago, I performed research on cell division, mapping genes on the chromosome of *Escherichia coli* bacteria.

This would seem to be a pretty radical turnabout. Had I renounced the Western world? Renunciation, at least as Buddhists use the term, is a much-misunderstood concept. It is not about giving up what is good and beautiful. How foolish that would be! Rather it is about disentangling oneself from the unsatisfactory and moving with determination toward what matters most. It is about freedom and meaning — freedom from mental confusion and self-centered afflictions, meaning through insight and loving-kindness.

When I was twenty I had an idea of what I did not want — a meaningless life — but could not figure out what I wanted. My adolescence had been far from boring. I remember the excitement I felt when, at sixteen, I had the opportunity to join a journalist friend of mine at lunch with Igor Stravinsky. I drank in everything he said. He autographed for me a copy of the score of *Agon,* a then lesser-known work that I was especially fond of. He wrote these words: "To Matthieu, *Agon,* which I like very much myself."

There was no shortage of enthralling encounters in the intellectual circle in which my parents moved. My mother, Yahne Le Toumelin, a well-known painter, full of life, poetry, and human warmth, who became a Buddhist nun herself, was friends with the great figures of surrealism and contemporary art — André Breton, Leonora Carrington, Maurice Béjart, for whom she painted vast theatrical sets. My father, who, under his pen name, Jean-François Revel, became one of the pillars of French intellectual life, held unforgettable dinners for the great thinkers and creative minds of the time: Luis Buñuel; Emmanuel Cioran, the despairing philosopher; Mario Suares, who liberated Portugal from the yoke of fascism; Henri Cartier-Bresson, the "eye of the century"; and many others.

In 1970 my father wrote *Without Marx or Jesus,* in which he expressed his rejection of political and religious totalitarianisms alike. The book stayed on the U.S. bestseller list for a whole year.

I was hired in 1967 as a young researcher at the Institut Pasteur, in the cellular genetics lab of François Jacob, who had recently won the Nobel Prize for medicine. There I worked with some of the great names of molecular biology, including Jacques Monod and André Lwoff, who lunched together every day at the communal table in a corner of the library, along with scientists from all over the world. François Jacob had only two doctoral students; he confided to a mutual friend that he had taken me on not only because of my university work, but also because he'd heard that I had plans to build a harpsichord, a dream I never brought to fruition but which earned me a place in a highly coveted laboratory.

I also loved astronomy, skiing, sailing, and ornithology. At the age of twenty, I published a book on migratory animals.[1] I learned photography from a friend who was a professional wildlife photographer, and spent many a weekend stalking grebes and wild geese in the Sologne marshes and along the beaches of the Atlantic. I spent winters coursing the slopes of my native Alps and summers on the ocean with friends of my uncle, the navigator Jacques-Yves Le Toumelin, who, shortly after World War II, undertook one of the first solo trips around the globe on his thirty-foot sailboat. He introduced me to all sorts of unusual people — adventurers, explorers, mystics, astrologers, and metaphysicians. One day we went to pay a call on one of his friends and found a note pinned to the door of his Paris studio: "Sorry to miss you — I'm off to Timbuktu on foot."

Life was far from dull, but something essential was missing. In 1972, when I was twenty-six and fed up with life in Paris, I decided to move to Darjeeling, in India, in the shadow of the Himalayas, to study with a great Tibetan master.

How had I reached this crossroads? The striking individuals with whom I'd crossed paths each had his or her own special genius. I'd have liked to play the piano like Glenn Gould or chess like Bobby Fisher, to have Baudelaire's poetic gift, but I did not feel inspired to *become* what they were at the human level. Despite their artistic, scientific, and intellectual qualities, when it came to altruism, openness to the world, resolve, and joie de vivre, their ability was neither better nor worse than that of any of us.

Everything changed when I met a few remarkable human beings who exemplified what a fulfilled human life can be. Prior to those meetings, I was inspired through my readings of great figures like Martin Luther King Jr. and Mohandas Gandhi, who by the sheer strength of their human qualities were able to inspire others to change their way of being. When I turned twenty, I saw a series of documentaries made by a friend of mine, Arnaud Desjardins, on the great spiritual masters who had fled the ruthless invasion of Tibet by communist China. They were now living as refugees in India and Bhutan. I was taken aback. They all had very diverse physical appearances, but there emanated from all of them a strikingly similar inner beauty, compassionate strength, and wisdom. I could not go and meet Socrates, listen to Plato debating, or sit at Saint Francis's feet, yet suddenly here were two dozen of them before my very eyes. It did not take me very long to decide to travel to India and meet them.

How to describe my first encounter with Kangyur Rinpoche, in June 1967, in a small wooden cottage a few miles from Darjeeling? He radiated inner goodness, sitting with his back to a window that looked out over a sea of clouds, through which the majestic Himalayas rose to an altitude of more than twenty-four thousand feet. Words are inadequate to describe the depth, serenity, and compassion that emanated from him. For three weeks, I sat opposite him all day long and had the impression that I was doing what people call meditating — in other words, simply collecting myself in his presence, trying to see what lay behind the screen of my thoughts.

But it was only after my return from India, during my first year at the Institut Pasteur, that I realized how important that meeting with Kangyur Rinpoche had been. I became aware that I'd found a reality that could inspire my whole life and give it direction and meaning. It was over the course of subsequent journeys I made every summer between 1967 and 1972 that I realized that I forgot all about my life in Europe every time I reached Darjeeling. Conversely, during the rest of the year, when I was at the Institut Pasteur, my thoughts were constantly flying off to the Himalayas. My teacher, Kangyur Rinpoche, had advised me to finish my doctoral studies, so I didn't rush things. But though I waited several years, it was not difficult for me to make a decision that I've never regretted: to go and live where I wanted to be.

My father was sorely disappointed to see me abruptly put an end to a career whose beginnings, he felt, were promising. Moreover, as a convinced agnostic he did not take Buddhism very seriously, even though, as he wrote, "I had nothing against it, for its unadulterated and straightforward approach give it a distinctive position among religious doctrines and have earned it the respect of some of the most exacting Western philosophers."[2] Although we did not see each other very often for many years — he came to visit me in Darjeeling and later in Bhutan — we remained close, and when asked by journalists, he remarked: "The only clouds that ever passed over our relationship were those of the Asian monsoon."

What I discovered never called for blind faith. It was a rich, pragmatic science of mind, an altruistic art of living, a meaningful philosophy, and a spiritual practice that led to genuine inner transformation. Over the past thirty-five years, I have never found myself in contradiction with the scientific spirit as I understand it — that is, as the empirical search for truth. I have also met human beings who were enduringly happy. More, in fact, than what we usually call happy: they were imbued with a deep insight into reality and the nature of mind, and filled with benevolence for others. I have also come to understand that although some people are naturally happier than others, their happiness is still vulnerable and incomplete, and that achieving durable happiness as a way of being is a skill. It requires sustained effort in training the mind and developing a set of human qualities, such as inner peace, mindfulness, and altruistic love.

All the ingredients for allowing me to find a way to a fulfilled life had come together: a profound and sane way of thinking and the living example of those who embodied wisdom in their words and actions. There wasn't any of the "do what I say, not what I do" that discourages so many seekers all over the world.

I remained in Darjeeling for the next seven years. I lived near Kangyur Rinpoche until his death in 1975 and then continued to study and meditate in a small hermitage just above the monastery. I learned Tibetan, which is now the language I mostly speak in my everyday life in the East. It was then that I met my second main teacher, Dilgo Khyentse Rinpoche, with whom I spent thirteen unforgettable years in Bhutan and India. He was one of the great luminaries of his time, revered by everyone from the king of Bhutan down to the humblest farmer, and became a close teacher to the Dalai Lama. He was someone whose inner journey led him to an extraordinary depth of knowledge and enabled him to be, for all who met him, a fount of loving-kindness, wisdom, and compassion.

There was a constant stream of other teachers and disciples who came to meet and study with him, so when I began translating Tibetan scriptures into Western languages, there were always living treasure-houses of knowledge from whom I could seek clarifications about the texts. I also served as Khyentse Rinpoche's interpreter and traveled with him to Europe and to Tibet when he first returned to the Land of Snows after thirty years in exile. In Tibet, all that was left was ruins. Six thousand monasteries had been destroyed, and many of the people who had survived — unlike the million Tibetans who died of famine and persecution — had spent fifteen or twenty years in labor camps. Khyentse Rinpoche's return was like the sun suddenly rising after a long, dark night.

In India and then in Bhutan, I lived a simple life. I would receive a letter every few months, had no radio, and knew little of what was going on in the world. In 1979 Khyentse Rinpoche began building a monastery in Nepal to preserve the Tibetan heritage. Artists, scholars, meditators, philanthropists, and many others flocked to Shechen Monastery. I have lived there more or less permanently since Khyentse Rinpoche's death in 1991, helping his grandson, Rabjam Rinpoche, the abbot of Shechen, to fulfill our teacher's vision.

One day someone called me from France to ask if I would like to publish a dialogue with my father. I did not take the proposal very seriously and replied: "That's fine with me. Just ask my father." I thought that would be the last I'd hear of it. I could not imagine my agnostic father agreeing to do a book of dialogue with a Buddhist monk, even one who was his son. I was wrong. At a lunch, the publisher proposed several book ideas to my father which he promptly rejected, remaining focused on the art of gastronomy. But when, over dessert, the publisher proposed the dialogue, my father froze and, after a few seconds of silence, replied: "I cannot refuse that." That was the end of my quiet, anonymous life.

When I learned of his answer, I was a little concerned that my father, famous for his relentless demolition of views that he considered wrongheaded, would tear me to pieces. Fortunately the encounter occurred on my turf. My father came to Nepal, and we spent ten days in a forest inn above Kathmandu Valley, recording our conversations, an hour and a half in the morning and another hour in the afternoon. The rest of the day we strolled together through the woods. He too must have been a bit worried, perhaps that the debate would not be up to his intellectual standards, since at the end of the first day he immediately faxed our publisher, Nicole Lattès, to say: "Everything is going well." From my side, I had drafted an exhaustive list of topics. When he first looked at it he exclaimed: "But that's everything philosophers have discussed for the past two thousand years!" Anyway, we went on, days passed, and at the final session he came back with the list and, pointing to a few remaining topics, said: "Well, we haven't discussed these yet."

Our book, *The Monk and the Philosopher,* was an instant success. Over 350,000 copies were printed in France, and it was translated into twenty-one languages. I was invited onto countless TV shows and swept up in a whirlpool of media activity. Although I was glad to share some ideas that I deeply valued and that had brought so much to my life, this episode also made me realize how artificial the making of celebrity is. I was the same old guy, but suddenly I had become a public figure.

It also dawned on me that much more money than I had ever envisioned having was going to come my way — quite a change from my many years living in India on $50 a month. Since I could not see myself getting a big house and a swimming pool, I decided to donate all the proceeds and rights of that and all subsequent books to a foundation that carries out humanitarian and educational projects in Asia. The decision eased my mind. Humanitarian projects have since become a central focus of my life, and with a few dedicated volunteer friends and generous benefactors, under the inspiration of my abbot, Rabjam Rinpoche, we have managed to build and run more than thirty clinics and schools in Tibet, Nepal, and India. We do this spending barely 1 percent on overhead expenses.

Then came the return to science. It happened in two steps: first physics and the nature of outer reality, then cognitive sciences and the nature of mind.

When Trinh Xuan Thuan, a renowned astrophysicist from the University of Virginia, suggested we have a dialogue on Buddhism and science, I could not resist, since I had many questions at the ready for a physicist about the nature of the world of phenomena. Thuan and I met at the Summer University, in Andorra, in 1997. During our long walks together through the majestic Pyrenean scenery, we had a series of fascinating conversations. Are atoms "things" or mere "observable phenomena"? Does the notion of a "first cause" to the universe stand up to analysis? Is there a solid reality behind the veil of appearances? Is the universe made of "interdependent events" or of "autonomous entities"? We found striking philosophical similarities between the Copenhagen school's interpretation of quantum physics and the Buddhist analysis of reality. Further encounters followed, and *The Quantum and the Lotus* was born.

This dialogue had mostly to do with the philosophical, ethical, and human aspects of science. The next step, in which I am still fully engaged, was to collaborate in scientific studies about the heart of Buddhist practice: transforming the mind.

My late spiritual friend Francisco Varela, a pioneer neuroscientist, had always told me that the collaboration between cognitive sciences and Buddhist contemplatives was the way to go, since it held vast potential not only for understanding the human mind but also for conducting actual scientific experimentation. Francisco himself had cofounded the Mind and Life Institute with the American businessman Adam Engle to facilitate and organize meetings between top scientists and the Dalai Lama, who has always been extremely interested in science.

I first joined the Mind and Life meetings in 2000, in Dharamsala, the seat of the Dalai Lama in India. The subject was "destructive emotions." It was a most fascinating meeting, with some of the best scientists in the field, including Francisco Varela, Richard J. Davidson, Paul Ekman, and others, and was chaired by Daniel Goleman. The five days of dialogue were pervaded with a unique brilliance, openness, and deeply felt aspiration to contribute something unique and beneficial to humankind. I was asked to present the Buddhist perspective on the various ways of dealing with emotions. Like a schoolboy taking an exam, I felt odd doing this in the presence of the Dalai Lama, who knew the subject matter a hundred times better than I did. I had been acting as the Dalai Lama's French interpreter for a decade, so I assumed in my mind my usual role of interpreter and tried to concentrate on the audience, the scientists and over fifty observers, and to convey the essence of what I had learned from my teachers. As the meeting progressed, it became clear that a research program could be put together. One could invite expert meditators to the labs and study the effect of years of mind training. How would their ability to deal with emotions and even their brains have changed? This kind of study had always been one of Francisco's dreams. An agenda was set with Richard Davidson and Paul Ekman. The story of that ongoing collaboration, of which I became an intimate part, is related in Daniel Goleman's *Destructive Emotions* and in Chapter 16 of the present book.

It was very exciting to return to science after some thirty years of absence, and to do so with such great scientists. I was intrigued to see if the latest methods of scientific investigation would reveal whether different meditative states, such as focused attention or compassion, would have distinct brain signatures. I was also very keen to find out if a group of experienced meditators would yield similar results and how they would differ from untrained subjects. Since then, I have thoroughly enjoyed the uplifting and warm atmosphere in which this collaboration is taking place. With the first scientific papers now coming out, I think that we are on the threshold of ground-breaking research.

I have also become increasingly involved in photography and have published five photography books over the years. I feel fortunate to be able to share through images the inner beauty of those with whom I live and the outer beauty of their world, and to offer a little hope for human nature.

Why now a book on happiness? It began with a typical example of the "French exception." Some French intellectuals despise happiness and are very vocal about it. I debated one of them for a French magazine and thought that if I ever wrote another book, I would include a chapter on the subject. In the meantime Paul Ekman, Richard Davidson, Alan Wallace, and I spent two days at a northern California coastal wilderness, writing an article titled "Buddhist and Psychological Perspectives on Emotions and Well-Being."[3] I realized that the subject was so central to human life that it deserved an in-depth exploration. For a year I read everything I could get my hands on about happiness and well-being in the works of Western philosophers, social psychologists, cognitive scientists, and even in the tabloid press, which regularly reports peoples' views on happiness, such as that of one French actress: "For me, happiness is eating a tasty plate of spaghetti"; or "Walking in the snow under the stars," and so on. The many definitions of happiness that I encountered contradicted one another and often seemed vague or superficial. So in the light of the analytical and contemplative science of mind that I had encountered through the kindness of my teachers, I embarked on trying to unravel the meaning and mechanism of genuine happiness, and of course of suffering.

When the book came out in France, it sparked a national debate. The same intellectuals confirmed that they were not interested in happiness and discarded the idea that it could be cultivated as a skill. One author wrote an article asking me to stop bugging people with the "dirty works of happiness." Another magazine did a feature on "the sorcerers of happiness." After spending a grueling month in Paris engaged in these debates and with the media, I felt like the scattered parts of a puzzle. I was happy to return to the mountains of Nepal and put the pieces back together.

Although my life has become more hectic, I am still based at Shechen Monastery in Nepal and spend two months a year in my hermitage facing the Himalayas.

I doubtless have a lot more practice and effort ahead of me before I achieve genuine inner freedom, but I am fully enjoying the journey. Simplifying one's life to extract its quintessence is the most rewarding of all the pursuits I have undertaken. It doesn't mean giving up what is truly beneficial, but finding out what really matters and what brings lasting fulfillment, joy, serenity, and, above all, the irreplaceable boon of altruistic love. It means transforming oneself to better transform the world.

As I write in the conclusion of this book, when I was twenty words like *happiness* and *benevolence* did not mean much to me. I was a typical young Parisian student, going to see Eisenstein and Marx Brothers movies, playing music, manning the barricades in May '68 near the Sorbonne, loving sports and nature. But I didn't have much sense of how to lead my life except playing it by ear, day in and day out. I somehow felt that there was a potential for flourishing in myself, and in others, but had no idea about how to actualize it. Thirty-five years later, I surely still have a long way to go, but at least the sense of direction is clear to me and I enjoy every step on the path.

That is why this book, though Buddhist in spirit, is not a "Buddhist" book as opposed to a "Christian" or an "agnostic" book. It was written from the perspective of "secular spirituality," a theme dear to the Dalai Lama. As such it is intended not for the Buddhist shelves of libraries, but for the heart and mind of anyone who aspires to a little more joie de vivre and to let wisdom and compassion reign in her or his life.

Shechen Monastery, Nepal
May 2005

1

TALKING ABOUT HAPPINESS

Every man wants to be happy, but in order to be so he needs first to understand what happiness is.

JEAN-JACQUES ROUSSEAU

An American friend of mine, a successful photography editor, once told me about a conversation she'd had with a group of friends after they'd finished their final college exams and were wondering what to do with their lives. When she'd said, "I want to be happy," there was an embarrassed silence, and then one of her friends had asked: "How could someone as smart as you want nothing more than to be happy?" My friend answered: "I didn't say *how* I want to be happy. There are so many ways to find happiness: start a family, have kids, build a career, seek adventure, help others, find inner peace.... Whatever I end up doing, I want my life to be a truly happy one."

The word *happiness,* writes Henri Bergson, "is commonly used to designate something intricate and ambiguous, one of those ideas which humanity has intentionally left vague, so that each individual might interpret it in his own way."[1] From a practical point of view, leaving the definition of happiness vague wouldn't matter if we were talking about some inconsequential feeling. But the truth is altogether different, since we're actually talking about a way of being that defines the quality of every moment of our lives. So what exactly is happiness?

Sociologists define happiness as "the degree to which a person evaluates the overall quality of his present life-as-a-whole positively. In other words, how much the person likes the life he or she leads."[2] This definition, however, does not distinguish between profound satisfaction and the mere appreciation of the outer conditions of our lives. For some, happiness is just "a momentary, fleeting impression, whose intensity and duration vary according to the availability of the resources that make it possible."[3] Such happiness must by nature be elusive and dependent on circumstances that are quite often beyond our control. For the philosopher Robert Misrahi, on the other hand, happiness is "the radiation of joy over one's entire existence or over the most vibrant part of one's active past, one's actual present, and one's conceivable future."[4] Maybe it is a more enduring condition. According to André Comte-Sponville, "By 'happiness' we mean any span of time in which joy would seem immediately possible."[5]

Is happiness a *skill* that, once acquired, endures through the ups and downs of life? There are a thousand ways of thinking about happiness, and countless philosophers have offered their own. For Saint Augustine, happiness is "a rejoicing in the truth." For Immanuel Kant, happiness must be rational and devoid of any personal taint, while for Marx it is about growth through work. "What constitutes happiness is a matter of dispute," Aristotle wrote, "and the popular account of it is not the same as that given by the philosophers."

Has the word *happiness* itself been so overused that people have given up on it, turned off by the illusions and platitudes it evokes? For some people, talking about the search for happiness seems almost in bad taste. Protected by their armor of intellectual complacency, they sneer at it as they would at a sentimental novel.

How did such a devaluation come about? Is it a reflection of the artificial happiness offered by the media? Is it a result of the failed efforts we use to find genuine happiness? Are we supposed to come to terms with unhappiness rather than make a genuine and intelligent attempt to untangle happiness from suffering?

What about the simple happiness we get from a child's smile or a nice cup of tea after a walk in the woods? As rich and comforting as such genuine glimpses of happiness might be, they are too circumstantial to shed light on our lives as a whole. Happiness can't be limited to a few pleasant sensations, to some intense pleasure, to an eruption of joy or a fleeting sense of serenity, to a cheery day or a magic moment that sneaks up on us in the labyrinth of our existence. Such diverse facets are not enough in themselves to build an accurate image of the profound and lasting fulfillment that characterizes true happiness.

By *happiness* I mean here a deep sense of flourishing that arises from an exceptionally healthy mind. This is not a mere pleasurable feeling, a fleeting emotion, or a mood, but an optimal state of being. Happiness is also a way of interpreting the world, since while it may be difficult to change the world, it is always possible to change the way we look at it.

A FORETASTE OF HAPPINESS

Although Bertha Young was thirty she still had moments like this when she wanted to run instead of walk, to take dancing steps on and off the pavement, to bowl a hoop, to throw something up in the air and catch it again, or to stand still and laugh at — nothing — at nothing, simply. . . . What can you do if you are thirty and, turning the corner of your own street, you are overcome, suddenly, by a feeling of bliss — absolute bliss! — as though you'd suddenly swallowed a bright piece of that late afternoon sun and it burned in your bosom, sending out a little shower of sparks into every particle, into every finger and toe?

KATHERINE MANSFIELD, "BLISS"[6]

Ask any number of people to describe a moment of "perfect" happiness. Some will talk about moments of deep peace experienced in a harmonious natural setting, of a forest dappled in sunshine, of a mountain summit looking out across a vast horizon, of the shores of a tranquil lake, of a night walk through snow under a starry sky, and so on. Others will refer to a long-awaited event: an exam they've aced, a sporting victory, meeting someone they've longed to meet, the birth of a child. Still others will speak of a moment of peaceful intimacy with their family or a loved one, or of having made someone else happy.

The common factor to all of these experiences would seem to be the momentary disappearance of inner conflicts. The person feels in harmony with the world and with herself. Someone enjoying such an experience, such as walking through a serene wilderness, has no particular expectations beyond the simple act of walking. She simply *is*, here and now, free and open.

For just a few moments, thoughts of the past are suppressed, the mind is not burdened with plans for the future, and the present moment is liberated from all mental constructs. This moment of respite, from which all sense of emotional urgency has vanished, is experienced as one of profound peace.

For someone who has achieved a goal, completed a task, or won a victory, the tension they have long carried with them relaxes. The ensuing sense of release is felt as a deep calm, free of all expectation and fear.

But this experience is just a passing glimpse brought on by a particular set of circumstances. We call it a magic moment, a state of grace. And yet the difference between these flashes of happiness seized on the fly and the immutable peacefulness of the sage, for instance, is as great as that between the tiny section of sky seen through the eye of a needle and the limitless expanses of outer space. The two conditions differ in dimension, duration, and depth.

Even so, we can learn something from these fleeting moments, these lulls in our ceaseless struggles; they can give us a sense of what true plenitude might be and help us to recognize the conditions that favor it.

A Way of Being

I remember one afternoon as I was sitting on the steps of our monastery in Nepal. The monsoon storms had turned the courtyard into an expanse of muddy water and we had set out a path of bricks to serve as stepping-stones. A friend of mine came to the edge of the water, surveyed the scene with a look of disgust, and complained about every single brick as she made her way across. When she got to me, she rolled her eyes and said, "Yuck! What if I'd fallen into that filthy muck? Everything's so dirty in this country!" Since I knew her well, I prudently nodded, hoping to offer her some comfort through my mute sympathy. A few minutes later, Raphaèle, another friend of mine, came to the path through the swamp. "Hup, hup, hup!" she sang as she hopped, reaching dry land with the cry "What fun!" Her eyes sparkling with joy, she added: "The great thing about the monsoon is that there's no dust." Two people, two ways of looking at things; six billion human beings, six billion worlds.

On a more somber note, Raphaèle once told me of a meeting she'd had on her first visit to Tibet, in 1986, with a man who had had an appalling time during the Chinese invasion. "He invited me to sit down on a bench and served me some tea he kept in a large thermos. It was his first time talking to a Westerner. We laughed a lot; he was really adorable. Children kept coming by to stare at us in astonishment, and he showered me with questions. Then he told me how he'd been jailed for twelve years by the Chinese invaders and condemned to cut stone for a dam being built in the Drak Yerpa valley. The dam was completely useless, since the riverbed was almost always dry! All his friends dropped dead of hunger and exhaustion around him, one by one. Despite the horror of his story, there wasn't the slightest trace of hatred in his words or the least bit of resentment in his eyes, which beamed with kindness. As I fell asleep that night, I wondered how a man who had suffered so much could seem so happy."

Anyone who enjoys inner peace is no more broken by failure than he is inflated by success. He is able to fully live his experiences in the context of a vast and profound serenity, since he understands that experiences are ephemeral and that it is useless to cling to them. There will be no "hard fall" when things turn bad and he is confronted with adversity. He does not sink into depression, since his happiness rests on a solid foundation. One year before her death at Auschwitz, the remarkable Etty Hillesum, a young Dutchwoman, affirmed: "When you have an interior life, it certainly doesn't matter what side of the prison fence you're on. . . . I've already died a thousand times in a thousand concentration camps. I know everything. There is no new information to trouble me. One way or another, I already know everything. And yet, I find this life beautiful and rich in meaning. At every moment."[7]

Once at an open meeting in Hong Kong, a young man rose from the audience to ask me: "Can you give me one reason why I should go on living?" This book is a humble response to that question, for happiness is above all a love of life. To have lost all reason for living is to open up an abyss of suffering. As influential as external conditions may be, suffering, like well-being, is essentially an interior state. Understanding that is the key prerequisite to a life worth living. What mental conditions will sap our joie de vivre, and which will nourish it?

Changing the way we see the world does not imply naive optimism or some artificial euphoria designed to counterbalance adversity. So long as we are slaves to the dissatisfaction and frustration that arise from the confusion that rules our minds, it will be just as futile to tell ourselves "I'm happy! I'm happy!" over and over again as it would be to repaint a wall in ruins. The search for happiness is not about looking at life through rose-colored glasses or blinding oneself to the pain and imperfections of the world. Nor is happiness a state of exaltation to be perpetuated at all costs; it is the purging of mental toxins, such as hatred and obsession, that literally poison the mind. It is also about learning how to put things in perspective and reduce the gap between appearances and reality. To that end we must acquire a better knowledge of how the mind works and a more accurate insight into the nature of things, for in its deepest sense, suffering is intimately linked to a misapprehension of the nature of reality.

REALITY AND INSIGHT

What do we mean by reality? In Buddhism the word connotes the true nature of things, unmodified by the mental constructs we superimpose upon them. Such concepts open up a gap between our perception and reality, and create a never-ending conflict with the world. "We read the world wrong and say that it deceives us," wrote Rabindranath Tagore.[8] We take for permanent that which is ephemeral and for happiness that which is but a source of suffering: the desire for wealth, for power, for fame, and for nagging pleasures.

By knowledge we mean not the mastery of masses of information and learning but an understanding of the true nature of things. Out of habit, we perceive the exterior world as a series of distinct, autonomous entities to which we attribute characteristics that we believe belong inherently to them. Our day-to-day experience tells us that things are "good" or "bad." The "I" that perceives them seems to us to be equally concrete and real. This error, which Buddhism calls *ignorance,* gives rise to powerful reflexes of attachment and aversion that generally lead to suffering. As Etty Hillesum says so tersely: "That great obstacle is always the representation and never the reality."[9] The world of ignorance and suffering — called *samsara* in Sanskrit — is not a fundamental condition of existence but a mental universe based on our mistaken conception of reality.

The world of appearances is created by the coming together of an infinite number of ever-changing causes and conditions. Like a rainbow that forms when the sun shines across a curtain of rain and then vanishes when any factor contributing to its formation disappears, phenomena exist in an essentially interdependent mode and have no autonomous and enduring existence. Everything is *relation;* nothing exists in and of itself, immune to the forces of cause and effect. Once this essential concept is understood and internalized, the erroneous perception of the world gives way to a correct understanding of the nature of things and beings: this is insight. Insight is not a mere philosophical construct; it emerges from a basic approach that allows us gradually to shed our mental blindness and the disturbing emotions it produces and hence the principal causes of our suffering.

Every being has the potential for perfection, just as every sesame seed is permeated with oil. *Ignorance*, in this context, means being unaware of that potential, like the beggar who is unaware of the treasure buried beneath his shack. Actualizing our true nature, coming into possession of that hidden wealth, allows us to live a life full of meaning. It is the surest way to find serenity and let genuine altruism flourish.

There exists a way of being that underlies and suffuses all emotional states, that embraces all the joys and sorrows that come to us. A happiness so deep that, as Georges Bernanos wrote, "nothing can change it, like the vast reserve of calm water beneath a storm."[10] The Sanskrit word for this state of being is *sukha.*

Sukha is the state of lasting well-being that manifests itself when we have freed ourselves of mental blindness and afflictive emotions. It is also the wisdom that allows us to see the world as it is, without veils or distortions. It is, finally, the joy of moving toward inner freedom and the loving-kindness that radiates toward others.

2

Is Happiness the Purpose of Life?

One must practice the things which produce happiness, since if that is present we have everything and if it is absent we do everything in order to have it.

Epicurus

Who wants to suffer? Who wakes up in the morning thinking: "I wish I could suffer all day"? We all strive, consciously or unconsciously, competently or clumsily, passionately or calmly, adventurously or routinely, to be happier and suffer less. Yet we so often confuse genuine happiness with merely seeking enjoyable emotions.

Every day of our lives, we find a thousand different ways to live intensely, forge bonds of friendship and love, enrich ourselves, protect those we love, and keep those who would harm us at arm's length. We devote our time and energies to these tasks, hoping they will provide us and others with a sense of fulfillment and well-being.

However we go about looking for it, and whether we call it joy or duty, passion or contentment, isn't happiness the goal of all goals? Aristotle called it the only goal "we always choose for its own sake and never as a means to something else." Anyone who says otherwise doesn't really know what he wants; he is simply seeking happiness under another name.

Stephen Kosslyn, a Harvard professor and one of the world's leading researchers in mental imagery, once told me that when he wakes up in the morning it is not the desire to be happy that gets him out of bed but the sense of duty, the sense of responsibility for his family, for the team he leads, for his work, for humanity. He maintained that happiness is not among his considerations. And yet when we think about it, the satisfaction of accomplishing what we consider to be worthy goals through a long-term effort strewn with obstacles undeniably reflects certain aspects of true happiness, *sukha*. It is what allows a sense of harmony within ourselves. In doing his "duty" — and even if he believes that suffering and hardship "build character" — such a man is clearly not seeking to cultivate his own unhappiness or that of humankind.

The tragedy lies in our frequent misidentification of the ways to achieve that well-being. Ignorance perverts our desire to improve ourselves. As the Tibetan master Chögyam Trungpa explains: "When we talk of ignorance, it has nothing to do with stupidity. In a way, ignorance is very intelligent, but it is an intelligence that works exclusively in one direction. That is, we react exclusively to our own projections instead of simply seeing what is there."[1]

Ignorance, in the Buddhist lexicon, is an inability to recognize the true nature of things and of the law of cause and effect that governs happiness and suffering. Supporters of ethnic cleansing, for instance, claim that they want to build the best of all possible worlds, and some appear to be deeply convinced of the rightness of their abomination. As paradoxical and unhealthy as it may seem, those who satisfy their selfish impulses by sowing death and destruction expect their actions to bring them a certain degree of gratification. Malevolence, delusion, contempt, and arrogance can never be means of achieving genuine happiness; and yet, even as they veer wildly astray, those who are cruel, obsessed, self-righteous, or conceited are still blindly pursuing happiness while being completely unaware of its true nature. Likewise, someone who commits suicide in order to end unbearable anguish is desperately reaching out for happiness.

How do we dispel this basic ignorance? The only way is through honesty and sincere introspection. There are two ways we can undertake this: analysis and contemplation. Analysis consists of a candid and systematic evaluation of every aspect of our own suffering and of the suffering we inflict on others. It involves understanding which thoughts, words, and actions inevitably lead to pain and which contribute to well-being. Of course, such an approach requires that we first come to see that something is not quite right with our way of being and acting. We then need to feel a burning desire to change.

The contemplative approach consists of rising above the whirlpool of our thoughts for a moment and looking calmly within, as if at an interior landscape, to find the embodiment of our deepest aspirations. For some this may be a life lived intensely at every moment, sampling the many delicacies of pleasure. For others it may be the attainment of goals: a family, social success, leisure, or, more modestly, a life without undue suffering. But these formulations are incomplete. If we go even deeper into ourselves, we may come to find that our primary aspiration, that which underlies all the others, is for some satisfaction powerful enough to nourish our love of life. This is the wish: "May every moment of my life and of the lives of others be one of wisdom, flourishing, and inner peace!"

A TASTE FOR SUFFERING?

Talking about drugs, a Parisian teenager once told me: "If you don't crash a little between doses, you don't appreciate the difference as much. I accept the really tough times for the moments of euphoria. Since I can't get rid of my pain, I prefer to embrace it. I have no interest in developing inner happiness; it's too hard and takes too long. I'd rather have instant happiness, even if it isn't real and even if it gets a little weaker every time I go for it." Hence the emphasis on sensation and momentary pleasures, and the dismissal of the search for deep and lasting serenity as utopian. And yet, while "lousy" or unhappy intervals give life a little more variety, they are never sought out for their own sake, but merely for the contrast they provide, the promise of change they hold out.

For the writer Dominique Noguez, misery is more interesting than happiness because it has a "vividness, an extremely seductive, Luciferian intensity. It has the additional attraction . . . of not being an end in itself, but of always leaving something to anticipate (happiness, that is)."[2] What a foolish merry-go-round: Here, just a bit more pain before your happiness! Like the madman who beats himself over the head with a hammer so that he can feel better when he stops. In short, lasting happiness is boring because it is always the same, while suffering is more exciting because it is always different. We may appreciate such contrasts for the variety and color they give life, but who wants to swap moments of joy for moments of suffering?

On the other hand, it would seem more resourceful, perhaps wise, to use suffering as a vehicle of transformation that allows us to open ourselves with compassion to those who suffer as we do, or even more than we do. It is in that sense, and that sense alone, that we should understand the Roman philosopher Seneca when he says: "Suffering may hurt, but it is not an evil." It is not an evil when, unable to avoid it, we turn it to profit to learn and to change, while recognizing that it is never a good thing in and of itself.

On the contrary, "the desire for happiness is essential to man. It is the motivator of all our acts. The most venerable, clearly understood, enlightened, and reliable constant in the world is not only that we want to be happy, but that we want only to be so. Our very nature requires it of us," wrote Saint Augustine in *On the Happy Life.* That desire inspires our every act, our every word, and our every thought so naturally that we are totally unaware of it, like the oxygen we breathe all our lives without thinking about it.

EVERYTHING YOU NEED TO BE HAPPY

To imagine happiness as the achievement of *all* our wishes and passions is to confuse the legitimate aspiration to inner fulfillment with a utopia that inevitably leads to frustration. In affirming that "happiness is the satisfaction of all our desires" in all their "multiplicity," "degree," and "duration,"[3] Kant dismisses it from the outset to the realm of the unachievable. When he insists that happiness is the condition of one for whom "everything goes according to his wish and will,"[4] we have to wonder about the mystery whereby anything might "go" according to our wishes and will. It reminds me of a line I once heard in a gangster movie.

"I want what's owed to me."

"What's owed to you, man?"

"The world, chico, and everything in it."

Even if, ideally, the satisfaction of all our desires were achievable, it would lead not to happiness but to the creation of new desires or, just as likely, to indifference, disgust, or even depression. Why depression? If we were to convince ourselves that satisfying all our whims would make us happy, the collapse of that delusion would make us doubt the very existence of happiness. If I have more than I could possibly need and I am still not happy, happiness must be impossible. That's a good example of how far we can go in fooling ourselves about the causes of happiness. The fact is that without inner peace and wisdom, *we have nothing we need to be happy*. Living on a pendulum between hope and doubt, excitement and boredom, desire and weariness, it's easy to fritter away our lives, bit by bit, without even noticing, running all over the place and getting nowhere. Happiness is a state of inner fulfillment, not the gratification of inexhaustible desires for outward things.

DOES OUR HAPPINESS DEPEND ON THAT OF OTHERS?

Among all the clumsy, blind, and extreme ways we go about building happiness, one of the most sterile is egocentrism. "When selfish happiness is the only goal in life, life soon becomes goalless," wrote Romain Rolland.[5] Even if we display every outward sign of happiness, we can never be truly happy if we dissociate ourselves from the happiness of others. This in no way requires us to neglect our own happiness. Our own desire for happiness is as legitimate as anyone else's. And in order to love others, we must learn to love ourselves. It's not about swooning over the color of our own eyes, our figure, or some personality trait, but about giving due recognition to the desire to live each moment of existence as a moment of meaning and fulfillment. To love oneself is to love life. It is essential to understand that we make ourselves happy in making others happy.

In brief, the goal of life is a deep state of well-being and wisdom at all moments, accompanied by love for every being. True happiness arises from the essential goodness that wholeheartedly desires everyone to find meaning in their lives. It is a love that is always available, without showiness or self-interest. The immutable simplicity of a good heart.

EXERCISE

Examining the causes of happiness

Take a quiet moment alone and try to find out what really makes you happy. Is your happiness derived mainly from outer circumstances? How much of it is due to your state of mind and the way you experience the world? If happiness comes from outer circumstances, check how stable or fragile they are. If it is due to a state of mind, consider how you can further cultivate it.

3

A TWO-WAY MIRROR:
LOOKING WITHIN, LOOKING WITHOUT

*Seeking happiness outside ourselves is like waiting for sunshine
in a cave facing north.*

TIBETAN SAYING

While everyone wants to be happy one way or another,
there's a big difference between aspiration and achievement. That is the tragedy of human beings. We fear misery but
run to it. We want happiness but turn away from it. The very
means used to ease suffering often fuel it. How could such a
misjudgment occur? Because we are confused about how to go
about it. We look for happiness outside ourselves when it is basically an inner state of being. If it were an exterior condition, it
would be forever beyond our reach. Our desires are boundless
and our control over the world is limited, temporary, and, more
often than not, illusory.

We forge bonds of friendship, start families, live in society,
work to improve the material conditions of our existence — is
that enough to define happiness? No. We can have "everything

we need" to be happy and yet be most unhappy; conversely, we can remain serene in adversity. It is naive to imagine that external conditions alone can ensure happiness. That is the surest way to a rude awakening. As the Dalai Lama has said: "If a man who has just moved into a luxury apartment on the hundredth floor of a brand-new building is deeply unhappy, the only thing he'll look for is a window to jump out of."[1] How many times do we have to hear that money can't buy happiness, that power corrupts the honest, and that fame ruins private life? Failure, separation, disease, and death can occur at any moment.

We willingly spend a dozen years in school, then go on to college or professional training for several more; we work out at the gym to stay healthy; we spend a lot of time enhancing our comfort, our wealth, and our social status. We put a great deal into all this, and yet we do so little to improve the inner condition that determines the very quality of our lives. What strange hesitancy, fear, or apathy stops us from looking within ourselves, from trying to grasp the true essence of joy and sadness, desire and hatred? Fear of the unknown prevails, and the courage to explore that inner world fails at the frontier of our mind. A Japanese astronomer once confided to me: "It takes a lot of daring to look within." This remark — made by a scientist at the height of his powers, a steady and open-minded man — intrigued me. Recently I also met a Californian teenager who told me: "I don't want to look inside myself. I'm afraid of what I'd find there." Why should he falter before what promised to be an absolutely fascinating research project? As Marcus Aurelius wrote: "Look within; within is the fountain of all good."[2]

It is something that we must learn how to do. When we are thrown into confusion by inner troubles, we have no idea how to soothe them and instinctively turn outward. We spend our lives cobbling together makeshift solutions, trying to imagine the conditions that will make us happy. By force of habit, this way of living becomes the norm and "that's life!" our motto. And although the search for temporary well-being may occasionally be successful, it is never possible to control the quantity, quality, or duration of exterior circumstances. That holds true for almos every aspect of life: love, family, health, wealth, power, comfort, pleasure. My friend the philosopher and Buddhist practitioner Alan Wallace has written: "If you bank on achieving genuine happiness and fulfillment by finding the perfect mate, getting a great car, having a big house, the best insurance, a fine reputation, the top job — if these are your focus, wish also for good luck in life's lottery."[3] When you spend your time trying to fill a leaky barrel, you neglect the *methods* and above all the *ways of being* that will allow you to find happiness within yourself.

The main culprit here is our muddled approach to the dynamic of happiness and suffering. No one would deny that it is eminently desirable to live long and in good health, to be free in a country at peace where justice is respected, to love and to be loved, to have access to education and information, to enjoy adequate means of subsistence, to be able to travel the world, to contribute as much as possible to the well-being of others, and to protect the environment. Sociological studies of entire populations clearly show that human beings enjoy their lives more in such conditions. Who would want anything else? In pinning all our hopes on the external world, however, we can only end up being disappointed.

For instance, in hoping that money will make us happier, we work to acquire it; once we have it, we become obsessed with making it grow and we suffer when we lose it. A friend from Hong Kong once told me that he'd promised himself that he'd save a million dollars, then quit work and enjoy life, and thereby become happy. Ten years later he had not one million but three million dollars. What about happiness? His answer was brief: "I wasted ten years of my life."

Wealth, pleasures, rank, and power are all sought for the sake of happiness. But as we strive, we forget the goal and spend our time pursuing the means for their own sake. In so doing, we miss the point and remain deeply unsatisfied. This substitution of means for ends is one of the main traps lying across the pursuit of a meaningful life. As the economist Richard Layard puts it: "Some people say you should not think about your own happiness, because you can only be happy as a by-product of something else. That is a dismal philosophy, a formula for keeping oneself occupied at all costs."[4]

If, conversely, happiness is a state that depends on inner conditions, each of us must recognize those conditions with awareness and then bring them together. Happiness is not given to us, nor is misery imposed. At every moment we are at a crossroads and must choose the direction we will take.

Can We Cultivate Happiness?

"Cultivate happiness!" I said briefly to the doctor: "do you cultivate happiness? How do you manage?" ... Happiness is not a potato, to be planted in mould, and tilled with manure.

Charlotte Brontë, *Villette*

Charlotte Brontë makes her point with great wit, yet it would be a pity to underestimate the mind's power of transformation. If we try resolutely over the course of years to master our thoughts as they come to us, to apply appropriate antidotes to negative emotions and to nourish positive ones, our efforts will undoubtedly yield results that would have seemed unattainable at first. We marvel at the idea of an athlete's being able to clear an eight-foot high jump, and if we hadn't seen it on television we wouldn't believe it possible, since we know that most of us can barely clear four. When it comes to physical performance we soon run into limitations, but the mind is far more flexible. Why, for instance, should there be any limit to love or to compassion? We may have varied dispositions to cultivate these human qualities, but we all have the potential to progress continually throughout our life, through persistent efforts.

Oddly, many modern thinkers are, in the words of one French author, dead set against "the construction of the self as a never-ending task."[5] If we were forced on principle to give up every long-term project, the very concepts of apprenticeship, education, culture, or self-improvement would become meaningless. Leaving aside the spiritual path, why bother reading books, undertaking scientific research, learning about the world? The acquisition of knowledge is a never-ending task too. Why accept that but neglect our own transformation, which determines the quality of our lived experience? Is it better just to allow ourselves to drift? Isn't that how we crash on the rocks?

MUST WE SETTLE FOR BEING OURSELVES?

Even so, some people think that in order to be really happy all we need do is learn to love ourselves as we are. This all depends on what is meant by "being ourselves." Is it being on a perpetual seesaw between satisfaction and displeasure, calm and excitability, enthusiasm and apathy? Resigning ourselves to this way of thinking while letting our impulses and tendencies run rampant is the easy way out, a compromise, even a kind of surrender.

Many formulas for happiness insist that by nature we are a blend of light and shadow and that we must learn to accept our faults along with our positive qualities. They claim that by giving up the fight against our own limitations we can resolve most of our inner conflicts and greet each day with confidence and ease. Setting our own natures free is the best way; muzzling them can only exacerbate our problems. If we have to choose, it is certainly better to live spontaneously than to spend our days champing at the bit, being bored to tears, or hating ourselves. But isn't that just a way of wrapping our habits up in a pretty package?

It may be true that "expressing ourselves," giving free rein to our "natural" impulses, gives us momentary relief from our inner tensions, but we remain trapped in the endless circle of our usual habits. Such a lax attitude doesn't solve any serious problems, since in being ordinarily oneself, one remains ordinary. As the French philosopher Alain has written, "You don't need to be a sorcerer to cast a spell over yourself by saying 'This is how I am. I can do nothing about it.' "[6]

We are very much like birds that have lived too long in a cage to which we return even when we get the chance to fly away. We have grown so accustomed to our faults that we can barely imagine what life would be like without them. The prospect of change makes us dizzy.

And yet it's not as if we lack energy. We're constantly striving in any number of different directions, tackling countless projects. A Tibetan proverb says, "They have the starry sky for a hat and the white frost for boots," because they're up late at night and awake before dawn. But if it does occur to us to think, "I should try to develop altruism, patience, humility," we hesitate and tell ourselves that these qualities will come to us naturally in the long run, or that it's not a big deal and that we've gotten along just fine without them up to now. Who without determined and methodic efforts could play Mozart? It certainly can't be done by plunking away at the keyboard with two fingers. Happiness is a skill, a manner of being, but skills must be learned. As the Persian proverb has it: "Patience turns the mulberry leaf into satin."

Exercise
Developing attention
Sit quietly in your meditation posture and focus all your attention upon a chosen object. It can be an object in your room, your breath, or your own mind. Inevitably as you do this, your mind will wander. Each time it does, gently bring it back to the object of concentration, like a butterfly that returns again and again to the flower it feeds on. As you persevere, your concentration will become more clear and stable. If you feel sleepy, assume a straighter posture and lift your gaze slightly upward to revive your awareness. Conversely, if your mind becomes agitated, relax your posture, direct your gaze slightly downward, and let any inner tension dissolve.

Cultivating attention and mindfulness in this way is a precious tool for all other kinds of meditation.

4

FALSE FRIENDS

Those who seek happiness in pleasure, wealth, glory, power, and heroics are as naive as the child who tries to catch a rainbow and wear it as a coat.

DILGO KHYENTSE RINPOCHE

If we wish to identify the external factors and mental attitudes that favor genuine happiness and those that are prejudicial to it, we must first learn to distinguish between happiness and certain conditions that may appear similar to it but are actually very different.

HAPPINESS AND PLEASURE: THE GREAT MIX-UP

The most common error is to confuse pleasure for happiness. Pleasure, says the Hindu proverb, "is only the shadow of happiness." It is the direct result of pleasurable sensual, esthetic, or intellectual stimuli. The fleeting experience of pleasure is dependent upon circumstance, on a specific location or moment in time. It is unstable by nature, and the sensation it evokes soon becomes neutral or even unpleasant. Likewise, when repeated it may grow insipid or even lead to disgust; savoring a delicious meal is a source of genuine pleasure, but we are indifferent to it once we've had our fill and would get sick of it if we continued eating. It is the same thing with a nice wood fire: coming in from the cold, it is pure pleasure to warm ourselves by it, but we soon have to move away if we don't want to burn ourselves.

Pleasure is exhausted by usage, like a candle consuming itself. It is almost always linked to an *activity* and naturally leads to boredom by dint of being repeated. Listening rapturously to a Bach prelude requires a focus of attention that, minimal as it is, cannot be maintained indefinitely. After a while fatigue kicks in and the music loses its charm. Were we forced to listen for days on end, it would become unbearable.

Furthermore pleasure is an individual experience, most often centered on the self, which is why it can easily descend into selfishness and sometimes conflict with the well-being of others. In sexual intimacy there can certainly be mutual pleasure through giving and receiving pleasurable sensations, but such pleasure can transcend the self and contribute to genuine happiness only if the very nature of mutuality and generous altruism lies at its core. You can experience pleasure at somebody else's expense, but you can never derive happiness from it. Pleasure can be joined to cruelty, violence, pride, greed, and other mental conditions that are incompatible with true happiness. "Pleasure is the happiness of madmen, while happiness is the pleasure of sages," wrote the French novelist and critic Jules Barbey d'Aurevilly.

Some people even enjoy vengeance and torturing other human beings. In the same vein, a businessman may rejoice in the ruin of a competitor, a thief revel in his booty, a spectator at a bullfight exult in the bull's death. But these are only passing, sometimes morbid states of elation that, like moments of positive euphoria, have nothing to do with happiness.

The fervid and almost mechanical quest for sensual pleasures is another example of gratification's going hand in hand
with obsession and, ultimately, disenchantment. More often
than not, pleasure does not keep its promises, as poet Robert
Burns describes in *Tam O'Shanter*:

But pleasures are like poppies spread,
You seize the flower, its bloom is shed;
Or like the snow falls in the river,
A moment white — then melts forever.

Unlike pleasure, genuine flourishing may be influenced by
circumstance, but it isn't dependent on it. It does not mutate
into its opposite but endures and grows with experience. It imparts a sense of fulfillment that in time becomes second nature.

Authentic happiness is not linked to an activity; it is a state
of being, a profound emotional balance struck by a subtle understanding of how the mind functions. While ordinary pleasures are produced by contact with pleasant objects and end
when that contact is broken, sukha — lasting well-being — is
felt so long as we remain in harmony with our inner nature.
One intrinsic aspect of it is selflessness, which radiates from
within rather than focusing on the self. One who is at peace with
herself will contribute spontaneously to establishing peace within
her family, her neighborhood, and, circumstances permitting,
society at large.

In brief, there is no direct relationship between pleasure and
happiness. This distinction does not suggest that we mustn't
seek out pleasurable sensations. There is no reason to deprive
ourselves of the enjoyment of a magnificent landscape, of
swimming in the sea, or of the scent of a rose. Pleasures become
obstacles only when they upset the mind's equilibrium and lead

to an obsession with gratification or an aversion to anything that thwarts them.

Although intrinsically different from happiness, pleasure is not its enemy. It all depends on how it is experienced. If it is tainted with grasping and impedes inner freedom, giving rise to avidity and dependence, it is an obstacle to happiness. On the other hand, if it is experienced in the present moment, in a state of inner peace and freedom, pleasure adorns happiness without overshadowing it.

HAPPINESS AND JOY

The difference between joy and happiness is more subtle. Genuine happiness radiates outward spontaneously as joy. Inner joy is not necessarily manifested exuberantly, but as a luminous appreciation of the present moment, which can extend itself into the next moment, creating a continuum that one might call joie de vivre. Sukha can also be enhanced by unexpected delights. And yet not all forms of joy proceed from sukha — far from it. As Christophe André stresses in his work on the psychology of happiness: "There are unhealthy joys, far removed from the serenity of happiness, such as that of vengeance. . . . There is also calm happiness, often far removed from the intrinsic excitation of joy. . . . We jump for joy, not for happiness."[1]

We have seen how hard it can be to agree on a definition of happiness and have tried to pin down the meaning of true happiness. The word *joy* is equally vague, since, as the psychologist Paul Ekman has shown, it is associated with feelings as varied as the pleasures of the five senses: amusement (from the chuckle to the belly laugh); contentment (a calmer kind of satisfaction); excitement (in response to novelty or challenge); relief (following upon another emotion, such as fear, anxiety, and sometimes even pleasure); wonder (before something astonishing and admirable, or that surpasses understanding); ecstasy or bliss (transporting us outside ourselves); exultation (at having accomplished a difficult task or undertaken a daring exploit); radiant pride (when our children earn a special honor); elevation (from having witnessed an act of great kindness, generosity, or compassion); gratitude (the appreciation of a selfless act of which one is the beneficiary); and unhealthy jubilation, schadenfreude (in relishing someone else's suffering, such as through revenge).[2] We might also throw in rejoicing (in someone else's happiness), delight or enchantment (a shining kind of contentment), and spiritual radiance (a serene joy born from deep well-being and benevolence), which is indeed more an enduring state of being than a fleeting emotion.

These emotions all possess an element of joy, generally bring a smile to the face, and are manifested by a specific expression and tone of voice. But in order to participate in or contribute to happiness, they must be free of all negative emotion. When anger or envy erupts, joy is abruptly extinguished. When attachment, egoism, or pride creeps in, it is slowly smothered.

If joy is to endure and mature serenely — if it is to be, in the words of Corneille, a "blossoming of the heart" — it must be linked to other aspects of true happiness: clarity of mind, loving-kindness, the gradual withering of negative emotions, and the disappearance of selfish whimsy.

LIVE IT UP!

"Living it up" has become the leitmotif of modern man — a compulsive hyperactivity without any downtime, no gap of unscheduled time, lest we end up alone with ourselves. The meaning doesn't matter, so long as it's intense. We feel that without constant activity, life would be fatally insipid. Friends of mine who lead cultural tours in Asia have told me how their clients can't bear the least gap in their itinerary. "Is there really nothing scheduled between five and seven?" they ask anxiously. We are, it seems, afraid to turn our gaze in upon ourselves. We are fully focused on the exterior world, as experienced through the five senses. It seems naive to believe that such a feverish search for intense experience can lead to a lasting enriched quality of life.

If we do take the time to explore our inner world, it's in the form of daydreams and imagination, dwelling on the past or fantasizing endlessly about the future. A genuine sense of fulfillment, associated with inner freedom, can also offer intensity to every living moment, but of an altogether different sort. It is a sparkling experience of inner well-being, in which the beauty of each thing shines through. It is knowing how to enjoy the present moment, the willingness to nurture altruism and serenity and to bring the best part of ourselves to mature — transforming oneself to better transform the world.

An Artificial High

We might imagine that achieving sudden fame or sudden wealth would satisfy all our desires, but more often than not the satisfaction provided by such achievements is short-lived and does nothing to improve our well-being. I met a famous Taiwanese singer who, having described her discomfort and disenchantment with fame and fortune, burst into tears, crying: "I wish I'd never become famous!" Studies have shown that an unexpected situation — winning the lottery jackpot, for instance — can lead to a temporary heightening of one's pleasure quotient but has little long-term effect on the happy or unhappy disposition of the subjects involved. In the case of lottery winners, it has been found that most experience a period of elation following their stroke of good luck but a year later have returned to their normal satisfaction level.[3] Sometimes, too, the event, which was presumably enviable, destabilizes the life of the "happy winner." The late psychologist Michael Argyle cites the case of a twenty-four-year-old Englishwoman who had won a jackpot of more than one million pounds sterling. She quit her job and was soon consigned to boredom; she bought a new house in a fashionable neighborhood and found herself cut off from her friends; she bought a fancy car, although she didn't know how to drive; she bought mountains of clothing, most of which never left the closet; she went to fine restaurants but preferred to eat fish and chips. Within a year she began to suffer from depression, her life empty and without satisfaction.[4]

We all know how very clever and tireless our consumer society is at inventing countless bogus pleasures, laboriously hyped stimulants designed to keep us in a state of emotional tension capable of triggering a kind of mental anesthesia. A Tibetan friend of mine who was contemplating the flashy advertising billboards in New York commented: "They are trying to steal our minds." There is a distinct difference between true joy, which is the natural manifestation of well-being, and euphoria, the elation caused by passing excitation. Any superficial thrill that is not anchored in enduring contentment is almost invariably followed by disappointment.

SUFFERING AND UNHAPPINESS

Just as we distinguished between happiness and pleasure, we must also make the distinction between affliction and suffering. We *incur* suffering but we *create* unhappiness. The Sanskrit word *dukkha*, the opposite of *sukha*, does not simply define an unpleasant sensation, but rather reflects a fundamental vulnerability to suffering and pain that can ultimately lead to worldweariness, the feeling that life is not worth living because there is no way to find meaning in it. Sartre put these noxious words into the mouth of the hero of his book *Nausea:*

> *If someone had asked me what it means to be alive, I would have answered in good faith that it means nothing, merely an empty vessel. . . . We were all just a pile of awkward lives, embarrassed by ourselves. We hadn't the slightest reason to be there, none of us. Every living being, confused, vaguely anxious, felt redundant. . . . I was redundant too. . . . I had vague notions of doing away with myself, to rid the world of at least one of these superfluous lives.*[5]

The belief that the world would be better off without us is a common cause of suicide.

Suffering can be triggered by numerous causes over which we sometimes have some power, and sometimes none. Being born with a handicap, falling ill, losing a loved one, or being caught up in war or in a natural disaster are all beyond our control. Unhappiness is altogether different, being *the way in which we experience our suffering.* Unhappiness may indeed be associated with physical or moral pain inflicted by exterior conditions, but it is not *essentially* linked to it.

A study of quadriplegics found that although most acknowledged having considered suicide at first, a year after having been paralyzed only 10 percent considered their lives to be miserable; most considered theirs to be good.[6] Just as it is the mind that translates suffering into unhappiness, it is the mind's responsibility to master its perception thereof. A change, even a tiny one, in the way we manage our thoughts and perceive and interpret the world can significantly change our existence. Changing the way we experience transitory emotions leads to a change in our moods and to a lasting transformation of our way of being. Such "therapy" targets the sufferings that afflict most of us and seeks to promote the optimal flourishing of the human being.

EXERCISE

Distinguishing happiness from pleasure

Bring to your mind a past experience of physical pleasure, with all its intensity. Remember how you enjoyed it at first and then how it gradually changed into a neutral feeling and maybe even waned into lassitude and lack of interest. Did it bring you a sense of inner or lasting fulfillment?

Then remember an occasion of inner joy and happiness. Recall how you felt, for example, when you made someone else really happy, or when you peacefully enjoyed the company of a loved one or the sight of beautiful natural scenery. Consider the lasting effect this experience had on your mind and how it still nourishes a sense of fulfillment. Compare the quality of such a state of being with that of a fleeting sensation of pleasure.

Learn to value these moments of deep well-being and aspire to find ways to develop them further.

5

IS HAPPINESS POSSIBLE?

The outward freedom that we shall attain will only be in exact proportion to the inward freedom to which we may have grown at a given moment. And if this is a correct view of freedom, our chief energy must be concentrated on achieving reform from within.

MAHATMA GANDHI

At some point in our lives, we have all met people who live and breathe happiness. This happiness seems to permeate all of their gestures and words with a quality and force that are impossible to ignore. Some declare unambiguously and without ostentation that they have attained a happiness that abides deep within them, whatever life may bring. For such people, according to Robert Misrahi, "happiness is the form and overall meaning of a life that considers itself to be full and meaningful, and which experiences itself as such."[1]

Although such a state of constant fulfillment is rare, surveys have shown that where the conditions of life are not especially oppressive, most people claim to be satisfied with the quality of their lives (75 percent in the developed countries).

It would be counterproductive to reject studies and surveys that reflect the opinions of hundreds of thousands of people interviewed over the course of a dozen years. But it does make sense to question the nature of the happiness that the subjects are referring to. The fact is, their average satisfaction remains relatively stable because the material conditions of life in the developed countries are generally excellent. On the other hand, it is eminently fragile. Should just one of these conditions suddenly vanish — due to the loss of a loved one or a job, for instance — that feeling of happiness would crumble. And in any case, declaring ourselves satisfied with life because there is no objective reason to complain about its conditions (of all the countries studied, Switzerland has the most "happy" people) in no way prevents us from feeling ill at ease deep within ourselves. By the age of thirty-five, 15 percent of North Americans have experienced a major depression. Since 1960, the divorce rate in the United States has doubled, while reported rapes have increased fourfold and juvenile violence fivefold.[2]

This distinction between exterior and interior well-being explains the apparent contradiction between some of these findings and the Buddhist assertion that suffering is omnipresent in the universe. When we speak about omnipresence, it means not that all people are *continuously* in a state of suffering, but that they are vulnerable to the latent suffering that can arise at any moment. They will remain vulnerable so long as they fail to dispel the mental toxins that cause unhappiness.

IS HAPPINESS A RESPITE FROM SUFFERING?

Many people think of happiness as merely a temporary lull, experienced as a positive contrast to suffering. For Schopenhauer, "all happiness is negative. . . . Ultimately, satisfaction and contentment are merely the interruption of pain and privation."[3] Freud writes that "what we call happiness, in the strictest sense of the word, arises from the fairly sudden satisfaction of pent-up needs. By its very nature it can be no more than an episodic phenomenon."[4] When suffering abates or ceases momentarily, the ensuing interlude is experienced by contrast as "happy." Happiness is thus viewed as being just a deceptively calm moment in the middle of a storm.

A friend of mine who spent many years in a Chinese concentration camp in Tibet told me that when he was being interrogated he was forced to stand motionless on a stool for days on end. When he collapsed, those brief moments lying on the icy cement floor of his cell, before he was dragged to his feet again, were delightful relief to him. While this may be an example — and an extreme one at that — of happiness resulting from the attenuation of suffering, my friend took pains to point out that only his stable condition of inner well-being allowed him to survive years of incarceration and torture.

On a far less somber note, I remember a train trip through India, undertaken in rather difficult and turbulent conditions. I had reserved my seat — a good idea for a thirty-six-hour journey — but my car was never attached to the train and I found myself in a substitute wagon, jam-packed, having no compartments and no glass in the windows. Huddling on a wooden berth with a half-dozen frozen travelers (it was January), I observed the hundreds of other passengers crammed into their seats and on the corridor floors. On top of it all, I had a high fever and lumbago. We were traveling through Bihar, a country of bandits, and the passengers had chained up their luggage wherever they could. I was used to traveling in India and stowed the briefcase containing my laptop and an entire month's work in an apparently secure corner of the upper berth. Nevertheless it was spirited away by an innovative thief from the neighboring berth, presumably with a hook. As night fell, I realized what had happened. Then the lights went out for several hours. There I was, wrapped in my sleeping bag, listening to the cursing of passengers frantically trying to keep tabs on their luggage in the dark. Suddenly I realized that, far from being upset, I felt incredibly light and experienced a feeling of total felicity and freedom. You may imagine that the fever was making me delirious, but I was absolutely clearheaded, and the contrast between the situation and my feelings was so comical that I began to laugh in the dark. This was definitely not a case of happiness via relief; rather it was an experience of innate serenity, brought into sharper focus by particularly unpleasant external circumstances. It was a moment of "letting go," that state of deep satisfaction found only within oneself and which is therefore independent of external circumstances. We cannot deny the existence of pleasant and unpleasant sensations, but they are trivial with respect to genuine well-being. Such experiences have helped me to see that it is certainly possible to live in a state of enduring happiness.

Once we have come to that conclusion, our goal becomes to determine levelheadedly the causes of unhappiness and to correct them. Since true happiness is not limited to momentary relief from life's ups and downs, it requires us to eliminate the major causes of unhappiness, which, as we have seen, are ignorance and mental toxins. If happiness is indeed a way of being, a state of consciousness and inner freedom, there is essentially nothing to prevent us from achieving it.

The denial of the possibility of happiness seems to have been influenced by the concept of the world and mankind as being fundamentally evil. This belief stems largely from the notion of original sin, which Freud, according to psychologist Martin Seligman, "dragged . . . into twentieth-century psychology, defining all of civilization (including modern morality, science, religion, and technological progress) as just an elaborate defense against basic conflicts over infantile sexuality and aggression." This kind of interpretation has led a great many contemporary intellectuals to conclude absurdly that any act of generosity or kindness comes from a negative impulse. Seligman quotes Doris Kearns Goodwin, the biographer of Franklin and Eleanor Roosevelt, according to whom the first lady devoted a great portion of her life to helping people of color because she was compensating for her mother's narcissism and her father's alcoholism. Goodwin, says Seligman, never even considers the possibility that Eleanor Roosevelt was simply acting out of pure kindness! For Seligman and his colleagues in the field of positive psychology, "there is not a shred of evidence that strength and virtue are derived from negative motivation."[5]

We also know that our constant bombardment with bad news by the media and the presentation of violence as the ultimate solution to any conflict encourages what sociologists call the "wicked world syndrome." One simple illustration of this was at the 1999 Visa pour l'Image, an international photojournalism festival in Perpignan, France, in which I participated as an exhibitor. Of the thirty-six exhibits mounted there, only two were devoted to subjects that put a constructive spin on human nature. The thirty-four others were about war, Mafia crimes in Palermo, drug dens in New York City, and other negative aspects of the world.

The "wicked world syndrome" calls into question the very possibility of actualizing happiness. The battle would appear to be lost before it's engaged. The belief that human nature is essentially corrupt taints our vision of life with pessimism and makes us question the very basis of the search for happiness, that is, every human being's potential for perfection. Trying to purify something that is fundamentally bad would be as pointless as trying to bleach a lump of coal. Conversely, the development of our deep human potential is like polishing a gold nugget to bring out its shine.

When the Messenger Becomes the Message

All of this is very nice in theory, but how does it translate into practice? As the American psychiatrist Howard Cutler puts it in *The Art of Happiness:* "I became convinced that the Dalai Lama had learned to live with a sense of fulfillment and a degree of serenity that I had never seen in other people."[6] Such an example might seem a little out of our league, but the truth is that as inaccessible as it may seem, the Dalai Lama is definitely not an isolated case. I myself have spent thirty-five years living among not only sages and spiritual masters, but also a number of "ordinary" people whose inner serenity and joy help them to withstand most of the ups and downs of life. These people have nothing further to gain for themselves and are therefore entirely available to others. My friend Alan Wallace relates the case of a Tibetan hermit whom he knew well and who told him, with no pretension whatsoever (he was living peacefully in his hermitage, making no demands on anyone), that he had lived for twenty years in a "state of continuous bliss."[7]

This is not about marveling over exceptional cases or proclaiming the so-called superiority of one approach — Buddhist, in this case — over other schools of thought. The main lesson I draw from it is this: *If the wise man can be happy, then happiness must be possible.* This is a crucial point, since so many people believe, in effect, that true happiness is impossible.

The wise man and the wisdom he embodies do not represent an inaccessible ideal, but a living example. It so happens that it is precisely such points of reference that we need in our daily lives so as to better understand what we can become. The point here is not that we need to reject wholesale the lives we are leading, but that we can benefit immensely from the wisdom of those who have elucidated the dynamics of happiness and suffering.

Fortunately, the idea of the happy wise man is alien neither to the Western world nor to the modern world, although it has become a rare commodity. According to the philosopher André Comte-Sponville: "The wise man has nothing left to expect or to hope for. Because he is entirely happy, he needs nothing. Because he needs nothing, he is entirely happy."[8] Such qualities do not fall from the sky, and if the image of the wise man is a little old-fashioned nowadays — at least in the West — whose fault is that? We are responsible for a scarcity that afflicts us all. One is not born wise; one becomes it.

From the Hermitage to the Office

This is all very inspiring, you might say, but what good is it to me in my daily life, where I have a family and a job and spend most of my time in circumstances very different from those enjoyed by sages and hermits? Yet the wise man is indeed relevant to our lives in that he strikes a note of hope: he shows me what I could become. He has trod a path open to all, each step of which is a source of enrichment. We can't all become Olympic javelin athletes, but we can all learn to throw the javelin and we can develop some ability to do so. You don't have to be Andre Agassi to love playing tennis, or Louis Armstrong to delight in playing a musical instrument. In every sphere of human activity there are sources of inspiration whose perfection, far from discouraging us, in fact whets our enthusiasm by holding out an admirable vision of that to which we aspire. Isn't that why the great artists, the men and women of conviction, the heroes, are beloved and respected?

Spiritual practice can be enormously beneficial. The fact is, it is possible to undergo serious spiritual training by devoting some time every day to meditation. More people than you might think do so, while leading regular family lives and doing absorbing work. The positive benefits of such a life far outweigh the few problems of schedule arrangement. In this way we can launch an inner transformation that is based in day-to-day reality.

When I was working at the Institut Pasteur and immersed in Parisian life, the few moments I reserved every day for contemplation brought me enormous benefits. They lingered like a scent in the day's activities and gave them an entirely new value. By contemplation I mean not merely a moment of relaxation, but an inward turning of the gaze. It is very fruitful to watch how thoughts arise, and to contemplate the state of serenity and simplicity that is always present behind the scrim of thoughts, be they gloomy or upbeat. This is not as complicated as it might seem at first glance. You need only give a little of your time to the exercise in order to feel its impact and appreciate its fruitfulness. By gradually acquiring through introspective experience a better understanding of how thoughts are born, we learn how to fend off mental toxins. Once we have found a little bit of inner peace, it is much easier to lead a flourishing emotional and professional life. Similarly, as we free ourselves of all insecurities and inner fears (which are often connected to excessive self-centeredness), we have less to dread and are naturally more open to others and better armed to face the vagaries of existence.

No state, church, or despot can insist on our obligation to develop human qualities. It is up to us to make that choice. As geneticist-demographer Luca Cavalli-Sforza and his son Francesco so eloquently put it:

> *Our inner freedom knows no limits other than those we impose on it or allow to be imposed on it. And that freedom also holds great power. It can transform an individual, allow him to nurture all his capacities and to live every moment of his life in utter fulfillment. When indi-*

viduals change by bringing their consciousness to matu-rity, the world changes too, because the world is made up of individuals.[9]

EXERCISE

How to begin to meditate

No matter what your outer circumstances might be, there is always, deep within you, a potential for flourishing. This is a potential for loving-kindness, compassion, and inner peace. Try to get in touch with and experience this potential that is always present, like a nugget of gold, in your heart and mind.

This potential needs to be developed and matured in order to achieve a more stable sense of well-being. However, this will not happen by itself. You need to develop it as a skill. For that, begin by becoming more familiar with your own mind. This is the beginning of meditation.

Sit quietly, in a comfortable but balanced posture. Whether you sit cross-legged on a cushion or more conventionally on a chair, try to keep your back straight, yet without being tense. Rest your hands on your knees or thighs or in your lap, keep your eyes lightly gazing in the space in front of you, and breathe naturally. Watch your mind, the coming and going of thoughts. At first it might seem that instead of diminishing, thoughts rush through your mind like a waterfall. Just watch them arising and let them come and go, without trying to stop them but without fueling them either.

Take a moment at the end of the practice to savor the warmth and joy that result from a calmer mind.

After a while your thoughts will become like a peaceful river. If you practice regularly, eventually your mind will easily become serene, like a calm ocean. Whenever new thoughts arise, like waves raised by the winds, do not be bothered by them. They will soon dissolve back into the ocean.

6

THE ALCHEMY OF SUFFERING

If there is a way to free ourselves from suffering
We must use every moment to find it.
Only a fool wants to go on suffering.
Isn't it sad to knowingly imbibe poison?

SEVENTH DALAI LAMA

A long time ago, the son of a king of Persia was raised along-side the son of the grand vizier, and their friendship was legendary. When the prince ascended to the throne, he said to his friend: "While I attend to the affairs of the kingdom, will you please write me a history of men and the world, so that I can draw the necessary lessons from it and thus know the proper way to act."

The king's friend consulted with the most famous historians, the most learned scholars, and the most respected sages. Five years later he presented himself proudly at the palace.

"Sire," he said, "here are thirty-six volumes relating the entire history of the world from creation to your accession."

"Thirty-six volumes!" cried the king. "How will I ever have time to read them? I have so much work administering my kingdom and seeing to my two hundred queens. Please, friend, condense your history."

Two years later, the friend returned to the palace with ten volumes. But the king was at war against the neighboring monarch. He was found on a mountaintop in the desert, directing the battle.

"The fate of our kingdom is being played out as we speak. Where would I find the time to read ten volumes? Abridge your history even further."

The vizier's son left and worked three years on a single volume that gave an accurate picture of the essence. The king was now caught up in legislating.

"How lucky you are to have the time to write quietly. While you've been doing that, I've been debating taxes and their collection. Bring me tenfold fewer pages — I'll spend an evening mining them."

Two years later, it was done. But when the friend returned, he found the king bedridden, in dreadful pain. The friend himself was no longer young; his wrinkled face was haloed by a mane of white hair.

"Well?" whispered the king with his dying breath. "The history of men?"

His friend gazed steadily at him and, as the king was about to die, he said:

"They suffer, Majesty."

Yes, they suffer, at every moment and throughout the world. Some die when they've just been born; some when they've just given birth. Every second, people are murdered, tortured, beaten, maimed, separated from their loved ones. Others are abandoned, betrayed, expelled, rejected. Some are killed out of hatred, greed, ignorance, ambition, pride, or envy. Mothers lose their children, children lose their parents. The ill pass in never-ending procession through the hospitals. Some suffer with no hope of being treated, others are treated with no hope of being cured. The dying endure their pain, and the survivors their mourning. Some die of hunger, cold, exhaustion; others are charred by fire, crushed by rocks, or swept away by the waters.

This is true not only for human beings. Animals devour each other in the forests, the savannahs, the oceans, and the skies. At any given moment tens of thousands of them are being killed by humans, torn to pieces, and canned. Others suffer endless torments at the hands of their owners, bearing heavy burdens, in chains their entire lives; still others are hunted, fished, trapped between teeth of steel, strangled in snares, smothered under nets, tortured for their flesh, their musk, their ivory, their bones, their fur, their skin, thrown into boiling water or flayed alive.

These are not mere words but a reality that is an intrinsic part of our daily lives: death, the transitory nature of all things, and suffering. Though we may feel overwhelmed by it all, powerless before so much pain, turning away from it is only indifference or cowardice. We must be intimately concerned with it, and do everything we possibly can to relieve the suffering.

THE MODALITIES OF SUFFERING

Buddhism speaks of pervasive suffering, the suffering of change, and the multiplicity of suffering. Pervasive suffering is comparable to a green fruit on the verge of ripening; the suffering of change, to a delicious meal laced with poison; and the multiplicity of suffering, to the eruption of an abscess on a tumor. Pervasive suffering is not yet recognized as such. The suffering of change begins with a feeling of pleasure and turns to pain. The multiplicity of suffering is associated with an increase in pain.

These correspond to three modes of suffering: visible suffering, hidden suffering, and invisible suffering. Visible suffering is evident everywhere. Hidden suffering is concealed beneath the appearance of pleasure, freedom from care, fun. A gourmet eats a fine dish and moments later is gripped by the spasms of food poisoning. A family is happily gathered for a picnic in the country when a child is suddenly bitten by a snake. Partygoers are merrily dancing at the county fair when the tent abruptly catches fire. This type of suffering may potentially arise at any moment in life, but it remains hidden to those who are taken in by the illusion of appearances and cling to the belief that people and things last, untouched by the change that affects everything.

There is also the suffering that underlies the most ordinary activities. It is not easy to identify or so readily localized as a toothache. It sends out no signal and does not prevent us from functioning in the world, since, on the contrary, it is an integral part of the daily routine. What could be more innocuous than a boiled egg? Farm-raised hens may not have it so bad, but let's take a brief look into the world of battery farming. Male chicks are separated at birth from the females and sent straight to the grinder. The hens are fed day and night under artificial lighting to make them grow faster and lay more eggs. Overcrowding makes them aggressive, and they continually tear at each other's feathers. None of this history is apparent in your breakfast egg.

Invisible suffering is the hardest to distinguish because it stems from the blindness of our own minds, where it remains so long as we are in the grip of ignorance and selfishness. Our confusion, born of a lack of judgment and wisdom, blinds us to what we must do and avoid doing to ensure that our thoughts, our words, and our actions engender happiness and not suffering. This confusion and the tendencies associated with it drive us to reenact again and again the behavior that lies at the source of our pain. If we want to counteract this harmful misjudgment, we have to awaken from the dream of ignorance and learn to identify the very subtle ways in which happiness and suffering are generated.

Are we capable of identifying ego-clinging as the cause of that suffering? Generally speaking, no. That is why we call this third type of suffering invisible. Selfishness, or rather the feeling that one is the center of the world — hence "self-centeredness" — is the source of most of our disruptive thoughts. From obsessive desire to hatred, not to mention jealousy, it attracts pain the way a magnet attracts iron filings.

So it would seem that there is no way to escape the suffering that prevails everywhere. Prophets have followed upon wise men and saints upon potentates, and still the rivers of suffering flow. Mother Teresa toiled for fifty years on behalf of the dying of Calcutta, but if the hospices she founded were to disappear, those patients would be back on the streets as if they'd never existed. In adjacent neighborhoods, they're still dying on the sidewalks. We gauge our impotence by the omnipresence, magnitude, and perpetuity of suffering. Buddhist texts say that in the cycle of death and rebirth, no place, not even one the size of a needle's point, is exempt from suffering.

Can we allow such a view to drive us to despair, discouragement, or worse yet, indifference? Unable to bear its intensity, must we be destroyed by it?

THE CAUSES OF SUFFERING

Is there any way to put an end to suffering? According to Buddhism, suffering will always exist as a *universal phenomenon,* but *every individual* has the potential for liberation from it.

As for human beings in general, we cannot expect suffering to simply vanish from the universe, because, in the Buddhist view, the universe is without beginning or end. There can be no real beginning because *nothing* cannot suddenly become *some-*

thing. Nothingness is a word that allows us to picture for ourselves the absence or even nonexistence of worldly phenomena, but a mere idea cannot give birth to anything at all.

As for a real end, in which *something* becomes *nothing,* it is equally impossible. As it happens, wherever life exists in the universe, so does suffering: disease, old age, death, separation from loved ones, forced coexistence with our oppressors, denial of basic necessities, confrontations with what we fear, and so on.

Despite all that, this vision does not lead Buddhism to the view held by certain Western philosophers for whom suffering is *inevitable* and happiness out of reach. The reason for that is simple: unhappiness has causes that can be identified and acted upon. It is only when we misidentify the nature of those causes that we come to doubt the possibility of healing.

The first mistake is believing that unhappiness is inevitable because it is the result of divine will or some other immutable principle and that it will therefore be forever out of our control. The second is the gratuitous idea that unhappiness has no identifiable cause, that it descends upon us randomly and has no relation to us personally. The third mistake draws on a confused fatalism that boils down to the idea that whatever the cause, the effect will always be the same.

If unhappiness had immutable causes, we would never be able to escape it. The laws of causality would have no meaning — anything could come from anything else, flowers could grow in the sky and light create darkness and, as the Dalai Lama says, it would be easier "not to go to all the trouble of constantly ruminating over our suffering. It would be better just to think about something else, go to the beach, and have a nice cold beer!" Because if there were no cure for suffering, it would be pointless to make it worse by stressing over it. It would be better to accept it fully and to distract oneself so as to feel it less harshly.

But everything that occurs *does* have a cause. What inferno does not start with a spark, what war without thoughts of hatred, fear, or greed? What inner pain has not grown from the fertile soil of envy, animosity, vanity, or, even more basically, ignorance? Any active cause must itself be a changing one; nothing can exist autonomously and unchanging. Arising from impermanent causes, unhappiness is itself subject to change and can be transformed. There is neither primordial nor eternal suffering.

We all have the ability to study the causes of suffering and gradually to free ourselves from them. We all have the potential to sweep away the veils of ignorance, to free ourselves of the selfishness and misplaced desires that trigger unhappiness, to work for the good of others and extract the essence from our human condition. It's not the magnitude of the task that matters, it's the magnitude of our courage.

THE FOUR TRUTHS OF SUFFERING

Over 2,500 years ago, seven weeks after attaining enlightenment under the Bodhi tree, the Buddha gave his first teaching in the Deer Park outside Varanasi. There he taught the Four Noble Truths. The first is the truth of suffering — not only the kind of suffering that is obvious to the eye, but also the kind, as we have seen, that exists in subtler forms. The second is the truth of the causes of suffering — ignorance that engenders craving, malice, pride, and many other thoughts that poison our lives and those of others. Since these mental poisons can be eliminated, an end to suffering — the third truth — is therefore possible. The fourth truth is the path that turns that potential into reality. The path is the process of using all available means to eliminate the fundamental causes of suffering. In brief, we must:

Recognize suffering,
Eliminate its source,
End it
By practicing the path.

WHEN AFFLICTION BECOMES SUFFERING

Just as we distinguished between happiness and pleasure, we also have to clarify the difference between unhappiness and ephemeral discomforts. The latter depend on external circumstances, while unhappiness is a profound state of dissatisfaction that endures even in favorable external conditions. Conversely, it's worth repeating that one can suffer physically or mentally — by feeling sad, for instance — without losing the sense of fulfillment that is founded on inner peace and selflessness. There are two levels of experience here, which can be compared respectively to the waves and the depths of the ocean. A storm may be raging at the surface, but the depths remain calm. The wise man always remains connected to the depths. On the other hand, he who knows only the surface and is unaware of the depths is lost when he is buffeted by the waves of suffering.

But how, you might ask, can I avoid being shattered when my child is sick and I know he's going to die? How can I not be torn up at the sight of thousands of civilian war victims being deported or mutilated? Am I supposed to stop feeling? What could ever make me accept something like that? Who wouldn't be affected by it, including the most serene of wise men? The difference between the sage and the ordinary person is that the former can feel unconditional love for those who suffer and do everything in his power to attenuate their pain without allowing his lucid vision of existence to be shaken. The essential thing is to be available to others without giving in to despair when the natural episodes of life and death follow their course.

For the past few years I've had a friend, a Sikh in his sixties with a fine white beard, who works at the Delhi airport. Every time I pass through, we have a cup of tea together and discuss philosophy and spirituality, taking up the conversation where we left off several months earlier. One day he told me: "My father died a few weeks ago. I'm devastated, because his death seems so unfair to me. I can't understand it and I can't accept it." And yet the world cannot in itself be called unfair; all it does is reflect the laws of cause and effect, and impermanence — the instability of all things — is a natural phenomenon.

As gently as possible, I told him the story of the woman who, overwhelmed by the death of her son, came to the Buddha and begged him to restore the boy to life. The Buddha told her that in order to do so, he needed a handful of earth from a house that had never experienced any death. Having visited every house in the village and come to see that none had escaped bereavement, the woman returned to the Buddha, who comforted her with words of love and wisdom.

I also told him the story of Dza Mura Tulku, a spiritual master who lived in the early twentieth century in eastern Tibet. He had a family, and throughout his life he felt a deep affection for his wife, which she reciprocated. He did nothing without her and always said that if anything should happen to her, he could not long outlive her. And then she died suddenly. The master's friends and disciples hurried to his side. Recalling what they had heard him say so often, none dared tell him the news. Finally, as tactfully as possible, one disciple told the master that his wife had died.

The tragic reaction they'd feared failed to occur. The master looked at them and said: "Why do you look so upset? How many times have I told you that phenomena and beings are impermanent? Even the Buddha had to leave the world." No matter how tenderly he'd felt for his wife, and despite the great sadness he most surely felt, allowing himself to be consumed by grief would have added nothing to his love for her. It was more important for him to pray serenely for the deceased and to make her an offering of that serenity.

Remaining painfully obsessed with a situation or the memory of a departed loved one, to the point of being paralyzed by grief for months or years on end, is evidence not of affection, but of an attachment that does no good to others or to oneself. If we can learn to acknowledge that death is a part of life, distress will gradually give way to understanding and peace. "Don't think you're paying me some kind of great tribute if you let my death become the great event of your life. The best tribute you can pay to me as a mother is to go on and have a good and fulfilling life." These words were spoken by a mother to her son only moments before her death.

So the way in which we experience these waves of suffering depends a great deal on our attitude. It is therefore always better to familiarize ourselves with and prepare ourselves for the kind of suffering we are likely to encounter, some of which will be unavoidable, such as illness, old age, and death, rather than to be caught off guard and sink into anguish. A physical or moral pain can be intense without destroying our positive outlook on life. Once we have acquired inner well-being, it is easier to maintain our fortitude or to recover it quickly, even when we are confronted externally by difficult circumstances.

Does such peace of mind come simply because we wish it to? Hardly. We don't earn our living just by wishing to. Likewise, peace is a treasure of the mind that is not acquired without effort. If we let ourselves be overwhelmed by our personal problems, no matter how tragic, we only increase our difficulties and become a burden on those around us. If our mind becomes accustomed to dwelling solely on the pain that events or people inflict on it, one day the most trivial incident will cause it infinite sorrow. As the intensity of this feeling grows with practice, everything that happens to us will eventually come to distress us, and peace will find no place within us. All manifestations will assume a hostile character and we will rebel bitterly against our fate, to the point of doubting the very meaning of life. It is essential to acquire a certain inner sense of well-being so that without in any way blunting our sensitivities, our love, and our altruism, we are able to connect with the depths of our being.

WOUNDED BEINGS

Some people have known so little affection and so much suffering in their early life that they are deeply wounded. It is hard for them to find a place of peace and love within themselves and consequently to trust others. Sometimes, however, they develop the healing and empowering faculty of *resilience*, which makes them less vulnerable to difficult situations and helps them to transform such situations into personal strengths and to find their way in life. But they may also carry these wounds for a long time in their relationships. It is well established that newborns and infants need a great deal of loving-kindness and affection to grow in an optimal way. Bulgarian and Chinese orphanages, where infants are rarely touched by their caretakers, let alone given affection and love, offer well-known and tragic evidence that the brains of neglected infants do not develop normally. I have witnessed extraordinary changes in infants from Nepalese orphanages, who at first seemed like inert, "absent" little beings and blossomed into wonderfully lively children within months of having been adopted by loving parents who constantly related to them with affection, touched them, and spoke to them.

Whether or not we benefit from affection and love at an early age thus greatly influences our ability to give and receive love later in life, and simultaneously our degree of inner peace. If we consider the categories first described by Mary Ainsworth and applied by Phil Shaver and his colleagues to adolescents and adults,[1] a "secure" person will not only enjoy a high degree of well-being but will be naturally open to and trusting of others. She is open to emotions and memories, exhibits high "coherence of mind," and is nonhostile during disagreements with others and able to compromise. She generally copes well with stress. An "anxious and insecure" person will lack self-confidence and doubt the possibility of encountering genuine benevolence and affection, while yearning deeply for it. Such a person will be less trusting, more possessive and jealous, and will fall prey to nagging suspicions, often on a purely imaginary basis. She is excessively ruminative and vulnerable to depression, and tends to become overly emotional when stressed. An "insecurely avoidant" person will rather keep others at bay than risk further suffering. Such a person will avoid becoming too intimate with others, either in a fearful way or by silencing all emotions in his mind and retreating within the cocoon of self-absorption. He has high self-esteem, but his self-esteem is defensive and brittle; he isn't very open to emotions and memories, and is often bored, distracted, "compulsively self-reliant," and not very caring.

According to Shaver and his colleagues, the emotional style of parents, principally the mother, influences considerably that of the child. If the mother has an "avoidant" style, there is a 70 percent chance that the child will "learn" the same style while interacting with his mother. The same is true for the secure and anxious styles. The best gift one can thus give to a child is to manifest loving, open, and peaceful qualities oneself and to let the emotional alchemy work its way.

Are such emotional styles acquired during the first years of life engraved in the stone of unchanging traits? Fortunately not. Phil Shaver and his colleagues have also shown that insecure anxious and avoidant persons can change considerably toward a more secure emotional style precisely by being exposed to affection and other positive emotions.[2]

How can we help deeply wounded persons? By giving them enough love so that some peace and trust can grow in their hearts. How can they help themselves? By engaging in a meaningful dialogue with a human and warmhearted psychologist using methods that have proven to be efficient, such as cognitive therapy, and by cultivating loving-kindness, compassion, and mindfulness.

Making the Best of Suffering

While suffering is never desirable, that does not mean that we can't make use of it, when it is inevitable, to progress humanly and spiritually. Suffering can provide an extraordinary lesson capable of making us aware of the superficiality of many of our daily concerns, of our own fragility, and, above all, of what really counts deep down within us.

Having lived several months on the verge of death in terrible pain, Guy Corneau, a Canadian psychiatrist, finally "let go." He stopped fighting a pain that could not be soothed and opened himself to the potential for serenity that is ever present in us.

This opening of the heart only became more marked in the following days and weeks. I was plunged into nameless beatitude. A vast fire of love burned within me. I only had to close my eyes to partake of it, long and satisfying draughts. . . . And then I understood that love was the very fabric of this universe, the common identity of each being and each thing. There was only love and nothing else. . . . In the long run, suffering helps us to discover a world where there is no real division between external and internal, between the body and the mind, between me and others.[3]

We can learn from suffering if we use it wisely. On the other hand, resigning ourselves to it with a simple "that's life!" is like renouncing from the get-go any possibility of the inner change that is available to everyone and that allows us to prevent suffering from being systematically converted into misery. Just because we are not defeated by such obstacles as illness, animosity, criticism, or bad luck in no way means that events do not affect us or that we have overcome these obstacles forever; it only means that they no longer block our progress toward inner freedom. If we do not wish to be confounded by suffering and we want to put it to the best use as a catalyst, we must not allow anxiety and despondency to conquer our mind. The eighth-century master Shantideva writes: "If there is a cure, what good is discontent? If there is no cure, what good is discontent?"

MANAGING SUFFERING

If it is possible to relieve mental anguish by transforming one's mind, how can this process be applied to physical suffering? How do we endure crippling, virtually intolerable pain? Here again we should distinguish between two types of suffering: physiological pain and the mental and emotional suffering it unleashes. There are certainly a number of ways to experience the same pain with more or less intensity.

Neurologically, we know, emotional reactions to pain vary significantly from person to person, and a considerable percentage of pain sensation is linked to the anxious desire to suppress it. If we allow that anxiety to overwhelm our mind, the most benign pain will soon become unbearable. So our assessment of pain also depends on our mind. It is the mind that reacts to pain with fear, rejection, despondency, or a feeling of powerlessness; instead of being subjected to a single agony, we accumulate a host of them.

Having come to grips with this idea, how do we learn to control pain instead of being its victim? Since we can't escape it, it is better to embrace it than to try to reject it. The pain persists whether we succumb to dejection or hold on to our resilience and desire to live, but in the latter case we maintain our dignity and self-confidence, and that makes a big difference.

There are various methods to achieve that end. One method uses mental imagery; another lets us transform pain by awakening ourselves to love and compassion; a third involves developing inner strength.

THE POWER OF IMAGES

Buddhism has traditionally turned to what modern psychology calls mental imagery to modify the perception of pain. We may visualize, for instance, a soothing, luminous nectar that soaks into the center of pain and gradually dissolves it into a feeling of well-being. The nectar then permeates our entire body and the pain fades away.

A synthesis of the results published in some fifty scientific articles has demonstrated that in 85 percent of cases recourse to mental methods enhances the capacity to endure pain.[4] Among these diverse techniques, mental imagery has proven to be the most effective, although its efficacy varies depending on the visual support. For instance, one may visualize a neutral situation or a pleasant one, such as a beautiful landscape. There are other ways for a patient to be distracted from pain, such as concentrating on an exterior object (watching a slide show, for instance), practicing a repetitive exercise (counting from one hundred to zero by threes), or consciously accepting the pain. The three methods cited, however, yield inferior results. The disparity is explained by the fact that mental imaging is a greater focuser of attention than methods based on exterior images, intellectual exercises, or an attitude. A group of researchers has found that within a month of guided practice of mental imaging, 21 percent of patients claim a notable improvement in their chronic migraines, as opposed to 7 percent of the control group that did not undergo training.[5]

EXERCISE

Using mental imagery

When a powerful feeling of desire, envy, pride, aggression, or greed plagues your mind, try to imagine situations that are sources of peace. Transport yourself mentally to the shores of a placid lake or to a high mountaintop overlooking a broad vista. Imagine yourself sitting serenely, your mind as vast and clear as a cloudless sky, as calm as a windless ocean. Experience this calmness. Watch your inner tempests subside and let this feeling of peace grow anew in your mind. Understand that even if your wounds are deep, they do not touch the essential nature of your mind, the fundamental luminosity of pure consciousness.

THE POWER OF COMPASSION

Another method that allows us to manage suffering, emotional as well as physical, is linked to the practice of compassion. Through compassion we take control of our own suffering, linked to that of all others, in the thought that "others besides me are afflicted by similar hardships to mine, and sometimes far worse. How I wish that they too could be free of their pain." After that, our pain does not feel as oppressive, and we stop asking the bitter question: "Why me?"

But why should we deliberately dwell on other people's suffering when we go to such extremes to avoid our own? In so doing, aren't we pointlessly increasing our own burden? We are not. When we are completely self-absorbed, we are vulnerable and fall easy prey to confusion, impotence, and anxiety. But when we experience a powerful sense of empathy with the suffering of others, our impotent resignation gives way to courage, depression to love, narrow-mindedness to openness toward all those around us. Increasing compassion and loving-kindness, the ultimate in positive emotions, develops our readiness to offer relief to the suffering of others while reducing the importance of our own problems.

DEVELOPING INNER STRENGTH

When we feel severe physical or emotional pain, we may simply look at the experience. Even when it is crippling, we must ponder whether it has any color, shape, or any other immutable characteristic. We find that the more we try to bring it into focus, the more the pain's definition becomes blurred. Ultimately we come to see that behind the pain there is a pristine awareness that does not change and that is beyond pain and pleasure. We may then relax our mind and try to allow our pain to rest in that state of pure awareness. This will allow us to stop being the passive victim of pain and to resist or reverse its devastation of our mind.

After the Chinese invasion of Tibet in 1959, Tenzin Choedrak, the personal physician of the Dalai Lama, was first sent to a forced labor camp in northeastern Tibet along with some one hundred others. Five prisoners, himself among them, survived. He was transferred from camp to camp for nearly twenty years and often thought that he would die of hunger or of the abuse inflicted on him.[6] A psychiatrist who specializes in post-traumatic stress and who treated Doctor Choedrak was astonished that he showed not the least sign of post-traumatic stress syndrome. He was not bitter, felt no resentment, displayed serene kindness, and had none of the usual psychological problems, such as anxiety, nightmares, and so on. Choedrak acknowledged that he occasionally felt hatred for his torturers, but that he always returned to the practice of meditation on inner peace and compassion. That was what sustained his desire to go on living and ultimately saved him.

Another example of someone who underwent physical ordeals that were scarcely imaginable is Ani Pachen. After twenty-one years in detention, Ani Pachen, a Tibetan princess, nun, and member of the resistance, was held in total darkness for nine months.[7] Only the birdsong that penetrated her cell allowed her to tell day from night. She insisted that while she certainly was not "happy" in the usual sense of the word, she was able to sustain the main aspects of sukha by looking within and relating again and again to her meditation practice and to her

spiritual teacher, by contemplating the meaning of impermanence and of the laws of cause and effect, and by becoming
more aware than ever of the devastating consequences of hatred, greed, and lack of compassion.

We are not talking here about an intellectual and moral
stance that differs culturally and philosophically from our own,
and which we could debate endlessly. The people just described
are proof that it is possible to maintain sukha even under repeated torture. They lived this experience for years on end, and
the authenticity of that experience is far more powerful than
any theory.

Another example is that of a man I have known for twenty
years who lives in Bumthang province at the heart of the Himalayan kingdom of Bhutan. He was born without arms or
legs, and he lives on the outskirts of a village in a little bamboo
hut of just a few square yards. He never goes out and barely
moves from his mattress on the floor. He came from Tibet forty
years ago, carried by fellow refugees, and has lived in this hut
ever since. The mere fact that he is still alive is extraordinary in
itself, but even more striking is the joy that radiates from him.
Every time I see him, he is in the same serene, simple, gentle,
and unaffected frame of mind. When we bring him small gifts
of food, blankets, a portable radio, he says that there was no
need to bring him anything. "What could I possibly need?" he
laughs.

There is usually somebody from the village to be found in
his cabin — a child, an elder, a man or woman who has brought
him water, a meal, some gossip. Most of all, they say, they come
because it does them good to spend a little time in his company.
They ask his advice. When a problem arises in the village, they
usually come to him to solve it.

Dilgo Khyentse Rinpoche, my spiritual father, would sometimes stop and visit him when he passed through Bumthang.

He would give him his blessing because our friend asked for it, but Khyentse Rinpoche knew that it was certainly less necessary for him than for most. The man had found happiness within himself, and nothing could take it from him.

EXERCISE
Training in the exchange of happiness and suffering
Begin by generating a powerful feeling of warmth, loving-kindness, and compassion for all beings. Then imagine those who are enduring suffering similar to or worse than your own. As you breathe out, visualize that you are sending them all your happiness, vitality, good fortune, health, and so on, on your breath in the form of cool, white, luminous nectar. Picture them fully absorbing the nectar, which soothes their pain and fulfills their aspirations. If their life is in danger of being cut short, imagine that it has been prolonged; if they are sick, imagine that they are healed; if they are poor and helpless, imagine that they have obtained what they need; if they are unhappy, that they have become full of joy.

When you inhale, visualize your heart as a bright, luminous sphere. Imagine that you are taking upon yourself, in the form of a gray cloud, the disease, confusion, and mental toxins of these people, which disappears into the white light of your heart without leaving any trace. This will transform both your own suffering and that of others. There is no sense that you are being burdened by them. When you are taking upon yourself and dissolving their sufferings, feel a great happiness, without attachment or clinging.

You can also imagine that your body is duplicating itself in countless forms that travel throughout the universe, transforming itself into clothing for those who are cold, food for the famished, or shelter for the homeless.

This visualization is a powerful means to develop benevolence and compassion. It can be carried out anytime and during your day-to-day activities. It does not require you to neglect your own well-being; instead it allows you to adjust your reaction to unavoidable suffering by assigning a new value to it. In fact, identifying clearly your own aspiration to well-being is the first step toward feeling genuine empathy for others' suffering. Furthermore, this attitude significantly increases your enthusiasm and readiness to work for the good of others.

7

The Veils of the Ego

First we conceive the "I" and grasp onto it.
Then we conceive the "mine" and cling to the material world.
Like water trapped on a waterwheel, we spin in circles, powerless.
I praise the compassion that embraces all beings.

CHANDRAKIRTI

Mental confusion is a veil that prevents us from seeing reality clearly and clouds our understanding of the true nature of things. Practically speaking, it is also the inability to identify the behavior that would allow us to find happiness and avoid suffering. When we look outward, we solidify the world by projecting onto it attributes that are in no way inherent to it. Looking inward, we freeze the flow of consciousness when we conceive of an "I" enthroned between a past that no longer exists and a future that does not yet exist. We take it for granted that we see things as they are and rarely question that opinion. We spontaneously assign intrinsic qualities to things and people, thinking "this is beautiful, that is ugly," without realizing that our mind superimposes these attributes upon what we perceive. We divide the entire world between "desirable" and "undesirable," we ascribe permanence to ephemera and see independent entities in what is actually a network of ceaselessly changing relations. We tend to isolate particular aspects of events, situations, and people, and to focus entirely upon these particularities. This is how we end up labeling others as "enemies," "good," "evil," et cetera, and clinging strongly to those attributions. However, if we consider reality carefully, its complexity becomes obvious.

If one thing were truly beautiful and pleasant, if those qualities genuinely belonged to it, we could consider it desirable at all times and in all places. But is anything on earth universally and unanimously recognized as beautiful? As the canonical Buddhist verse has it: "For the lover, a beautiful woman is an object of desire; for the hermit, a distraction; for the wolf, a good meal." Likewise, if an object were inherently repulsive, everyone would have good reason to avoid it. But it changes everything to recognize that we are merely *attributing* these qualities to things and people. There is no intrinsic quality in a beautiful object that makes it beneficial to the mind, and nothing in an ugly object to harm it.

In the same way, a person whom we consider today to be an enemy is most certainly somebody else's object of affection, and we may one day forge bonds of friendship with that selfsame enemy. We react as if characteristics were inseparable from the object we assign them to. Thus we distance ourselves from reality and are dragged into the machinery of attraction and repulsion that is kept relentlessly in motion by our mental projections. Our concepts freeze things into artificial entities and we lose our inner freedom, just as water loses its fluidity when it turns to ice.

THE CRYSTALLIZATION OF THE EGO

Among the many aspects of our confusion, the most radically disruptive is the insistence on the concept of a personal identity: the ego. Buddhism distinguishes between an innate, instinctive "I" — when we think, for instance, "I'm awake" or "I'm cold" — and a conceptual "self" shaped by the force of habit. We attribute various qualities to it and posit it as the core of our being, autonomous and enduring.

At every moment between birth and death, the body undergoes ceaseless transformations and the mind becomes the theater of countless emotional and conceptual experiences. And yet we obstinately assign qualities of permanence, uniqueness, and autonomy to the self. Furthermore, as we begin to feel that this self is highly vulnerable and must be protected and satisfied, aversion and attraction soon come into play — aversion for anything that threatens the self, attraction to all that pleases it, comforts it, boosts its confidence, or puts it at ease. These two basic feelings, attraction and repulsion, are the fonts of a whole sea of conflicting emotions.

The ego, writes Buddhist philosopher Han de Wit, "is also an affective reaction to our field of experience, a mental withdrawal based on *fear.*"[1] Out of fear of the world and of others, out of dread of suffering, out of anxiety about living and dying, we imagine that by hiding inside a bubble — the ego — we will be protected. We create the illusion of being separate from the world, hoping thereby to avert suffering. In fact, what happens is just the opposite, since ego-grasping and self-importance are the best magnets to attract suffering.

Genuine fearlessness arises with the confidence that we will be able to gather the inner resources necessary to deal with any situation that comes our way. This is altogether different from withdrawing into self-absorption, a fearful reaction that perpetuates deep feelings of insecurity.

Each of us is indeed a unique person, and it is fine to recognize and appreciate who we are. But in reinforcing the separate identity of the self, we fall out of sync with reality. The truth is, we are fundamentally interdependent with other people and our environment. Our experience is simply the content of the mental flow, the continuum of consciousness, and there is no justification for seeing the self as an entirely distinct entity within that flow. Imagine a spreading wave that affects its environment and is affected by it but is not the medium of transmission for any particular entity. We are so accustomed to affixing the "I" label to that mental flow, however, that we come to identify with it and to fear its disappearance. There follows a powerful attachment to the self and thus to the notion of "mine" — *my* body, *my* name, *my* mind, *my* possessions, *my* friends, and so on — which leads either to the desire to possess or to the feeling of repulsion for the "other."

This is how the concepts of the self and of the other crystallize in our minds. The erroneous sense of duality becomes inevitable, forming the basis of all mental affliction, be it alienating desire, hatred, jealousy, pride, or selfishness. From that point on, we see the world through the distorting mirror of our illusions. We find ourselves in disharmony with the true nature of things, which inevitably leads to frustration and suffering.

We can see this crystallization of "I" and "mine" in many situations of daily life. You are napping peacefully in a boat in the middle of a lake. Another craft bumps into yours and wakes you with a start. Thinking that a clumsy or prankish boater has crashed into you, you leap up furious, ready to curse him out, only to find that the boat in question is empty. You laugh at your own mistake and return peaceably to your nap. The *only* difference between the two reactions is that in the first case, you'd thought yourself the target of someone's malice, while in the second you realized that your "I" was not a target.

Likewise, if someone punches you, your irritation will be long-lasting. But consider the physical pain — it fades quickly and is soon imperceptible. The only thing that continues to hurt is the ego's wound. A friend of mine had come to Nepal from Hong Kong to attend some teachings. Thousands of people had gathered and were jam-packed on the floor of our monastery's vast courtyard. As my friend was moving back and forth trying to seat herself a bit more comfortably, cross-legged on her cushion, someone punched her in the back. As she told me later: "I felt irritated for a whole hour. How could someone attending Buddhist teachings behave in such a rude and un-compassionate way toward me, who had come so far to receive these teachings! But after a while I realized that although my ir-ritation had been long-lasting, the actual physical pain had faded quickly and had soon become imperceptible. The only thing that continued to hurt was my wounded ego! I had one minute of body pain and fifty-nine minutes of ego pain!" When we see the self as a mere concept and not as an autonomous en-tity that we must protect and satisfy at all costs, we react in completely different ways.

Here is another example to illustrate our attachment to the idea of "mine." You are looking at a beautiful porcelain vase in a shopwindow when a clumsy salesman knocks it over. "What a shame! Such a lovely vase!" you sigh, and continue calmly on your way. On the other hand, if you had just bought that vase and had placed it proudly on the mantle, only to see it fall and smash to smithereens, you would cry out in horror, "My vase is broken!" and be deeply affected by the accident. The sole dif-ference is the label "my" that you had stuck to the vase.

This erroneous sense of a real and independent self is of course based on egocentricity, which persuades us that our own fate is of greater value than that of others. If your boss scolds a colleague you hate, berates another you have no feelings about, or reprimands you bitterly, you will feel pleased or delighted in the first case, indifferent in the second, and deeply hurt in the third. But in reality, what could possibly make the well-being of any one of these three people more valuable than that of the others? The egocentricity that places the self at the center of the world has an entirely *relative* point of view. Our mistake is in fixing our own point of view and hoping, or worse yet, insisting, that "our" world prevail over that of others.

On a visit to Mexico, the Dalai Lama was shown a map of the world and told: "If you look at how the continents are arranged, you'll see that Mexico is at the center of the world." (When I was a child, a Breton friend of mine told me that the little island of Dumet was the center of the known world!) The Dalai Lama answered: "If you follow that line of reasoning, you'll find that Mexico City is at the center of Mexico, my house is at the center of the city, my family is at the center of the house, and within my family *I* am the center of the world."

WHAT TO DO WITH THE EGO?

Unlike Buddhism, very few psychological treatments address the problem of how to reduce the feeling of self-centeredness — a reduction that, for the wise man, extends all the way to eradicating the ego. This is certainly a new, even subversive idea in the West, which holds the self to be the fundamental building block of the personality. Surely, if I eliminate my ego I will cease to exist as a person. How can you have an individual without an I, an ego? Isn't such a concept psychically dangerous? Isn't there a risk of sinking into some kind of schizophrenia? Isn't a weak or nonexistent ego the clinical sign of a potentially forceful pathology? Don't you need a fully developed personality before you can renounce the ego? These are the kinds of defensive reactions most Westerners have to such unfamiliar notions. The idea that one needs a robust ego comes from the fact that some people who suffer from mental problems are said to have a fragmented, fragile, or deficient sense of self.

The psychology of infancy describes how a baby learns about the world; how she figures out her relationship to her mother, her father, and those around her; how, at the age of one, she comes to understand that she and her mother are two distinct beings, that the world is not simply an extension of herself, and that she can be the cause of unfolding events. This growing awareness is called psychological birth. That is when we begin to see the individual as a personality, ideally stable, self-assured, and anchored to its belief in the existence of its self. Parental and then academic education reinforce that notion, which is prevalent throughout our literature and our history. In a way, you might say that the belief in an established self is one of the dominant characteristics of our civilization. Do we not speak of building strong, resilient, adaptable, and assertive personalities?

This confuses ego and self-confidence. The ego can attain only a contrived confidence built on insubstantial attributes — power, success, beauty and physical strength, intellectual brilliance, the opinions of others — and on whatever we believe to constitute our "identity," our image, as we see it and as others see it. When things change and the gap with reality becomes too wide, the ego becomes irritated, freezes up, and falters. Self-confidence collapses and all that is left is frustration and suffering.

For Buddhism, paradoxically, genuine self-confidence is the *natural quality of egolessness.* To dispel the illusion of the ego is to free oneself from a fundamental vulnerability. The fact is, the sense of security derived from that illusion is eminently fragile. Genuine confidence comes from an awareness of a basic quality of our mind and of our potential for transformation and flourishing, what Buddhism calls buddha nature, which is present in all of us. Such recognition imparts peaceful strength that cannot be threatened by external circumstances or inner fears, a freedom that transcends self-absorption and anxiety.

Another widespread idea is that without a vigorous sense of self we would barely feel emotions and life would become incredibly dreary. We would lack creativity, the spirit of adventure — in a word, personality. Think about those around you who are endowed with a well-developed, not to say hyperdeveloped, ego. There are plenty to choose from. On the other hand, who are the people who, though differing in sex, age, and race, have manifested a genuine inner confidence that is not based on an "oversized" ego? Socrates, the Buddha, Jesus, Gandhi, Martin Luther King, Mother Teresa, the Dalai Lama, Nelson Mandela, and countless unsung heroes working in anonymity. Is there really any need to explain the difference?

Experience tells us that those who have managed, even partially, to free themselves of the ego's diktat think and act with spontaneity and freedom. This is in contrast with the constant paranoia provoked by the whims of a triumphant sense of self. Paul Ekman, one of the world's specialists in the science of emotion, has been inspired to study "people gifted with exceptionally human qualities." Among the most remarkable traits shared by such people, he notes, are "an impression of kindness, a way of being that others can sense and appreciate, and, unlike so many charismatic charlatans, perfect harmony between their private and public lives." They emanate goodness.

Above all, writes Ekman, they exhibit "an absence of ego. These people inspire others by how little they make of their status, their fame — in short, their self. They never give a second thought to whether their position or importance is recognized." Such a lack of egocentricity, he adds, "is altogether perplexing from a psychological point of view." Ekman also stresses how "people instinctively want to be in their company and how, even if they can't always explain why, they find their presence enriching. In essence, they emanate goodness."[2] Such qualities offer a striking contrast to the champions of the ego, whose presence can be really aggravating. Between the theatrics and occasional ferocity of the rampant ego and the warm simplicity of the egoless, the choice is not a hard one.

Psychopaths, who are unable to feel any empathy for others or any regret for the suffering they inflict upon them, are also ego-supremacists. As Aaron Beck, the founder of cognitive therapy, observes: "Professionals who have worked with psychopaths have been struck by their extreme egocentricity. They are totally self-serving, feel that they are superior to others, and, above all, think that they have innate rights and prerogatives that transcend or preempt those of other people."[3]

The idea that a powerful ego is necessary to succeed in life undoubtedly stems from the confusion between attachment to our own image and the resolve to achieve our deepest aspirations. The fact is, the less influenced we are by the sense of our self's importance, the easier it is to acquire lasting inner strength. The reason for this is simple: self-importance is a target open to all sorts of mental projectiles — jealousy, fear, greed, repulsion — that perpetually destabilize it.

THE DECEPTIVE EGO

In our day-to-day lives, we experience the self through its vulnerability. A simple smile gives it instant pleasure and a scowl achieves the contrary. The self is always "there," ready to be wounded or gratified. Rather than seeing it as multiple and elusive, we make it a unitary, central, and permanent bastion. But let's consider what it is we suppose contributes to our identity. Our body? An assemblage of bones and flesh. Our consciousness? A continuous stream of instants. Our history? The memory of what is no more. Our name? We attach all sorts of concepts to it — our heritage, our reputation, and our social status — but ultimately it's nothing more than a grouping of letters. When we see the word JOHN, our spirits leap, we think, "That's me!" But we only need to separate the letters, J-O-H-N, to lose all interest. The idea of "our" name is just a mental fabrication.

It is the deep sense of self lying at the heart of our being that we have to examine honestly. When we explore the body, the speech, and the mind, we come to see that this self is nothing but a word, a label, a convention, a designation. The problem is, this label thinks it's the real deal. To unmask the ego's deception, we have to pursue our inquiry to the very end. When you suspect the presence of a thief in your house, you have to inspect every room, every corner, every potential hiding place, just to make sure there's really no one there. Only then can you rest easy. We need introspective investigation to find out what's hiding behind the illusion of the self that we think defines our being.

Rigorous analysis leads us to conclude that the self does not reside in any part of the body, nor is it some diffuse entity permeating the entire body. We willingly believe that the self is associated with consciousness, but consciousness too is an elusive current: in terms of living experience, the past moment of consciousness is dead (only its *impact* remains), the future is not yet, and the present doesn't last. How could a distinct self exist, suspended like a flower in the sky, between something that no longer exists and something that does not yet exist? It cannot be detected in either the body or the mind; it is neither a distinct entity in a combination of the two, nor one outside of them. No serious analysis or direct introspective experience can lead to a strong conviction that we possess a self. Someone may believe himself to be tall, young, and intelligent, but neither height nor youth nor intelligence is the self. Buddhism therefore concludes that the self is just a name we give to a *continuum,* just as we name a river the Ganges or the Mississippi. Such a continuum certainly exists, but only as a convention based upon the interdependence of the consciousness, the body, and the environment. It is entirely without autonomous existence.

THE DECONSTRUCTION OF THE SELF

To get a better handle on this, let's resume our analysis in greater detail. The concept of personal identity has three aspects: the "I," the "person," and the "self." These three aspects are not fundamentally different from one another, but reflect the different ways we cling to our perception of personal identity.

The "I" lives in the present; it is the "I" that thinks "I'm hungry" or "I exist." It is the locus of consciousness, thoughts, judgment, and will. It is the experience of our current state.

As the neuropsychiatrist David Galin clearly summarizes, the notion of the "person" is broader. It is a dynamic continuum extending through time and incorporating various aspects of our corporeal, mental, and social existence.[4] Its boundaries are more fluid. The person can refer to the body ("personal fitness"), intimate thoughts ("a very personal feeling"), character ("a nice person"), social relations ("separating one's personal from one's professional life"), or the human being in general ("respect for one's person"). Its continuity through time allows us to link the representations of ourselves from the past to projections into the future. It denotes how each of us differs from others and reflects our unique qualities. The notion of the person is valid and healthy so long as we consider it simply as connoting the overall relationship between the consciousness, the body, and the environment. It becomes inappropriate and unhealthy when we consider it to be an autonomous entity.

As to the "self," we've already seen how it is believed to be the very core of our being. We imagine it as an invisible and permanent thing that characterizes us from birth to death. The self is not merely the sum of "my" limbs, "my" organs, "my" skin, "my" name, "my" consciousness, but their exclusive owner. We speak of "my arm" and not of an "elongated extension of my self." If our arm is cut off, the self has simply lost an arm but remains intact. A person without limbs feels his physical integrity to be diminished, but clearly believes he has preserved his self. If the body is cut into cross sections, at what point does the self begin to vanish? We perceive a self so long as we retain the power of thought. This leads us to Descartes' celebrated phrase underlying the entire Western concept of the self: "I think, therefore I am." But the fact of thought proves absolutely nothing about the existence of the self, because the "I" is nothing more than the current contents of our mental flow, which changes from moment to moment. It is not enough for something to be perceived or conceived of for that thing to exist. We clearly see a mirage or an illusion, neither of which has any reality.

The idea that the self might be nothing but a concept runs counter to the intuition of most Western thinkers. Descartes, again, is categorical on the subject. "When I consider my mind — that is, myself, given that I am merely a thing that thinks — I can identify no distinct parts to it, but conceive of myself as a single and complete thing." The neurologist Charles Scott Sherrington adds: "The self is a unity. . . . It regards itself as one, others treat it as one. It is addressed as one, by a name to which it answers."[5] Indisputably, we instinctively see the self as unitary, but as soon as we try to pin it down, we have a hard time coming to grips with it.

IN SEARCH OF THE LOST SELF

Where then is the self? It cannot be exclusively in my body, because when I say "I am proud," it is my consciousness that is proud, not my body. So is it exclusively in my consciousness? That is far from certain. When I say: "Someone pushed me," was it my consciousness being pushed? Of course not. The self obviously cannot be outside the body and the consciousness. If it were an autonomous entity independent of one and the other, it could not be of their essence. Is it simply, as we explained above, the sum of their parts, their structure and their continuity? Is the concept of the self simply associated with the body and the consciousness in their entirety? You may notice that we have begun to move away from the notion of the self as owner or essence, and toward a more abstract notion, a concept. The only way out of this dilemma is to consider the self as a *mental or verbal designation* linked to a dynamic process, to a series of changing relations that incorporate the perception of the outer world, sensations, mental images, emotions, and concepts. *The self is merely an idea.*

It emerges when we combine the "I," the experience of the present moment, with the "person," the continuity of our existence. As David Galin explains, we actually have an innate tendency to simplify complex groupings by making "entities" of them and then to conclude that these entities are enduring. It is easier to function in the world by taking for granted that most of our environment remains unchanging minute by minute and by treating most things as if they were more or less constant. I would lose all notion of what "my body" is were I to perceive it as a whirlwind of atoms that is never the same for even a millionth of a second. But how quickly I forget that my ordinary perception of my body and of all phenomena is just an approximation and that in fact *everything* is changing *at every moment.*

This is how we reify the self and the world. The self is not nonexistent — as we are constantly reminded by experience — but it exists as a concept. It is in that sense that Buddhism says that the self has no autonomy or permanence, that it is like a mirage. Seen from afar, the mirage of a lake seems real, but we would have a hard time wringing any water out of it. Things are neither as they appear to exist nor are they entirely nonexistent. Like an illusion, they appear without having any ultimate reality. This is how the Buddha taught it:

> *Like a shooting star, a mirage, a flame,*
> *A magic trick, a dewdrop, a water bubble,*
> *Like a dream, lightning, or a cloud —*
> *Consider all things thus.*

THE FRAGILE FACES OF IDENTITY

The notion of the "person" includes the image we keep of ourselves. The idea of our identity, our status in life, is deeply rooted in our mind and continuously influences our relations with others. The least word that threatens our image of ourselves is unbearable, although we have no trouble with the same qualifier applied to someone else in different circumstances. If you shout insults or flattery at a cliff and the words are echoed back to you, you remain unaffected. But if someone else shouts the very same insults at you, you feel deeply upset. If we have a strong image of ourselves, we will constantly be trying to assure ourselves that it is recognized and accepted. Nothing is more painful than to see it opened up to doubt.

But what is this identity worth? The word *personality* comes from the Latin *persona*, for an actor's mask — the mask through which (*per*) the actor's voice resounds (*sonat*). While the actor is aware of wearing a mask, we often forget to distinguish between the role we play in society and an honest appreciation of our state of being.

We are generally afraid to tackle the world without reference points and are seized with vertigo whenever masks and epithets come down. If I am no longer a musician, a writer, sophisticated, handsome, or strong, what am I? And yet flouting all labels is the best guarantee of freedom and the most flexible, lighthearted, and joyful way of moving through the world. Refusing to be deceived by the ego in no way prevents us from nurturing a firm resolve to achieve the goals we've set for ourselves and at every instant to relish the richness of our relations with the world and with others. The effect, in fact, is quite the contrary.

THROUGH THE INVISIBLE WALL

How can I expect this understanding of the illusory nature of the ego to change my relationships with my family and the world around me? Wouldn't such a U-turn be unsettling? Experience shows that it will do you nothing but good. Indeed when the ego is predominant, the mind is like a bird constantly slamming into a glass wall — belief in the ego — that shrinks our world and encloses it within narrow confines. Perplexed and stunned by the wall, the mind cannot pass through it. But the wall is invisible because it does not really exist. It is an invention of the mind. Nevertheless, it functions as a wall by partitioning our inner world and damming the flow of our selflessness and joie de vivre. Our attachment to the ego is fundamentally linked to the suffering we feel and the suffering we inflict on others. Renouncing our fixation on our own intimate image and stripping the ego of all its importance is tantamount to winning incredible inner freedom. It allows us to approach every person and every situation with natural ease, benevolence, fortitude, and serenity. With no expectation of gain and no fear of loss, we are free to give and to receive. We no longer have the need to think, speak, or act in an affected and selfish way.

In clinging to the cramped universe of the ego, we have a tendency to be concerned exclusively with ourselves. The least setback upsets and discourages us. We are obsessed with our success, our failure, our hopes, and our anxieties, and thereby give happiness every opportunity to elude us. The narrow world of the self is like a glass of water into which a handful of salt is thrown — the water becomes undrinkable. If, on the other hand, we breach the barriers of the self and the mind becomes a vast lake, that same handful of salt will have no affect on its taste.

When the self ceases to be the most important thing in the world, we find it easier to focus our concern on others. The sight of their suffering bolsters our courage and resolve to work on their behalf, instead of crippling us with our own emotional distress.

If the ego were really our deepest essence, it would be easy to understand our apprehension about dropping it. But if it is merely an illusion, ridding ourselves of it is not ripping the heart out of our being, but simply opening our eyes.

So it's worthwhile to devote a few moments of our life to

letting the mind rest in inner calm and to understanding, through analysis and direct experience, the place of the ego in our lives. So long as the sense of the ego's importance has control over our being, we will never know lasting peace. The very source of pain remains intact deep within us and deprives us of that most essential of freedoms.

8

WHEN OUR THOUGHTS BECOME
OUR WORST ENEMIES

When we are unhappy, we can't help thinking that certain
images are armed with claws and stingers to torture us with.

ALAIN

Stricken by the death of a loved one, distraught over a
breakup, laid low by failure, heartbroken by the suffering of
others, or consumed by negative thoughts, we sometimes get
the feeling that life as a whole is spinning apart. There seems to
be no safe way out at all. Sadness settles like a pall over the
mind. "Just one person has left us, and the world is emptied of
people," lamented Lamartine. Unable to imagine an end to our
pain, we withdraw into ourselves and dread every coming moment. "When I tried to think clearly about this, I felt that my
mind was immured, that it couldn't expand in any direction. I
knew that the sun was rising and setting, but little of its light
reached me," writes Andrew Solomon.[1] As harrowing as the
situation may be — the death of a close friend, for instance —
there are countless ways to experience the ordeal. Happiness is
bound up with distress when we lack adequate inner resources

to sustain certain basic elements of sukha: the joy of being alive, the conviction that we still have the ability to flourish, an understanding of the ephemeral nature of all things.

Great external upheavals aren't necessarily what distress us most. It has been observed that depression and suicide rates decline considerably in times of war. Natural disasters, too, sometimes bring out the best in humankind in terms of courage, solidarity, and the will to live. Altruism and mutual assistance contribute greatly to reducing the post-traumatic stress associated with tragedies. Most of the time it is not outward events but our own mind and negative emotions that make us unable to maintain our inner stability and drag us down.

The conflictive emotions tie knots in our chest that obstinately refuse to be unraveled. In vain we try to fight them or reduce them to silence. We've only just gotten out from under them, we imagine, when they erupt again with renewed vigor. Such emotional distress is notably resistant to soothing, and every attempt to be rid of it seems doomed to failure. During such conflicts, our world shatters into a multitude of contradictions that generate adversity, oppression, and anguish. What went wrong?

Thoughts can be our best friends and our worst enemies. When they make us feel that the entire world is against us, every perception, every encounter, and the world's very existence become sources of torment. It is our thoughts themselves that rise up as enemies. They stampede through our mind in droves, each one creating its own little drama of ever-increasing confusion. Nothing is right outside because nothing is right inside.

When we get a close look at the tenor of our everyday thoughts, we realize the extent to which they color the inner film that we project onto the world. The worrier fears the least event — if he needs to take a plane, he thinks it will crash; if he has to drive, he'll have an accident; if he's seeing the doctor, he's sure he has cancer. For a jealous man, his lover's most innocuous travels are suspect, the smile directed elsewhere is a source of pain, and the least absence sends a host of senseless doubts raging through his mind. For these two subjects, as for the hot-tempered, the miserly, the obsessive, thoughts swell into daily tempests that cast a shadow over life by destroying their own joie de vivre and that of the people around them.

Yet this knot in our chest was tied not by our unfaithful husband, our object of desire, our dishonest colleague, or our unjust accuser, but by our own mind. It is the result of mental constructs that, as they accumulate and solidify, give the illusion of being external and real. What provides the raw material for that knot and allows it to form within us is an exacerbated sense of self-importance. Anything that does not respond to the self's demands becomes a disturbance, a threat, or an insult. The past is painful, we are unable to enjoy the present, and we tremble before the projection of our future anguish. According to Andrew Solomon, "In depression, all that is happening in the present is the anticipation of pain in the future, and the present qua present no longer exists at all."[2] The inability to manage our thoughts proves to be the principal cause of suffering. Learning to tone down the ceaseless racket of disturbing thoughts is a decisive stage on the road to inner peace. As Dilgo Khyentse Rinpoche explains:

> These trains of thought and states of mind are constantly changing, like the shapes of clouds in the wind, but we attach great importance to them. An old man watching children at play knows very well that their games are of little consequence. He feels neither elated nor upset at

*what happens in their game, while the children take it all
very seriously. We are just exactly them.*[3]

We must acknowledge that so long as we have not actualized sukha, our well-being is at the mercy of the storm. We can
respond to heartbreaks by trying to forget them, distracting
ourselves, moving away, going on a trip, and so on, but these
are merely plaster casts on a wooden leg. As Nicolas Boileau
put it:

*In vain he flees his troubles on a horse —
They share the saddle and see him on his course.*[4]

FIRST THINGS FIRST

How do we go about making peace with our own emotions?
First, we have to focus our mind on the raw power of inner suffering. Instead of avoiding it or burying it away in some dark
corner of our mind, we should make it the object of our meditation, without ruminating over the events that caused the pain
or reviewing every freeze-frame from the movie of our life.
Why is it unnecessary at this stage to dwell on the distant
causes of our suffering? The Buddha offered the following image. Will a man who has just been struck in the chest by an arrow ask himself, "What wood is the arrow made of? What kind
of bird do the feathers come from? What craftsman made it?
Was he a good man or a scoundrel?" He certainly won't. His
first concern will be to tear the arrow from his chest.

When a painful emotion strikes us, the most urgent thing is
to look at it head-on and to identify the immediate thoughts
that triggered and are fanning it. Then by fixing our inner gaze
on the emotion itself, we can gradually dissolve it like snow in
sunshine. Furthermore, once the strength of the emotion has

been sapped, the causes that triggered it will seem less tragic and we will have won ourselves the chance to break free from the vicious circle of negative thoughts.

CONTEMPLATING THE NATURE OF THE MIND

How can we prevent the perpetual reemergence of disturbing thoughts? If we resign ourselves to being the perpetual victims of our thoughts, we are like dogs who run after every stick thrown for them. Closely identifying with every thought, we follow it and reinforce it with boundless emotional entanglements.

So we need to take a closer look at mind itself. The first things we notice are the currents of thought that are continuously flowing without our even being aware of them. Like it or not, countless thoughts born of our sensations, our memories, and our imagination are forever streaming through our mind. But there is also a quality of mind that is always present no matter what kind of thoughts we entertain. That quality is the primary consciousness underlying all thought. It is what remains in the rare moment when the mind is at rest, almost motionless, even as it retains its ability to know. That faculty, that simple open presence, is what we may call *pure consciousness,* because it exists even in the absence of mental constructs.

In pursuing the mind's observation of itself even further, we will find ourselves experiencing this pure consciousness and the thoughts that emerge from it. It does exist. But what else can we say besides that? Do these thoughts have any inherent characteristics? Do they have a particular localization? No. A color? A shape? Neither. All we find is the quality of *knowing,* but no intrinsic features of their own. In pure consciousness we experience the mind as empty of inherent existence. This notion of emptiness of thought is undoubtedly very foreign to

Western psychology. What purpose does it serve? First of all, when a powerful emotion or thought arises — anger, for instance — what normally occurs? We are very easily overwhelmed by this thought, which multiplies into numerous new thoughts that disturb and blind us, and prompt us to utter words and commit acts, sometimes violent ones, that can make others suffer and soon become a source of regret. Instead of unleashing that avalanche, we can examine the angry thought itself and come to see that it has been nothing but smoke and mirrors from the start.

Thoughts emerge from pure consciousness and are then reabsorbed in it, just as waves emerge from the ocean and dissolve into it again. Once we understand this, we have taken a great leap toward inner peace. From that moment, our thoughts have lost much of their power to disturb us. To familiarize yourself with this method, when a thought arises, try to see where it came from; when it disappears, ask yourself where it went. In that brief moment when your mind is not encumbered by discursive thoughts, contemplate its nature. In that instant when past thoughts have fallen silent and future ones have yet to emerge, you can perceive a pure and luminous consciousness unadulterated by your conceptual constructs. Proceeding by direct experience, you will gradually come to understand what Buddhism means by the nature of mind.

It is not easy to experience pure consciousness, but it is possible. My dearly missed friend Francisco Varela, a leading researcher in the cognitive sciences and practitioner of Buddhist meditation, confided in me, when we spoke at length a few weeks before his death of cancer, that he had lately managed to spend practically all his time in that pure awareness. The physical pain seemed very distant to him and was no hindrance to his inner peace. Moreover he needed only the weakest doses of painkillers. His wife, Amy, told me later that he maintained that contemplative serenity until his very last breath.

Exercise

Resting in awareness

Look at what is behind the curtain of discursive thoughts. Try to find a waking presence there, free of mental fabrications, transparent, luminous, untroubled by thoughts of the past, the present, or the future. Try to rest in the present moment, free of concepts. Watch the nature of the gap between thoughts, which is free from mental constructs. Gradually extend the interval between the disappearance of one thought and the emergence of the next.

Remain in a state of simplicity that is free of mental constructs, yet perfectly aware; beyond effort, yet alert and mindful.

As you thus observe the wellspring of thoughts, it is possible to break their endless proliferation.

Having More Than One String to Your Bow

As the pain that afflicts us grows stronger, our mental universe contracts. Events and thoughts continually rebound off the walls of our circumscribed inner prison. They speed up and gather force, every ricochet inflicting new wounds. We must therefore broaden our inner horizons to the point where there are no walls for negative emotion to bounce off of. When these walls, built brick by brick by the self, come tumbling down, suffering's bullets will miss their mark and vanish in the vast openness of inner freedom. We realize that our suffering was simply forgetfulness of our true nature, which remains unchanged beneath the fog of emotions. It is essential to develop and sustain this broadening of the inner horizons. External events and thoughts will then emerge like stars that reflect off the calm surface of a vast ocean without disturbing it.

One of the best ways to achieve that state is to meditate on feelings that transcend our mental afflictions. If, for instance, we gradually let our mind be invaded by a feeling of love and compassion for *all* beings, the warmth of such a thought will very likely melt the ice of our frustrations, while its gentleness will cool the fire of our desires. We will have succeeded in raising ourselves above our personal pain to the point where it becomes almost imperceptible.

EXERCISE

When you feel overwhelmed by emotions

Imagine a stormy sea with breakers as big as houses. Each wave is more monstrous than the last. They are about to engulf your boat, your very life hangs on those few extra yards in the rushing wall of water. Then imagine observing the same scene from a high-flying plane. From that perspective, the waves seem to form a delicate blue-and-white mosaic, barely trembling on the surface of the water. From that height in the silence of space, your eye sees these almost motionless patterns, and your mind immerses itself in clear and luminous sky.

The waves of anger or obsession seem real enough, but remind yourself that they are merely fabrications of your mind; that they will rise and also again disappear. Why stay on the boat of mental anxiety? Make your mind as vast as the sky and you will find that the waves of afflictive emotions have lost all the strength you had attributed to them.

WHY BLAME THE ENTIRE WORLD?

It is tempting to systematically pass the blame on to the world and other people. When we feel anxious, depressed, cranky, envious, or emotionally exhausted, we're quick to pass the buck to the outside world; tensions with colleagues at work, arguments with our spouse — anything, even the color of the sky, can be a source of upset. This reflex is far more than a mere psychological evasion. It reflects the mistaken perception that causes us to attribute inherent qualities to external objects when in fact those qualities are *dependent* on our own minds. Systematically blaming others and holding them responsible for our suffering is the surest way to lead an unhappy life. It is by transforming our minds that we can transform our world.

We should not underestimate the consequences of our acts, words, and thoughts. If we sow the seeds of poisonous plants along with those of flowers, we should not be surprised when the harvest is mixed. If we alternate between selfless and harmful behaviors, we ought to expect to get a sharply contrasting blend of joys and sufferings.

It is easier to work with the disturbing effects of a strong emotion when we are in the midst of experiencing it, rather than when it lies dormant in the shadow of our unconscious. At the precise moment of the experience, we will have an invaluable opportunity to investigate the process of mental suffering.

To cite a personal example, I am not by nature an angry person, but over the course of the past twenty years, the times that I have lost my temper have taught me more about the nature of that destructive emotion than years of tranquillity. As the saying goes, "A single dog barking makes more noise than a hundred silent dogs." In the 1980s, I had just acquired my first laptop computer, which I used to translate Tibetan texts. One morning as I was working, sitting on the wooden floor in a monastery at the far end of Bhutan, a friend thought it would make a cute joke to spill a handful of *tsampa* (roast barley flour) on my keyboard as he passed by. I saw red and shot him a filthy look, saying, "Was that supposed to be funny?" Seeing that I was truly angry, he stopped and tersely replied, "One moment of anger can destroy years of patience." His gesture hadn't been especially clever, but he was essentially right.

Another time, in Nepal, a person who had swindled the monastery of a large sum of money came by to lecture me on morality. Again my blood boiled. My voice trembling with anger, I told her to get lost, and helped her out the door with a nudge. At the time, I was convinced that my anger was perfectly justified. It was only hours later that I came to see how destructive an emotion anger really is, reducing our clarity and inner peace and turning us into veritable puppets.

More constructive responses to these events would have been, in the first case, to simply explain to my friend how useful the laptop was for my work and how fragile it was, and in the second case, to firmly remind the person of the sheer facts, try to understand what was going on in her disturbed mind, and if possible gently help her out of her confusion.

Cultivating Serenity

In Tibet in the 1820s, a bandit much feared for his cruelty once came to the cave of the hermit Jigme Gyalwai Nyugu, intending to steal his meager provisions. Entering the cave, he found himself in the presence of a serene old man meditating with his eyes closed, his hair a mane of white, his face radiating peace, love, and compassion. At the very moment when the thief saw the sage, his aggression vanished and he stood several minutes watching him with wonder. Then he withdrew after asking the sage for his blessing. From then on, whenever the thief saw the opportunity to do wrong to anyone, the serene face of the white-haired old man came to his mind and he abandoned his evil plan. Visualizing such scenes is not about having fun with autosuggestion, but about being in resonance with the basic goodness lying at our very core.

The Power of Experience

When we emerge from that moment of blindness during which we are completely in the grip of a strong emotion, and our mind has been freed from its disruptive emotional burden, it is hard to believe that an emotion had dominated us to such an extent. There's an important lesson to be learned here: never underestimate the power of the mind, which is capable of reifying vast worlds of hatred, desire, elation, and sadness. The problems we experience contain a precious potential for transformation, a fountainhead of energy from which we can tirelessly draw the living force that makes us able to build where indifference or apathy prevent it. And every difficulty can become the wicker which we weave into an inner basket that can accommodate all the trials of life.

THE RIVER OF EMOTION

The burning flames of anger have parched the stream of my being.
The thick darkness of illusion has blinded my intelligence.
My consciousness drowns in torrents of desire.
The mountain of pride has flung me into the nether worlds.
The driving blizzard of envy has dragged me into samsara.
The demon of belief in the ego has me firmly by the throat.

DILGO KHYENTSE RINPOCHE

If the passions are the mind's great dramas, the emotions are its actors. Throughout our lives they rush through our minds like an unruly river, determining countless states of happiness and unhappiness. Should we try to tame this river? Is it even possible, and if so, how? Some emotions make us flourish, others sap our well-being, others make us wither. Let us recall that *eudaimonia*, one of the Greek words translated as "happiness," implies flourishing, fulfillment, accomplishment. Love directed toward the well-being of others, compassion focused on their suffering, in thought and deed, are examples of nourishing emotions that help to generate happiness. Obsessive desire, greed, and hatred are examples of draining emotions. How can we develop the constructive emotions while freeing ourselves of the destructive ones?

Despite their rich terminology for describing a wide range of mental events, the traditional languages of Buddhism have no word for emotion as such. That may be because according to Buddhism all types of mental activity, including rational thought, are associated with some kind of feeling, be it one of pleasure, pain, or indifference. And most affective states, such as love and hatred, arise together with discursive thought. Rather than distinguishing between emotions and thoughts, Buddhism is more concerned with understanding which types of mental activity are conducive to one's own and others' well-being, and which are harmful, especially in the long run. This is actually quite consistent with what cognitive science tells us about the brain and emotion. Every region in the brain that has been identified with some aspect of emotion has also been identified with aspects of cognition.[1] There are no "emotion centers" in the brain. The neuronal circuits that support emotions are completely intertwined with those that support cognition. This anatomical arrangement is consistent with the Buddhist view that these processes cannot be separated: emotions appear in a context of action and thought, and almost never in isolation from the other aspects of our experience. It should be noted that this runs counter to Freudian theory, which holds that powerful feelings of anger or jealousy, for instance, can arise without any particular cognitive or conceptual content.

THE IMPACT OF THE EMOTIONS

Derived from the Latin verb *emovere,* meaning "to move," the word *emotion* covers any feeling that moves the mind, be it toward a harmful, a neutral, or a positive thought. Emotion is that which conditions the mind and prompts it to adopt a particular perspective, a certain way of seeing things. It does not necessarily imply an affective outburst suddenly erupting in the mind, which is closer in definition to what scientists study as emotion.

The easiest way to distinguish between our emotions is to examine their motivation (mental attitude and objective) and their results. If an emotion strengthens our inner peace and seeks the good of others, it is *positive,* or constructive; if it shatters our serenity, deeply disturbs our mind, and is intended to harm others, it is *negative,* or afflictive. As for the outcome, the only criterion is the good or the suffering that we create by our acts, words, and thoughts, for ourselves as well as for others. That is what differentiates, for instance, indignation caused by injustice from rage born of the desire to hurt someone. The former has freed people from slavery and domination and moves us to march in the streets to change the world; it seeks to end the injustice as soon as possible or to make someone aware of the error of his ways. The second generates nothing but sorrow.

As the Tibetan poet Shabkar said: "One with compassion is kind even when angry; one without compassion will kill even as he smiles."

THE SCIENTIFIC PERSPECTIVE

According to the cognitive scientists Paul Ekman and Richard Davidson:

> *An evaluation of whether an emotion is beneficial or harmful is not the way mental states are divided by most psychologists. Instead there are two traditions for describing emotion: distinguishing among discrete emotions (e.g., anger, fear, disgust, enjoyment, etc.[2]) and distinguishing dimensions that are thought to underlie those emotions (e.g., pleasant-unpleasant, approach-avoid, etc.). Curios-*

ity and love are typical examples of emotions of approach; fear and loathing, of avoidance.[3]

The same authors also say:

Even the theorists who categorize emotions as simply positive or negative do not propose that all of the negative emotions are harmful to oneself or to others. While most theorists acknowledge that emotions can on some occasions be harmful, this is not thought to be intrinsic to any particular emotion. The goal is not to rid oneself or transcend an emotion, not even hatred, but to regulate experience and action once an emotion is felt.[4]

Psychologists who study emotions from the evolutionary angle[5] believe that they have evolved on the basis of their usefulness to our survival through their capacity to see us through life's major exercises: reproduction, care for offspring, relations with competitors and predators. Jealousy, for instance, can be thought of as the expression of a very ancient instinct that helps to maintain the cohesiveness of a couple, inasmuch as the jealous party will keep rivals at a distance and increase his progeny's odds of survival. Anger can help us rapidly overcome an obstacle that may be preventing us from achieving our desires or that may be threatening us. At the same time, none of these theoreticians has suggested that anger, or any other human emotion that has emerged in the course of evolution, may no longer be adapted to our current way of life. And yet they all agree that chronic or impulsive violence is pathological and acknowledge that hostility is destructive to one's health.[6] In one study, 255 medical students took a personality test designed to measure their level of hostility. Twenty-five years later, it was found that the most aggressive among them had suffered *five times* more cardiac events than those who were less irritable.[7]

For authors who consider *when* an emotional episode is dysfunctional, two issues predominate.[8] In the first case, an episode is considered to be dysfunctional or disruptive when the subject expresses an appropriate emotion with disproportionate intensity. If a child does something foolish, his parents' anger can have educational value; fury or hatred are completely disproportionate. Likewise, as Andrew Solomon writes, "grief is depression in proportion to circumstance; depression is grief out of proportion to circumstance."[9]

In the second case, the emotional episode is harmful when the subject expresses an emotion that is inappropriate to a given situation. If a little child thumbs her nose at you, it's better to laugh it off than to be sad or angry. As Aristotle pointed out, anyone can get angry. That's easy. But to get angry "on the right grounds and against the right persons and also in the right manner and at the right moment and for the right length of time" — that's not easy.

Whatever the scenario, for these psychologists the goal in dealing with our emotions is not to rid ourselves entirely of an emotion or to transcend it, but to manage our experience of it and the way in which it translates into action. Hostility, for instance, must be controlled in a way that effectively neutralizes a threatening individual while not giving free rein to unjustified cruel violence. Buddhism, however, goes further by saying that hostility is always negative because it generates and perpetuates hatred. It is entirely possible to act firmly and resolutely to overpower a dangerous person without feeling the slightest trace of hatred. The Dalai Lama was once asked about the best course of action to take when an intruder enters a room and threatens its occupants with a gun. He responded in a tone that was half serious and half playful: "I'd shoot him in the legs to neutralize him, then I'd go over and stroke his head and take care of him." Although he knew full well that reality isn't always that simple, he wanted to make it clear that vigorous action is enough and that it is not only pointless but harmful to inject hostility or hatred into it.

Ekman and Davidson conclude: "Rather than focusing on increasing consciousness of one's inner state, as Buddhism does, the emphasis in psychology has instead been on learning how to reappraise situations, or control (regulate) emotional behavior and expressions."[10] Psychoanalysis tries to make the patient aware of past tendencies and events, fixations, and blocks that lead to the miseries of neurosis and prevent her from functioning normally in the world.

Buddhism takes a different position. It stresses enhanced awareness of the formation of thoughts, which allows for the immediate identification of an angry thought as it arises, and for its deconstruction the next instant, the way a picture drawn on the surface of water melts away as it is sketched. We repeat the same process with the next thought, and so on. So we need to work on our thoughts one by one, analyzing the way they emerge and evolve and gradually learning to free them as they arise, defusing the chain reactions that allow thoughts to invade the mind. This method, which presents some similarities with those developed in the West in the cognitive therapies of Aaron Beck and the Mindfulness-Based Stress Reduction Program of Jon Kabat-Zinn, is essentially centered on the present moment. It is therefore important, from the standpoint of mental health, to be alert to the way thoughts form and to learn to move beyond their constraints, instead of developing and analyzing the endless film loop of our psychic history.

The essential point here is that we can never truly bring past events back to life. They survive only through the impact they have on our present experience. What really matters is the nature of our living experience, whether it is optimal or afflictive. If we become expert at freeing ourselves of all afflictive mental states as they take form, the actual content of the past events that might have triggered them becomes quite irrelevant. Furthermore, being able to repeatedly free oneself of such afflictive thoughts as they occur gradually erodes their very tendency to form again, until they stop appearing altogether. Just as our emotions, moods, and tendencies have been shaped by the accumulation of countless instantaneous thoughts, they can be transformed through time by dealing in a mindful way with such thoughts. "Take care of the minutes, for the hours will take care of themselves," Lord Chesterfield once told his son. This is the best path to gradual change.

TOWARD A POSITIVE PSYCHOLOGY

Until the 1980s, few researchers had focused on how to develop the positive aspects of our temperament. In 1998 a group of American psychologists was brought together by Martin Seligman, past president of the American Psychological Association, to form the Positive Psychology Center and to coordinate the various spheres of study that it involves. It was an attempt to broaden psychology's field of study beyond its longstanding traditional vocation to investigate and, where possible, correct emotional dysfunction and mental pathologies. An analysis in *Psychological Abstracts* of the books and articles published on psychology since 1887 finds 136,728 titles referring to anger, anxiety, or depression, but only 9,510 referring to joy, satisfaction, or happiness![11] While it is certainly important to treat psychological problems that handicap or even paralyze people's lives, it is essential to note that happiness is not the mere absence of unhappiness. Positive psychology, as represented by this new generation of researchers, seeks to study and reinforce the positive emotions that allow us to become better human beings and to get more joy out of life. We may progress from a pathological state to a so-called "normal" one, and from a normal state to an optimal one.

There are several justifications for such an approach. In 1969 the psychologist Norman Bradburn showed that pleasant and unpleasant affects derive from different mechanisms and must therefore be studied separately. Merely eliminating sadness and depression is no automatic guarantee of joy and happiness. The suppression of pain doesn't necessarily lead to pleasure. It is therefore necessary not only to rid oneself of negative emotions but also to develop positive ones.

We can take this a step further by asserting that it is not enough to abstain from harming others (the elimination of malice), and that this abstention must be augmented by a determined effort to help them (the development and implementation of altruism). According to Barbara Fredrickson of the University of Michigan, one of the founders of positive psychology, positive emotions broaden our thought-action repertoire, widening the array of the thoughts and actions that come to mind, including joy, interest, contentment, and love. These scientists believe that developing such positive thoughts therefore offers an indisputable evolutionary advantage, inasmuch as it helps us to broaden our intellectual and affective universe and to open ourselves to new ideas and experiences. Unlike depression, which often sends us into a tailspin, positive emotions create an upward spiral "by building resilience and influencing the ways people cope with adversity."[12]

What We Mean by "Negative" Emotions

The Tibetan word *nyön-mong* (*klesha* in Sanskrit) refers to a state of mental disturbance, torment, and confusion that "afflicts us from within." Consider hatred, jealousy, or obsession at the moment they form — there is no question that they make us deeply uncomfortable. Moreover, the actions and words they inspire are usually intended to hurt others. Conversely, thoughts of kindness, affection, and tolerance give us joy and courage, open our minds, and free us inside. They also spur us on to benevolence and empathy.

In addition, the disturbing emotions tend to distort our perception of reality and to prevent us from seeing it as it really is. Attachment idealizes its object, hatred demonizes it. These emotions make us believe that beauty or ugliness is inherent in people and in things, even though it is the mind that decides if they are "attractive" or "repulsive." This misapprehension opens a gap between the way things appear and the way they are. It clouds our judgment and makes us think and act as if these qualities were not largely based on how we see them. On the other hand, positive emotions and mental factors strengthen the clarity of our thinking and the accuracy of our reasoning, since they are based on a more accurate appreciation of reality. Selfless love reflects some understanding of the intimate interdependence of beings, of our happiness and that of others, a notion that is attuned to reality, while selfishness opens an ever wider abyss between us and other people.

The essential thing, therefore, is to identify the types of mental activity that lead to well-being and those that lead to suffering, even when the latter afford us brief instances of pleasure. This investigation calls for a subtle assessment of the nature of the emotions. For instance our delight in making a clever but malicious remark is considered to be negative. Conversely, our frustration or even sadness at being unable to ease the suffering we witness in no way hinders the quest for sukha, since it leads us to selflessly cultivate our capacity to help and inspires our determination to put it into action. Whatever the case may be, the best means of analysis is introspection and self-observation.

The first phase of that analysis is to identify the way in which the emotions arise. This requires the cultivation of watchful attention to the unfolding of our mental activity, along with mindfulness of the distinction between destructive emotions and those that nourish happiness. This analysis, undertaken over and over again, is the critical prelude to the transformation of a state of mental disturbance. To accomplish this, Buddhism prescribes rigorous training in introspection, a practice that involves stabilizing the attention and heightening clarity of thought. This discipline is close to the concept of "sustained, voluntary attention" developed by William James, the founder of modern psychology.[13] But while James questioned whether it was possible to develop and maintain that voluntary attention for more than a few seconds, Buddhist meditators have found that it can be developed significantly. When our discursive thoughts have been calmed through practice and our mind is clear and focused, we can examine the nature of our emotions and other mental states with great efficacy.

In the short term, certain mental processes — such as greed, hostility, and envy — can help us to attain what we think is desirable or attractive. We have also spoken about the advantages of anger and jealousy in terms of the survival of the species. In the long term, however, they hinder our development and that of others. Every incident of aggression and jealousy represents a setback in our quest for serenity and happiness. Buddhism's sole objective in treating the emotions is to free us from the fundamental causes of suffering. It starts with the principle that certain mental events are afflictive regardless of the intensity or context of their formation. That is particularly true for the three mental processes considered to be basic mental "poisons": desire (in the sense of craving or tormenting greed), hatred (the wish to harm), and delusion (which distorts our perception of reality). Buddhism usually includes pride and envy as well; together, these are the five major poisons associated with some sixty negative mental states. The texts also refer to "84,000 negative emotions." These are not all specified in detail, but the symbolic figure gives a sense of the complexity of the human mind and helps us to understand that our methods of transforming the mind must be adapted to the enormous variety of mental dispositions. That is why Buddhism speaks of the "84,000 doors" that lead to inner transformation.

EXERCISE
Calming the mind and looking within
Sit in a comfortable position. Your body remains in an erect but not tense posture with eyes gently open. For five minutes, breathe calmly, noticing the in-and-out flow of your breath. Experience the gradual calming of chaotic thoughts. When thoughts arise, neither attempt to block them nor let them multiply. Simply continue to watch your breath.

Next, instead of paying attention to outer sights, sounds, and events, turn your "gaze" inward and "look" at the mind itself. "Looking" here means observing your awareness itself, not the content of your thoughts. Let the mind gently come to rest, as a tired traveler finds a pleasant meadow in which to sit for a while.

Then, with a deep feeling of appreciation, think of the value of human existence and of its extraordinary potential for flourishing. Be aware, too, that this precious life will not last forever and that it is essential to make the best possible use of it. Sincerely examine what counts most in life for you. What do you need to accomplish or discard in order to achieve authentic well-being and live a meaningful existence? When the factors that contribute to true happiness have become clear to you, imagine that they begin to bloom in your mind. Resolve to nurture them day after day.

End your meditation by letting thoughts of pure kindness embrace all living beings.

10

DISTURBING EMOTIONS:
THE REMEDIES

Craving, hatred, and the other passions are enemies without hands or feet; they are neither brave nor intelligent. How have I become their slave? Entrenched in my heart, they strike at me at will. Fie on such ridiculous patience!

SHANTIDEVA

How do we strip the alienating emotions of their power without becoming insensitive to the world, without draining life of its richness? If we merely consign them to the depths of the unconscious, they will reemerge with renewed force at the first opportunity, continuing to strengthen the tendencies that perpetuate inner conflict. The ideal, contrarily, is to allow negative emotions to form and dissipate without leaving any trace in the mind. Thoughts and emotions will continue to surface, but they will not proliferate and will lose their power to enslave us.

One might argue that the conflictive emotions — anger, jealousy, greed — are acceptable because they are natural, and that there is no need to interfere with them. But disease is a natural phenomenon too. We do not resign ourselves to it or welcome it as a desirable ingredient of life. It is just as legitimate to act against afflictive emotions as it is to treat disease. Are these negative emotions really diseases? At first glance the parallel may seem excessive, but a closer look reveals that it is far from baseless, since most inner confusion and suffering arise from an array of disturbing emotions that weaken our "mental immune system." Conversely, lasting well-being arises from cultivating positive emotions and wisdom.

THE SPIRAL OF EMOTIONS

Why can't we simply allow the negative emotions to wear themselves down? Experience shows that, like an infection that goes untreated, the disturbing emotions gain in strength when allowed to take their course. Unleashing anger whenever it arises, for instance, tends to create a state of psychological instability that only increases irascibility. The results of various psychological studies contradict the notion that giving free rein to the emotions temporarily relieves bottled-up tensions.[1] By systematically allowing our negative emotions to express themselves, we develop habits to which we are vulnerable every time the emotional charge reaches the critical threshold. In addition, the threshold will gradually become lower and anger will erupt ever more easily. The result will be what is commonly called a bad temper, accompanied by chronic suffering. From the physiological point of view, arterial tension diminishes if we prevent anger from openly expressing itself, but it increases when we fly into a rage.[2]

Behavioral studies have also shown that those who are best able to balance their emotions (by controlling them without repressing them) also demonstrate the greatest selflessness in the face of the suffering of others.[3] Most hyperemotive people are more concerned with their own distress at the sight of suffering than with the ways in which they might help to relieve that suffering.

It does not follow, however, that we need to stifle our emotions. Preventing them from expressing themselves while leaving them intact, like a time bomb in a dark corner of our mind, is both a stopgap and an unhealthy solution. Psychologists aver that suppressed emotion can cause serious mental and physical damage, and that we should at all costs avoid turning our emotions against ourselves. On the other hand, the unbridled and extreme expression of emotions can also give rise to grave psychological conditions. We can die of a stroke in a fit of rage or consume ourselves in obsessive desire. In all such cases, it is because we haven't been able to establish the right dialogue between our intelligence and our emotions.

Is It Possible to Free Ourselves of Negative Emotions?

You might think that ignorance and negative emotions are inherent to the flow of consciousness, and that trying to rid yourself of them is like fighting against a part of yourself. But the most fundamental aspect of consciousness, the pure faculty of knowing — what has been called the "luminous" quality of the mind — contains no hatred or desire at its core. A mirror, for instance, will reflect both angry faces and smiling ones. The very quality of the mirror allows countless images to arise, yet none of them belongs to the mirror. In fact, if the angry face were intrinsic to the mirror, it could be seen at all times and would prevent other images from arising. Similarly, the most fundamental quality of cognition, the luminous quality of the mind, is what allows the arising of thoughts and underlies all of them. Yet none of these thoughts belongs intrinsically to the fundamental nature of the mind. The experience of introspection shows, on the contrary, that the negative emotions are transitory mental events that can be obliterated by their opposites, the positive emotions, acting as antidotes.

To that end, we have to begin by recognizing that the afflictive emotions are harmful to our well-being. This assessment is based not on some dogmatic distinction between good and bad, but on observation of the short- and long-term repercussions of certain emotions on oneself and on others. But the mere fact of recognizing the harmful effects of mental afflictions is not enough to overcome them. Having come to this awareness, you still have gradually to familiarize yourself with each antidote — loving-kindness as antidote to hatred, for instance — until the absence of hatred becomes second nature. The Tibetan word *gom*, which is usually translated as "meditation," more precisely denotes "familiarization," while the Sanskrit word *bhavana*, also translated as "meditation," means "cultivation." Indeed, meditation is not about sitting quietly in the shade of a tree and relaxing in a moment of respite from the daily grind; it is about familiarizing yourself with a new vision of things, a new way to manage your thoughts, of perceiving people and experiencing the world.

Buddhism teaches various ways of making this "familiarization" work. The three principal ways are *antidotes, liberation,* and *utilization.* The first consists of applying a specific antidote to each negative emotion. The second allows us to unravel, or "liberate," the emotion by looking straight at it and letting it dissolve as it arises. The third uses the raw power of emotion as a catalyst for inner change. The choice of one method over another will depend on the moment, the circumstances, and the capacities of the person using them. All share a common aspect and the same goal: to help us stop being victims of conflicting emotions.

The Use of Antidotes

The first method consists of neutralizing afflictive emotions with a specific antidote, just as we neutralize the destructive effects of poison with antivenom, or of acid with an alkali. One fundamental point emphasized by Buddhism is that two diametrically opposed mental processes cannot form simultaneously. We may fluctuate rapidly between love and hatred, but we cannot feel *in the same instant of consciousness* the desire to hurt someone and to do him good. The two impulses are as opposed to each other as water and fire. As the philosopher Alain has written: "One movement precludes the other; when you extend a friendly hand, you cannot make a fist."[4]

In the same way, by habituating your mind to altruistic love, you gradually eliminate hatred, because the two states of mind can alternate but cannot coexist. So the more we cultivate loving-kindness, the less space there will be for hatred in our mental landscape. It is therefore important to begin by learning the antidotes that correspond to each negative emotion, and then to cultivate them. These antidotes are to the psyche what antibodies are to the body.

Since altruistic love acts as a direct antidote to hatred, the more we develop it, the more the desire to harm will wither and finally disappear. It is not a question of suppressing hatred but of turning the mind to something diametrically opposed to it: love and compassion. Following a traditional Buddhist practice, you begin by recognizing your own aspiration to happiness, then extend that aspiration to those you love, and ultimately to all people — friends, strangers, and enemies. Little by little, altruism and benevolence will saturate your mind until it becomes second nature. In this way, training yourself in altruistic thought can offer lasting protection against chronic animosity and aggression. This will also be accompanied by a genuine readiness to act for the benefit of others.

It is equally impossible for greed or desire to coexist with inner freedom. Desire can fully develop only when it is allowed to run rampant to the point where it monopolizes the mind. The trap here is the fact that desire, and its ally pleasure, are not ugly like hatred. They are even extremely seductive. But the silken threads of desire, which seem so light at first, soon tighten, and the soft garment they had woven becomes a straitjacket. The more you struggle, the tighter it becomes.

In the worst cases, desire can drive us continuously to seek satisfaction at any cost; the more satisfaction seems to elude us, the more it obsesses us. On the other hand, when we contemplate its disturbing aspects and turn our minds toward developing inner calm, the obsession of desire can begin to melt like snow in the sun. Make no mistake — there's no question here of ceasing to love those whose lives we share, or of becoming indifferent to them. When we stop projecting the insatiable demands of our attachments onto people, we are able to love them more and to feel genuine concern for their true well-being.

As for anger, it can be neutralized by patience. This does not require us to remain passive, but to steer clear of being overwhelmed by destructive emotions. As the Dalai Lama explains: "Patience safeguards our peace of mind in the face of adversity. . . . It is a deliberate response (as opposed to an unreasoned reaction) to the strong negative thoughts and emotions that tend to arise when we encounter harm."[5]

You may object: "That's all very well in a perfect world, but human feelings are ambivalent by nature. We can love and envy at the same time. The complexity and richness of our feelings let us experience conflicting emotions simultaneously." We can feel deep love for a companion and despise him at the same time because he is betraying us. But is that really love? In the sense by which we have defined it, love is the wish for the person we love to be happy and to understand the causes of that happiness. True love and hatred cannot coexist, because the former wish is for the other's happiness, and the latter for his unhappiness. Attachment, desire, and possessiveness often accompany love but are not love. They can coexist with hatred because it is not their opposite. There definitely are mental states that are completely incompatible: pride and humility, envy and joy, generosity and avarice, calm and agitation. No ambivalence between these pairs is possible. With introspection we will be able to distinguish between the emotions that enhance our joy in living from those that diminish it.

FREEING THE EMOTIONS

The second method is liberation, in which, rather than trying to stem each emotion that afflicts us with its specific antidote, we use a single antidote that acts at a more basic level on all our mental afflictions. It is neither possible nor desirable to suppress the mind's natural activities, and it would be futile and unhealthy to try to block its thoughts. When we examine the emotions, we find that they are dynamic flows without any inherent substance of their own — in Buddhist terms, "empty" of real existence. What would happen if, instead of counteracting a disturbing emotion with its opposite — anger with patience, for instance — we were simply to contemplate the nature of the emotion itself?

You are overwhelmed by a sudden tide of anger. You feel as if there's no choice but to let it sweep you away. But look closely. It is nothing more than a thought. When you see a great black cloud in a stormy sky, it seems so solid that you could sit on it. But when you approach it, there's nothing to grab on to;

it is only vapor and wind. The experience of anger is like having a high fever. It is a temporary condition, and you do not need to identify with it. The more you look at anger in this manner, the more it evaporates under your gaze, like white frost under the sun's rays.

Where does anger come from, how does it evolve, where does it disappear to? All we can say for sure is that it is born in the mind, lingers there a moment or two, and then dissolves there, like waves that arise from the ocean and dissolve back into it. But a close examination of anger finds nothing substantial, nothing that can explain its tyrannical influence over our lives. Unless we pursue this investigation, we end up being fixated on the object of anger and overtaken by destructive emotion. If, on the other hand, we come to see that anger has no substance of its own, it rapidly loses all power. This is what Khyentse Rinpoche has to say on the matter:

> Remember that a thought is only the fleeting conjunction of myriad factors and circumstances. It does not exist by itself. When a thought arises, recognize its empty nature. It will immediately lose its power to elicit the next thought, and the chain of delusion will be broken. Recognize that emptiness of thoughts and allow your thoughts to rest a moment in the relaxed mind so that the mind's natural clarity remains limpid and unchanged.[6]

This is what Buddhism calls *liberation from anger at the moment it arises* by recognizing its emptiness, its lack of its own existence. This liberation happens spontaneously, like the image I evoked earlier of a sketch drawn on the surface of the water. In so doing, we have not suppressed our anger but neutralized its power to become a cause of suffering.

More often than not, we come to understand this only after

the crisis has passed. It is at the very moment of anger's emergence that we must recognize its empty nature. That understanding will strip thoughts of their power to build into a stream of obsession and oppression. They cross the mind without leaving a trace, like the trackless flight of a bird through the sky.

This technique can be used for all mental afflictions; it helps us to build a bridge between the exercise of meditation and our daily concerns. Once we get used to looking at thoughts the moment they appear and then allowing them to dissipate before they overwhelm the mind, it is much easier to maintain control over the mind and to manage the conflictive emotions in our active lives. To spur our vigilance and hard work, we should try to recall the bitter suffering that destructive emotions have caused us.

USING THE EMOTIONS AS CATALYSTS

The third technique for neutralizing afflictive emotions is the most subtle and the trickiest. When we look closely at our emotions, we find that, like musical notes, they are made up of numerous elements, or harmonics. Anger rouses us to action and often allows us to overcome obstacles. It also contains aspects of clarity, focus, and effectiveness that are not harmful in and of themselves. Desire has an element of bliss that is distinct from attachment; pride, an element of self-confidence that can be firm without lapsing into arrogance; envy, a drive to act that cannot be confused with the unhealthy dissatisfaction it entails.

As difficult as it is to separate these various aspects, it is possible to recognize and use the positive facets of a thought generally considered to be negative. In effect, what gives an emotion its noxious quality is the way we identify with and cling to it. This triggers a chain reaction during which the initial spark of clarity and focus becomes anger and hostility. The skills we gain from meditation experience help us to intervene before the reaction is initiated.

Emotions are not inherently disturbing, though they seem so the moment we identify with and hold on to them. The pure consciousness of which we have spoken, and which is the source of all mental events, is neither good nor bad in and of itself. Thoughts become disturbing only once the process of "fixation" is set in motion, when we attach ourselves to the qualities we attribute to the object of the emotion and to the self that is feeling it.

Once we learn to avoid that fixation, we do not need to bring in antidotes from the outside; the emotions themselves act as catalysts for freeing ourselves of their baneful influence. This happens because our point of view changes. When we fall into the sea, it is the water itself that buoys us and allows us to swim to shore. But we still need to know how to swim — that is, to have enough skill to exploit the emotions to good effect without drowning in their negative aspects.

This kind of practice requires great command of the language of the emotions. Allowing powerful emotions to express themselves without falling prey to them is playing with fire, or rather, trying to snatch a jewel from a snake's head. If we succeed, our understanding of the nature of the mind will grow accordingly; if we fail, we will find ourselves overwhelmed by the negative qualities of anger and its hold on us will be strengthened.

THREE TECHNIQUES, ONE GOAL

We have seen first how we can counteract each negative emotion with its specific antidote; then, how recognizing the empty nature of thoughts can neutralize any afflictive emotion; and, finally, how we can also use the negative emotion in a positive way. The contradictions here are only apparent ones. These techniques are simply different ways of tackling the same problem and achieving the same result: not to fall victim to the afflictive emotions and the suffering they lead to. In the same vein, it is easy to imagine several ways to avoid being poisoned by a toxic plant. We can use antidotes developed to neutralize the effects of specific poisons. We can also identify the source of our vulnerability to such poisons, our immune system, and then, in a single operation, strengthen that system with a universal resistance to all of them. We can, finally, analyze the poisons, isolate their component elements, and discover that some, applied in appropriate dosage, have medicinal qualities.

The important thing is that in each case we reach the same goal of freeing ourselves from negative emotions and progressing toward freedom from suffering. Each of these techniques is like a key; it makes little difference whether it be made of iron, silver, or gold, so long as it opens the door to freedom.

We must never forget, however, that the source of disturbing emotions is attachment to the self. If we want to be free of inner suffering once and for all, it is not enough to rid ourselves of the emotions themselves; we must eliminate our attachment to the ego. Is that possible? It is, because as we've seen, the ego exists merely as mental imputation. A concept can be dispelled, but only by the wisdom that perceives that the ego is devoid of intrinsic existence.

EMOTIONS IN TIME

The emotions can sometimes be so powerful that they allow no space for reflection and cannot be controlled at the moment they express themselves. Paul Ekman writes of the "refractory" period during which we are aware only of what justifies our anger or any other strong emotion.[7] We are completely impervious to anything that might help us see that the object of our anger is not as hateful as we think it is.

This is how Alain describes the process: "The passions entrap us. A really angry man performs a truly dramatic, brightly lit tragedy in his own head, laying out all his enemy's faults, ruses, preparations, scorn, plans for the future. Everything is interpreted through the lens of anger, and the anger is thereby strengthened."[8] In such cases there is no choice other than to work on these emotions *after* they have subsided. It is only once the tides of passion have receded that we come to see how biased our vision of things has been. It is only then that we are surprised to find how our emotions have manipulated and led us into error. We had imagined that our anger was entirely justified, but in order to be legitimate it ought to have done more good than bad, which it rarely does. "Positive anger," or rather indignation, can disrupt the status quo of an unacceptable situation or make someone understand that she is acting hurtfully, but such anger, inspired solely by selflessness, is rare. More often than not, our anger will have hurt someone while leaving us in a state of deep dissatisfaction. We should never underestimate the power of the mind to create and crystallize worlds of hatred, greed, jealousy, euphoria, or despair.

With the help of experience, we can deal with negative emotions *before* they surface. We can "see them coming" and learn to distinguish those that bring suffering from those that contribute to happiness. The techniques we have described can help us to better manage our emotions, which will gradually stop overwhelming us. In order to prevent forest fires in times of drought, the forester cuts firebreaks, lays up stores of water, and remains alert. He knows very well that it's easier to extinguish a spark than an inferno.

At a later stage, growing knowledge and mastery of the

mind will allow us to deal with our emotions at the very moment they appear, as they express themselves. That, as we've seen, is how the emotions that assail us are "liberated" as they form. They become incapable of sowing confusion in the mind and of being converted into words and acts that generate suffering. This method calls for perseverance, because we are not accustomed to dealing with thoughts in this manner.

Contrary to what one might imagine, inner freedom with respect to the emotions leads to neither apathy nor indifference. Life does not lose its color. It is simply that instead of being the plaything of our afflictive thoughts, moods, and disposition, we become their master. Not like a tyrant who exerts relentless and obsessive control over his subjects, but like a free human being who is master of his own fate.

At this point conflictive mental states give way to a rich palette of wholesome emotions that interact with other people on the basis of a fluid apprehension of reality. Wisdom and compassion become the predominant influences on our thoughts, words, and deeds.

EXERCISE
Freeing Emotions Directly
Bring to mind a situation in which you felt very angry and try to relive this experience. When anger arises, focus your attention on the anger itself instead of on its object. Don't unite with the anger but look at it as a separate phenomenon. As you keep on just observing the anger, it will gradually evaporate under your gaze.

It may keep on surging in your mind and you may feel unable to pacify it. It remains so vivid because your mind is drawn helplessly and repeatedly back toward the object of your resentment. The object becomes like a target, and each time you return to it, a mental spark is triggered and the emotion gets rekindled. You feel as if it has invaded your mind and that you are caught in a vicious circle. Instead of turning your attention to the "target," simply stare attentively at the emotion itself. You will see that it cannot sustain itself and soon runs out of steam.

Using the experience you gain during meditation sessions, try to apply this process of liberation in your daily life. With time, your anger will grow ever more transparent and your irritability will wane.

Practice in the same way with obsessive desire, envy, and other painful emotions.

A LONG-TERM ENDEAVOR

Most contemporary psychological research into the regulation of the emotions has focused on how to control and modulate the emotions *after* they have flooded the mind. What seems to be missing is the recognition of the central role that heightened awareness and clarity of mind — the "mindfulness" of Buddhism — can play in the process. *Recognizing* the emotion at the very moment it forms, *understanding* that it is but a thought, devoid of intrinsic existence, and *allowing it to dissipate* spontaneously so as to avoid the chain reaction it would normally unleash are all at the heart of Buddhist contemplative practice.

The mastery of any discipline — music, medicine, mathematics, and so on — requires intensive training. And yet it would seem that in the West — with the exception of psycho-analysis, whose results are at best uncertain — long-term, persistent efforts are not readily undertaken to transform emotional conditions. The very goal of psychoanalysis is different from that of positive psychology and Buddhism, which strive not merely to "normalize" our neurotic way of functioning in the world. The condition generally considered to be "normal" is just the starting point, not the goal. Our life is worth far more than that! Martin Seligman once told me, "The best it [psychoanalysis] can do is to bring us from minus ten to zero."

Most methods derived by Western psychology to effect lasting change in affective states focus above all on treating manifestly pathological conditions. According to a recent article by Western and Buddhist psychologists,

> With a few notable exceptions — among which the development of "positive psychology" — no effort has been invested in cultivating positive attributes of mind for individuals not suffering from mental disorders. It is important to underscore the fact that training for expertise in virtually any domain requires considerable practice. . . . Western approaches to bringing about changes in enduring emotional states or traits do not include such long-term persistent effort. Not even psychoanalysis typically involves the decades Buddhists consider required to cultivate sukha.[9]

Such effort, however, is eminently desirable. We need to get rid of mental toxins and at the same time to cultivate states of mind that contribute to emotional balance and ensure the optimal flourishing of a truly healthy mind. A great many conflictive emotions *are* mental disorders. A person in the grip of fierce hatred or obsessive envy cannot reasonably be considered sound-minded, even if he is not obviously a candidate for psychiatry. Because such emotions are integrated into our daily lives, the importance or even urgency of dealing with them seems less clear. As a result, the idea of training the mind is not among modern man's pressing concerns on the order of work, cultural activities, physical exercise, and leisure.

We have to understand that we are enormously resistant to change. I am talking not about the alacrity with which our society embraces superficial novelty trends, but about a profound inertia with respect to any genuine transformation of our way of being. Most of the time we don't even want to hear about the possibility of change, and we prefer to sneer at those who seek alternative solutions. Nobody really wants to be angry, jealous, or swollen with pride, but every time we give in to those emotions, our excuse is that it's perfectly normal, just a part of life's ups and downs. So what's the point of changing? Be yourself! Have fun, get a new car, a new lover, have it all, get high, but whatever you do don't touch the essence, because that calls for real work. An attitude like that would be perfectly justified if we were really satisfied with our lot. But are we? As Alain, again, has written: "The insane are proselytizers and, above all, are reluctant to be cured."

And yet once we've begun our work of introspection, we find that the transformation isn't nearly so painful as we'd imagined. On the contrary, as soon we've decided to undergo such an inner metamorphosis, even if we inevitably run into a few difficulties, we soon discover a joy in the work that makes each step a new satisfaction. We feel freedom and strength growing within us, crowding out our anxieties and fears. The sense of insecurity gives way to confidence tinged with joie de vivre, and chronic selfishness to friendly altruism.

A late teacher of mine, Sengdrak Rinpoche, lived on the mountainous border between Nepal and Tibet for more than thirty years. He told me that when he began his retreats as a teenager, he experienced some very hard years. His emotions were so powerful he thought he would go mad. And then, little by little, as he learned the various ways of dealing with the emotions, he acquired inner freedom. Ever since, every moment had been nothing but pure joy for him. And it showed! He was one of the most simple, lighthearted, and comforting people I've ever met. I felt as if outward difficulties would slide off him like water off a rose petal. When he spoke, his eyes sparkled with delight and he gave such an impression of buoyancy that I expected him to fly off like a bird.

Few of us would regret the years it takes to complete an education or master a crucial skill. So why complain about the perseverance needed to become a well-balanced and truly compassionate human being?

11

DESIRE

It is rare that happiness alights just so on the desire that called for it.

MARCEL PROUST

No one will dispute the fact that it is natural to have desire and that desire plays a motivating role in our lives. But there is a crucial difference between the deep aspirations that we generate throughout our lives and the desire that is solely concentrated on craving and obsession. Desire can assume infinitely varied forms: we can desire a glass of cool water, someone to love, a moment of peace, the happiness of others; we can also desire our own death. Desire can nourish our existence and can poison it.

It can also mature, free itself, and deepen into the aspiration of making oneself a better human being, of working for the good of others or of achieving spiritual awakening. It is important to make the distinction between desire, which is essentially a blind force, and aspiration, which is inspired by motivation and attitude. If the motivation is vast and selfless, it can be the source of the greatest human qualities and the greatest accomplishments. When it is narrow and egocentric, it fuels the endless preoccupations of daily life, which follow upon one another like waves, from birth to death, and offer no guarantee of deep satisfaction. When it is negative, it can wreak devastating damage.

As natural as it is, desire degenerates into a mental toxin as soon as it becomes craving, an obsession, or an unmitigated attachment. Such desire is all the more frustrating and alienating in that it is out of sync with reality. When we are obsessed by a thing or a person, we misconstrue them as being one hundred percent desirable, and possessing or enjoying them becomes an absolute necessity. Not only is greed a source of distress, but the "possession" of what we desire can, in any case, only be precarious, momentary, and constantly threatened. It is also illusory, in the sense that we ultimately have very little control over what we think we possess.

Desires come in different degrees of duration and intensity. A minor desire, such as for a cup of tea or a nice hot shower, is usually easily satisfied and thwarted only by extremely adverse conditions. There is also the desire to pass a test, to buy a house, the achievement of which may present certain difficulties that can generally be overcome with perseverance and ingenuity. Finally, there is a more basic level of desire, such as that of starting a family, of being happy with the companion of one's choice, of doing work one enjoys. The attainment of such desires takes a great deal of time, and the quality of life it engenders depends on our deepest aspirations, on the direction we want our lives to take. Do we want our actions to promote joy in our lives, or do we just want to make money and achieve a certain status in society? Do we picture our relationship in a couple as an instance of possession or of altruistic reciprocity?

Whatever we choose, we always participate in the dynamic of desire.

In Hong Kong I knew some of the young lions of the stock exchange, who bed down on the floor in the office in their sleeping bags so they can get up in the middle of the night and hit the computers to "catch" the New York exchange before it closes. They too are trying to be happy in their own way, but without much success. One of them told me that he goes down to the beach once or twice a year and looks at how beautiful the ocean is. At such times, he said, he can't help thinking, "What a strange life I lead. And yet I'll start all over again come Monday morning." Lack of priorities? Of courage? We perch at the mirrored surface of illusion without taking the extra time to allow the question to rise from our inner depths: "What do I really want out of life?" Once we've found an answer, there will always be time to think about how to attain it. But isn't it sad to stifle the question itself?

THE MECHANISM OF DESIRE

The craving for pleasant sensations is readily implanted in the mind, since pleasure is accommodating and always ready to offer its services. It is attractive, instills confidence, and with a few convincing images sweeps away all hesitation. What could we possibly have to fear from such a tempting offer? Nothing is easier than setting off down the path of pleasure. But the breeziness of those first few steps doesn't last long, and soon gives way to the disappointment of naive expectations and the loneliness that goes with the satiation of the senses. It's hardly realistic to hope that such pleasures will bring us lasting happiness one day.

The great pessimist Arthur Schopenhauer stated: "All striving springs from want or deficiency, from dissatisfaction with one's condition, and is therefore suffering so long as it is not satisfied. No satisfaction, however, is lasting; on the contrary, it is always merely the starting point of fresh striving. We see striving everywhere impeded in many ways, everywhere struggling and fighting, and hence always as suffering."[1] This assertion is true but incomplete. It assumes that we cannot escape desire and the suffering it perpetuates. If we want to escape it, we have to know how it is created.

The first thing to note is that all passionate desire — as opposed to such primary sensations as hunger or thirst — is foreshadowed by a feeling and a mental representation. The formation of that image can be set in motion by an outward object (a shape, a sound, a touch, a smell, or a taste) or an inward one (a memory or a daydream). Even if we are influenced by latent tendencies, even if desire — primarily sexual — is branded onto our physical constitution, it cannot express itself without a mental representation. It can be voluntary or seem to impose itself on our imagination; it can form slowly or with lightning speed, surreptitiously or openly; but the representation always precedes the active desire because its object must be reflected in our thoughts. It considers desirability to be an inherent characteristic of a given person, whose qualities it exaggerates and whose defects it minimizes. "Desire embellishes the objects on which it rests its wings of fire," wrote Anatole France.

Understanding this process helps us to accelerate the inner dialogue that allows us to overcome afflictive desire.

Generally, once mental images linked to a desire begin to build up in the mind, one either satisfies the desire or suppresses it. The former action represents a surrender of self-control, the second initiates a conflict. The inner conflict created by suppression is always a source of distress. On the other hand, the option of indulging a desire is like saying: "Why make everything so complicated? Let's satisfy the desire and have done with it." The problem is, you're never done with it: satiation is merely a respite. The mental imagery that desire is continuously creating very quickly reemerges. The more frequently we assuage our desires, the more these images multiply, intrude, and constrain us. The more salt water we drink, the thirstier we become. The repeated reinforcement of mental images leads to addiction and dependency, mental and physical. Once we reach that stage, the experience of desire is felt more like servitude than pleasure. We have lost our freedom.

FROM DESIRE TO OBSESSION

The obsessive desire that often accompanies passionate love can degrade affection, tenderness, and the joy of appreciating and sharing the life of another. It is the diametric opposite of altruistic love. It arises from egocentrism that merely cherishes itself in the other or, worse still, seeks to forge its own happiness at the other's expense. This kind of desire wants only to appropriate and control the people, objects, and situations that attract it.

This is how one dictionary defines passion: "Powerful, exclusive, and obsessive love. Violent affectivity that hampers the judgment." It is fueled by exaggeration and illusion, and insists that things be other than the way they actually are.

What about sexual infatuation? We may agree with Christian Boiron, an author and CEO, that "sexual attraction is not pathological, but it is not an emotion either. It is the normal expression of a desire, like hunger and thirst."[2] Nonetheless, it arouses the most powerful emotions in us because it draws its strength from all five senses combined: sight, touch, sound, taste, and smell. In the absence of inner freedom, any intense sensory experience unleashes its succession of attachments and subjugates us ever more cruelly. It's like a whirlpool in a river: we pay it little heed, we think it's safe to swim, but when the eddy suddenly accelerates and deepens, we're sucked in without hope of rescue. Conversely, the person who can maintain perfect inner freedom feels all these sensations in the simplicity of the present moment, with the delight of a mind free of attachment and expectation.

Obsessive desire exaggerates the intensity and frequency of the mental images that trigger it. Like a scratched record, it endlessly replays the same leitmotif. It is a polarization of the mental universe, a loss of flow that paralyzes inner freedom. Alain writes: "What would be left of the sorrow of the thwarted lover, tossing and turning in his bed and fantasizing devious schemes of revenge, if he were to stop mulling over the past and the future?"[3] Such obsessions become extremely painful when they are not assuaged and grow in power when they are. The universe of obsession is one in which the sense of urgency is bound to powerlessness.

Another characteristic of obsession is the fundamental dissatisfaction it elicits. It knows no joy, much less fulfillment. It couldn't be otherwise, since the victim of obsession stubbornly seeks relief in the very situations that torment him. The junkie reinforces his dependency, the alcoholic drinks to delirium, the scorned lover stares at his beloved's picture all day long. Obsession generates a state of chronic and anxious suffering made up of equal parts desire and repulsion, insatiability and exhaustion. In truth, it is an addiction to the causes of suffering.

Studies indicate that different regions of the brain and neuronal circuits are in play when we "want" something and when we "like" it. This helps us to understand how, once we grow used to feeling certain desires, we become dependent on them — we continue to feel the need to satisfy them even after we stop enjoying the feeling they give us. We reach the point of wanting without liking.[4] At the same time, we may wish to be free of the obsession, which hurts by compelling us to desire that which no longer pleases us. Conversely, we can also love something or somebody without necessarily desiring them.

In the same vein, scientists have implanted electrodes in a region of the brain in rats that produces sensations of pleasure when stimulated. The rats can stimulate themselves by pressing on a bar. The pleasure is so intense that they soon abandon all other activities, including food and sex. The pursuit of this feeling becomes an insatiable hunger, an uncontrollable need, and the rats press the bar until they drop from exhaustion and die.

DESIRE, LOVE, AND ATTACHMENT

How do we tell true love from possessive attachment? Altruistic love might be compared to the pure tone of a crystal glass, and attachment to the finger on the rim of the glass that stifles the sound. It must be said that the idea of love without attachment is relatively foreign to the Western sensibility. Not being attached means not that we love the person less, but that we are not primarily focused on self-love through the love we claim to have for the other. Altruistic love is the joy of sharing life with those around us — our friends, our lovers and companions, our wife or husband — and of contributing to their happiness. We love them for who they are and not through the distorting lens of self-centeredness. We are concerned for the other's happiness, and instead of wanting to possess him, we feel responsible for his well-being. Instead of anxiously awaiting some gratification from him, we can receive his reciprocal love joyfully.

And then gradually we try to extend that love even further. We must be capable of loving all people, unconditionally. Is it asking too much to love an enemy? It may seem like an impossible undertaking, but it is based on a very simple observation: all beings without exception wish to avoid suffering and to know happiness. Genuinely altruistic love is the desire for that wish to be granted. If the love we offer depends exclusively on how we are treated, we won't be able to love our enemy. However, it is otherwise certainly possible to hope that he will stop suffering and be happy!

How do we reconcile this unconditional and impartial love with the fact that we have preferential relationships with certain people in our lives? Look at the sun. It shines over all people impartially even though it may be hotter and brighter to those who are nearer to it. Despite the limitations inherent in any metaphor, we get the idea that it is possible to develop within ourselves the kind of goodness that embraces all living beings. In Nepal, for example, all women older than oneself are addressed as "big sister" and those younger as "little sister." Such open, altruistic, and caring kindness, far from diminishing the love we bear for our nearest and dearest, only increases and ornaments it.

We have to be realistic, of course — we can't very well overtly express our affection and love in the same way to everyone. It is normal that the effects of our love should involve some people more than others. Nonetheless, there is no reason why a special relationship with a friend or lover should limit the love and compassion we may feel for all people. When it arises, that limitation is called attachment. It is harmful to the extent that it pointlessly restricts selfless love's field of play. The sun ceases to shine in all directions; it is reduced to a narrow beam of light. Such attachment is a source of suffering, because selfish love constantly butts up against the barriers it has itself erected. The truth is, possessive and exclusive desire, obsession, and jealousy have meaning only in the closed universe of attachment. Selfless love is the highest expression of human nature that has not been obscured and distorted by the manipulations of the ego. Selfless love opens an inner door that renders self-importance, and hence fear, inoperative. It allows us to give joyfully and to receive gratefully.

12

HATRED

Hatred is the winter of the heart.

VICTOR HUGO

O f all the mental poisons, hatred is the most toxic. It is one of the chief causes of unhappiness and the driving force of all violence, all genocide, all assaults on human dignity. When someone hits us, instinct would have us hit back, so human societies give their members the right to retaliate in varying degrees of justice, depending on their level of civility. Tolerance, forgiveness, and understanding of the aggressor's situation are generally considered to be optional. We are rarely able to see the criminal as a victim of his own hatred. It is even harder to understand that the desire for vengeance stems from basically the same emotion that led the aggressor to assault us. So long as one person's hatred generates another's, the cycle of resentment, reprisal, and suffering will never be broken. "If hatred responds to hatred, hatred will never end," taught the

Buddha Shakyamuni. Eliminating hatred from our mind stream is therefore a critical step in our journey to happiness.

THE UGLY FACES OF HATRED

Negative anger, the precursor to hatred, obeys the impulse to shove aside anyone who stands in the way of what the self demands, without consideration of anyone else's well-being. It is also reflected in the hostility felt when the self is threatened, and in resentment when it is wounded, scorned, or ignored. Malice is less violent than hatred but more insidious and equally pernicious. It can be fanned into hatred, which is both the desire to harm someone and the act of doing so, directly or by circuitous means.

Hatred exaggerates the faults of its object and ignores its good qualities. As Aaron Beck notes: "Biased perceptions and thinking become set in a mental vise in response to threat, real or imaginary. This rigid frame, the prison of the mind, is responsible for much of the hate and violence that plague us."[1] The mind, steeped in animosity and resentment, encloses itself in illusion and is convinced that the source of its dissatisfaction is entirely exterior to itself. Our perception of being wronged or threatened leads us to focus exclusively on the negative aspects of a person or a group. We fail to see people and events in the context of a much vaster web of interrelated causes and conditions. Forming the image of the "enemy" as despicable, we generalize it to the whole person or the entire group. We solidify the "evil" or "disgusting" attributes we see in them as being permanent and intrinsic traits, and turn away from any reevaluation of the situation. We thus feel justified in expressing our animosity and retaliating. Self-righteousness can also make us feel the need to "cleanse" our entourage, society, and the world at large from such "evil." Hence discrimination, persecution, genocide, blind retaliation, and also the death penalty, the ultimate legal retaliation. By then we have obscured the basic benevolence that makes us appreciate everyone's aspiration to avoid suffering and achieve happiness.

Hatred is not expressed solely through anger, but the latter erupts the moment circumstances permit. It is linked to other negative emotions and attitudes: aggression, resentment, bitterness, intolerance, slander, and above all, ignorance. It can also stem from fear when we or those we love are threatened.

We also have to learn to identify "everyday" hatred connected to our immediate circle. What can we do when we hate our brother, our colleague, or our ex-husband? They obsess us. We brood over their faces, their habits, and their quirks until they make us sick; our obsession relentlessly converts mundane aversion into persecution. I knew a man who turned red with anger at the slightest mention of the wife who had left him twenty years earlier.

The undesirable effects of hatred are obvious. We need only peek within ourselves. Under its influence our mind sees things in an unrealistic way, the source of endless frustration. The Dalai Lama has an answer:

> By giving in to anger, we are not necessarily harming our enemy but we are definitely harming ourselves. We lose our sense of inner peace, we do everything wrong, we cannot sleep well, we put off our guests or we cast furious glances at those who have the impudence of being in our way. If we have a pet, we forget to feed it. We make life impossible for those who live with us, and even our dearest friends are kept at a distance. Since there are fewer and fewer people who sympathize with us, we feel more and more lonely. . . . To what end? Even if we allow our

*rage to go all the way, we will never eliminate all our en-
emies. Do you know of anyone who ever has? As long as
we harbor that inner enemy of anger or hatred, however
successful we are at destroying our outer enemies today,
others will emerge tomorrow.*"2

Hatred is clearly corrosive, whatever the intensity and circumstances behind it. Once hatred has overwhelmed us, we are
no longer masters of ourselves and are incapable of thinking in
terms of love and compassion. And yet hatred always begins
with a simple thought. This is the precise moment to jump in
with one of the techniques for dispelling negative emotions
that are discussed in Chapter 10.

THE DESIRE FOR VENGEANCE

It is important to stress that we can be deeply opposed to injustice, cruelty, oppression, and fanaticism, and do everything in
our power to counteract them, without succumbing to hatred.

When we consider an individual in the clutches of hatred,
anger, and aggression, we should consider him more as a sick
patient than as an enemy. Someone who should be healed, not
punished. If an insane patient attacks a doctor, the latter must
bring him under control and try his best to cure him without
feeling reciprocal hatred. One does not expect a doctor to start
beating up his patients. One can feel boundless repulsion for
the misdeeds of an individual or group of individuals, as well as
deep sadness for the suffering they have caused, without giving
in to the desire for revenge. Sadness and repulsion need to be
mingled with broad-minded compassion for the miserable condition to which the person has sunk. The patient should be distinguished from his disease. This is not just cheap pity for the
murderer, but vast compassion for *all* sentient beings, whoever

they might be, and the wish that they may become free from hatred and ignorance. In short, contemplating the horror of other people's crimes should enhance in one's own mind a boundless love and compassion for all, rather than hatred of a few.

It is therefore important not to confuse repulsion for despicable behavior with the irrevocable condemnation of a person. Of course the act does not commit itself, but although he may currently think and behave in the most noxious way, even the cruelest torturer was not born cruel, and who knows what he will be in twenty years? Who can say for sure that he will not change? A friend of mine told me about an inmate in an American prison for repeat offenders, who very often go on to kill one another within the institution itself. This inmate decided to pass some time by attending a meditation class offered to prisoners. This is his testimony: "One day, it felt like a wall collapsing inside me. I realized that up to then I had never thought or behaved in any other terms but hatred and violence, almost as if I'd been crazy. I suddenly understood the inhumanity of my actions and began to look at the world and other people in a totally different light."

Over the course of a year, he struggled to function on a more altruistic plane and to encourage his peers to renounce violence. Such transformations are rare only because the conditions conducive to them are not usually made available to prisoners. Someone who has lost all intent and power to cause harm can be considered to be a new person.

Just as an individual can fall prey to hatred, so too can a whole society. Yet hatred can disappear from people's minds. A clean stream can become polluted, yet it can be purified and become drinkable again. Without the possibility of inner change, we would be caught in a self-defeating despair bereft of all hope. A Buddhist saying goes, "The only good thing about evil is that it can be purified." Human beings can change, and if someone has truly changed, forgiveness is not indulgence toward his past deeds but an acknowledgment of what he has become. Forgiveness is intimately linked to the possibility of human transformation.

It is widely believed that responding to evil with violence is a "human" reaction dictated by suffering and the need for "justice." But doesn't genuine humanity avoid reacting with hatred? After the bomb attack that claimed hundreds of victims in Oklahoma City in 1995, the father of a three-year-old girl who was killed in the bombing was asked if he wanted to see the chief perpetrator, Timothy McVeigh, executed. He answered simply: "Another death isn't going to ease my sorrow." Such an attitude has nothing to do with weakness, cowardice, or any kind of compromise. It is possible to be acutely sensitive to intolerable situations and the need to redress them without being driven by hatred.

One day the Dalai Lama received a visit from a monk arriving from Tibet after spending twenty-five years in Chinese labor camps. His torturers had brought him to the brink of death several times. The Dalai Lama talked at length with the monk, deeply moved to find him so serene after so much suffering. He asked him if he had ever been afraid. The monk answered: "I was often afraid of hating my torturers, for in so doing I would have destroyed myself." A few months before she died at Auschwitz, Etty Hillesum wrote: "I can see no way around it. Each of us must look inside himself and excise and destroy everything he finds there which he believes should be excised and destroyed in others. We may be quite certain that the least iota of hatred that we bring into the world will make it even more inhospitable to us than it already is."[3]

Would such an attitude be tenable if a criminal broke into your house, raped your wife, killed your little boy, and kidnapped your sixteen-year-old daughter? As hateful and intolerable as such a situation may be, the inescapable question that arises is: What do I do now? In no instance is vengeance the most appropriate solution. Why not? Because in the long run it cannot bring us lasting well-being. It offers no consolation and fuels further violence.

As Gandhi said, "If we practice an eye for an eye and a tooth for a tooth, soon the whole world will be blind and toothless." Rather than applying the law of retaliation, wouldn't it be better to relieve your mind of the resentment that is corroding it? Even if such about-faces are rare — only one of the indictees at Nuremberg, Albert Speer, regretted his actions — there's no reason not to hope for them.

To react spontaneously with anger and violence when harm has been inflicted is sometimes considered heroic, but in truth those who remain free from hatred display much greater courage. An American couple, both lawyers, went to South Africa in 1998 to attend the trial of five teenagers who had savagely and gratuitously killed their daughter in the street. They looked the murderers in the eyes and told them: "We do not want to do to you what you did to our daughter." These were not insensitive parents. They simply saw the pointlessness of perpetuating hatred. In that sense, forgiveness is not excusing the wrong that has been done; it is completely giving up the idea of taking revenge.

Miguel Benasayag, writer, mathematician, and psychiatrist, spent seven years in Argentine military prisons, including months on end of solitary confinement. He was often tortured to the point of being nothing but a locus of pain. "What they were trying to do," he told me, "was to make us forget the very notion of human dignity." His wife and brother were thrown from a plane into the sea. His stepson was given to a high-ranking officer, a common practice at that time with the children of the regime's opponents. Twenty years later, when Miguel tracked down the general who in all probability had appropriated his stepson, he found himself unable to hate him. He realized that in such circumstances hatred made no sense and wouldn't fix or contribute to anything.

Our compassion and love usually depend on the benevolent or aggressive attitude of others toward us and our loved ones. That is why it is extremely difficult for us to feel compassionate toward those who harm us. Buddhist compassion, however, is based on the wholehearted desire for all beings without exception to be liberated from suffering and its causes, hatred in particular. One can also go further by wishing that all beings, criminals included, may find the causes of happiness. Studies on forgiveness have shown that nursing everlasting resentment against a wrongdoer, never forgiving, and taking revenge do not restore peace of mind to the victims or to their kin. On the contrary, forgiving, in the sense of renouncing hatred for the criminal, has been shown to have by far the best regenerating effect in restoring some sense of inner peace.

As for the death penalty, we know that it isn't even an effective deterrent. Its elimination in Europe was not followed by a rise in crime, and its reestablishment in some American states was not followed by a drop. Since life imprisonment is enough to prevent a murderer from committing further crimes, the death penalty is therefore nothing but legalized revenge. Whether it is murder or legal execution, any killing is simply wrong.

Society does not need the kind of forgiveness that reflects a lack of concern or leniency or, even worse, that endorses the evil that has been done to others. That would leave the door open for the same horrors to happen again. Society needs forgiveness and healing so that grudges, venom, and hatred are not perpetuated. Hatred devastates our minds and causes us to devastate others' lives. Forgiving means breaking the cycle of hatred.

Hating Hatred

The only target of resentment possible is hatred itself. It is a deceitful, relentless, and unbending enemy that tirelessly disrupts and destroys lives. As appropriate as patience without weakness may be toward those we consider to be our enemies, it is entirely inappropriate to be patient with hatred itself, regardless of the circumstances. As Khyentse Rinpoche said: "It is time to redirect hatred away from its usual targets, your so-called enemies, and toward itself. Indeed, hatred is your real enemy and it is hatred that you should destroy." It is futile to try to repress or reverse it; we must go straight to the roots of hatred and rip them up. Etty Hillesum, again, speaks to this issue: "They speak of extermination. Better to exterminate the evil within a man than the man himself."[4]

There are no remedies other than personal awareness, inner transformation, and perseverance. Evil is a pathological condition. A society prey to blind fury toward another sector of humanity is merely a group of individuals alienated by ignorance and hatred. Conversely, when enough individuals have accomplished this selfless change, society can evolve toward a more humane collective attitude, integrate the repudiation of hatred and vengeance into its laws, abolish the death penalty, and promulgate respect for human rights. We must never forget, however, that there can be no outer disarmament without inner disarmament. Each and every one must change, and this process begins with oneself.

EXERCISE

Meditate on love and compassion

Meditating is a method of learning to experience things in a new way. Bring realistically to mind the suffering of someone who is dear to you. You will soon feel a deep wish and resolve to ease her suffering and remove its cause. Let this feeling of compassion fill your mind and remain in it for a while.

Then extend that same feeling to all beings, realizing that they all aspire to be free from suffering. Combine this boundless compassion with a sense of readiness to do whatever is necessary to remedy their sufferings. Dwell as long as you can in that feeling of all-embracing experience of compassion.

If while contemplating on the countless sufferings of living beings you feel powerless and lose courage, shift your attention to those who enjoy some form of happiness and have admirable human qualities. Fully rejoice in these and cultivate enthusiastic joy. This will act as an antidote to depression and envy.

Another method is to shift your meditation to impartiality. Extend your feelings of love and compassion to all beings equally — dear ones, strangers, and enemies. Remember that no matter how they might threaten you, they all strive to achieve happiness and avoid suffering.

You can also focus on selfless love, the fervent wish that all beings may find happiness and the causes of happiness. Let loving-kindness permeate your mind and rest in this all-encompassing feeling of altruistic love.

At the end of your meditation, ponder awhile the interdependence of all things. Understand that just as a bird needs two wings to fly, you need to develop both wisdom and compassion. Before engaging in your daily activities, dedicate to all sentient beings all the good you have accrued from your meditation.

13

ENVY

What cowardice it is to be dismayed by the happiness of others and devastated by their good fortune.

MONTESQUIEU

A strange sentiment, envy. We are envious of other people's happiness and certainly not of their unhappiness. Isn't that ridiculous? Wouldn't it be natural to desire their happiness? Why be uneasy when they're happy? Why feel spiteful of their good qualities? The opposite of envy is rejoicing at all the joys, little and great, experienced by others. Their happiness becomes our own.

Envy does not have desire's attractive side; it does not come disguised as a righter of wrongs, like anger; it does not adorn itself with showy ornaments, like pride; and it isn't even lazy, like ignorance. No matter what light you look at it in, it always comes across as detestable.

There are, of course, several degrees of envy and jealousy, a broad palette ranging from envy to blind, destructive rage. Benign, everyday envy distilled into half-conscious thoughts that emerge as disparaging remarks. Envy reflected in mild malice toward a colleague who's doing better than us, in caustic reflections on a friend who always seems to meet with good fortune. *Envy and jealousy derive from the fundamental inability to rejoice in someone else's happiness or success.* The jealous man rehearses the injury in his mind, rubbing salt in the wound over and over again. There is no chance of happiness whatsoever at that moment.

In every instance, envy is the product of a wound to self-importance and the fruit of an illusion. What's more, envy and jealousy are absurd for whoever feels them, since unless he resorts to violence, he is their only victim. His pique does not prevent those he's jealous of from enjoying further success, wealth, or distinction.

The truth is, what can other people's happiness possibly deprive us of? Nothing, of course. Only the ego can be wounded by it and feel it as pain. It is the ego that can't bear other people's good cheer when we're depressed or their good health when we're sick. Why not take their joy as a source of inspiration instead of making it a source of vexation and frustration?

What about the jealousy born of a sense of injustice or betrayal? It's heartbreaking to be deceived by someone we are deeply attached to, but it is again self-love that is responsible for the ensuing suffering. La Rochefoucauld observes in his *Maxims* that "there is more self-love than love in jealousy."

A friend of mine recently confided in me. "My husband's infidelity hurts me on the deepest level. I can't stand the idea of his being happier with another woman. I keep asking myself the same question: 'Why not me? What does he find in her that I don't have?'"

It's extremely difficult to maintain one's equanimity in such circumstances. Fear of abandonment and a sense of insecurity are closely linked to the lack of inner freedom. Self-absorption, with its inseparable posse of fear and hope, attraction and rejection, is the foremost enemy of inner peace. If we *really* want someone else to be happy, we can't very well insist on telling them how they have to go about it. Only the ego has the nerve to say: "Your happiness depends on mine." As Swami Prajnanpad has written: "When you love someone, you cannot expect him to do as you please. That would be tantamount to loving yourself."[1]

If we are even remotely able to think clearly, we should courageously try to set aside the mental images that torture us and the obsessiveness that makes us dream of cruel reprisals against the "usurper" of whom we are jealous, and refrain from reinforcing them. These are the direct results of our having forgotten our innermost potential for affection and peace. It will be helpful to generate empathy and altruistic love for all people, including our rivals. This antidote will heal the wound, and in time envy and jealousy will come to seem like merely a bad dream.

14

THE GREAT LEAP TO FREEDOM

What a relief it is for the burdened man who has long walked through the world of suffering to lay down his heavy and useless load.

LONGCHEN RABJAM

To be free is to be master of oneself. For many people such mastery involves freedom of action, movement, and opinion, the opportunity to achieve the goals they have set themselves. This conviction locates freedom primarily outside oneself and overlooks the tyranny of thoughts. Indeed it is a commonplace in the West that freedom means being able to do whatever we want and to act on any of our impulses. It's a strange idea, since in so doing we become the plaything of thoughts that disturb our mind, the way a mountaintop wind bends the grass in every direction.

"For me, happiness would be doing anything I want with no one having to say anything about it," said one young Englishwoman interviewed by the BBC. Can anarchic freedom, in which the only goal is the immediate fulfillment of desires, bring happiness? There is every reason to doubt it. Spontaneity is a precious quality so long as it is not confused with mental chaos. If we let the hounds of craving, jealousy, arrogance, and resentment run amok in our mind, they will soon take over. Conversely, inner freedom is a vast, clear, and serene space that dispels pain and nourishes peace.

Inner freedom is above all freedom from the dictatorship of "me" and "mine," of the ego that clashes with whatever it dislikes and seeks desperately to appropriate whatever it covets. So being free comes down to breaking the bonds of afflictions that dominate and cloud the mind. It means taking life into one's own hand, instead of abandoning it to tendencies created by habit and mental confusion. If a sailor looses the tiller and lets the sails flap in the wind and the boat drift wherever the currents take it, it is not called freedom — it is called drifting. Freedom here means taking the helm and sailing toward the chosen destination.

In daily life this freedom allows us to be open and patient with others while remaining committed to the direction we have chosen to take in life. Indeed it is essential to have a sense of direction. When trekking in the Himalayas, you often have to walk for days or even weeks. You suffer from the cold, the altitude, snowstorms, but since every step brings you closer to your goal, there is joy in making the effort to attain it. If you get lost and find yourself without bearings in an unknown valley or forest, your courage instantly vanishes; the weight of exhaustion and solitude is suddenly crushing, anxiety mounts, and every step is an ordeal. You lose the will to walk; you want to sit down in despair. Perhaps the anxiety that some people feel likewise comes from a lack of direction in their lives, from having failed to grasp their own inner potential for change.

Understanding that we are neither perfect nor completely happy is not a weakness. It is a very healthy acknowledgment that has nothing to do with self-pity, pessimism, or a lack of self-confidence. Such understanding leads to a new appreciation of life's priorities and a surge of energy that Buddhism calls renunciation — a word that is often misunderstood and that really expresses a profound desire for freedom.

THE PARADOX OF RENUNCIATION

For many people, the idea of renunciation and nonattachment implies a descent into a dank dungeon of asceticism and discipline. The depressing privation of life's pleasures. A series of injunctions and bans that restrict one's freedom to enjoy life. A Tibetan proverb says: "Speaking to someone about renunciation is like hitting a pig on the nose with a stick. He doesn't like it at all."

But true renunciation is more like a bird soaring into the sky when its cage is opened. Suddenly the endless concerns that had oppressed the mind are gone, allowing the free expression of inner potential. We are like weary marchers, carrying heavy bags filled with a combination of provisions and stones. Wouldn't the smart thing be to set our bag down for a moment to sort it out and lighten our load?

Renunciation is not about depriving ourselves of that which brings us joy and happiness — that would be absurd; it is about abandoning what causes us inexhaustible and relentless distress. It is about having the courage to rid ourselves of dependency on the root causes of suffering. To do this, we first have to identify and recognize these causes and then become mindful of them in our daily life. If we do not take the time to do this, we can easily fool ourselves by overlooking the relevant causes.

Renunciation, then, does not come down to saying no to all that is pleasant, to giving up strawberry ice cream or a nice hot shower after a long walk in the hills. It comes down to asking ourselves, with respect to certain aspects of our lives: "Is this going to make me happier?" Genuine happiness — as opposed to contrived euphoria — endures through life's ups and downs. To renounce is to have the daring and intelligence to scrutinize what we usually consider to be pleasures in order to determine if they really enhance our well-being. The renunciant is not a masochist who considers everything that is good to be bad. Who could put up with this? The renunciant has taken the time to look within herself and has found that she does not need to cling to certain aspects of her life.

FREE FROM THE PAST, FREE FROM THE FUTURE

One day a Tibetan came to see an old wise man whom I happened to be visiting with at the time, at Ghoom near Darjeeling in India. He began by telling him all about his past misfortunes, then went on to list everything he feared for the future. All this time the wise man calmly roasted potatoes in a little brazier on the floor before him. After a while he told his plaintive visitor: "What's the point of worrying about things that no longer exist and things that do not yet exist?" Nonplussed, the visitor stopped talking and remained silent for quite some time alongside the sage, who occasionally handed him a hot, crusty potato.

Inner freedom allows us to savor the lucid simplicity of the present moment, free from the past and emancipated from the future. Freeing ourselves from the intrusion of memories of the past does not mean that we are unable to draw useful lessons from our experience. Freeing ourselves from fear of the future does not make us incapable of approaching it clearly, but saves us from getting bogged down by pointless fretting.

Such freedom has aspects of clearheadedness, and joy that allow us to accept things peacefully without sinking into passivity or weakness. It also allows us to use *all* life's circumstances, favorable and adverse, as catalysts for personal change, and to avoid becoming arrogant when they are favorable and depressed when they are not.

THE INTELLIGENCE OF RENUNCIATION

Renunciation is a way of taking one's life into one's own hands, that is, of becoming fed up with being manipulated like a puppet by selfishness, the scramble for power and possessions, and the never-ending quest for pleasure. She who practices genuine renunciation is well informed of all that goes on around her. She does not flee the world because she's unable to control it, but knowing how prejudicial pointless worries are, she has no interest in entertaining them. Her approach is eminently pragmatic. The renunciant shows no weakness, only daring.

Renunciation also conveys the delicious taste of simplicity and profound well-being. Once you have sampled it, it becomes easier and easier. But there is no question of forcing oneself into renunciation, which would be doomed to failure. First you must clearly see its advantages and aspire to free yourself from that which you want to renounce. Once you've done that, renunciation is experienced as an act of liberation.

While we must never neglect those with whom we share our lives, we can get off the endless roller coaster of happiness and suffering. In so doing, we reject nothing but simplify everything.

THE BALM OF SIMPLICITY

"Our life is frittered away by detail.... Simplify, simplify," wrote the American moralist Henry David Thoreau. Renunciation involves simplifying our acts, our speech, and our thoughts to rid ourselves of the superfluous. Simplifying our activities doesn't mean sinking into laziness; on the contrary, it means acquiring a growing freedom and counteracting the most subtle aspect of inertia — the impulse that, even when we know what really counts in life, prompts us instead to pursue a thousand trivial activities, one after the other, like ripples in the water.

To simplify our speech is to curtail the stream of pointless talk that continuously flows from our mouths. It is, above all, to abstain from directing hurtful remarks at others. Ordinary conversations, rued the hermit Patrul Rinpoche, are "echoes of echoes." You need only turn on the TV or go to any social gathering to be engulfed in a torrent of words that not only are often useless, but also aggravate covetousness, hostility, and vanity. You don't have to wrap yourself in aloof silence but simply be aware of what is appropriate speech and of the value of time. Appropriate speech avoids self-serving lies, cruel words, and the gossip whose only effect is to distract us and sow discord. It is always adapted to circumstance, gentle or firm as required, and the product of an altruistic and controlled mind.

Having a simple mind is not the same as being simple-minded. On the contrary, simplicity of mind is reflected in clarity of thought. Like clear water that lets us see all the way to the lake bottom, simplicity reveals the nature of the mind behind the veil of restless thought.

André Comte-Sponville has found an inspiring way of describing it:

> *The simple person lives the way he breathes, with no more effort or glory, with no more affectation and without shame.... Simplicity is freedom, buoyancy, transparency. As simple as the air, as free as the air.... The simple person does not take himself too seriously or too tragically. He goes on his merry way, his heart light, his*

soul at peace, without a goal, without nostalgia, without impatience. The world is his kingdom, and suffices him. The present is his eternity, and delights him. He has nothing to prove, since he has no appearances to keep up, and nothing to seek, since everything is before him. What is more simple than simplicity? What lighter? It is the virtue of wise men and the wisdom of saints.[1]

A WANDERER UNLIKE ANY OTHER

I cannot resist the pleasure of relating an episode from the life of Patrul Rinpoche, a Tibetan hermit of the nineteenth century. At first sight, no outward sign distinguished him as a great spiritual master. All his worldly possessions consisted of a walking stick; a little cloth bag containing an earthenware pot for boiling his tea and a copy of *Way of the Bodhisattva*, a classic text on love and compassion; and the clothes on his back. He stopped wherever he pleased — caves, forests, huts — and stayed however long he liked. Whenever he stopped at a monastery, he came unannounced so as to avoid any preparations being made in honor of his arrival. During his stay, he slept in a monk's cell or camped outdoors.

One day Patrul Rinpoche was sharing his learning with several thousand people near the Dzamthang monastery in eastern Tibet. Instead of sitting in a temple or on a throne, he sat on a grass-covered mound in a meadow. Although everyone knew that he never accepted gifts, at the end of the lesson an old man insisted on presenting him with a silver ingot, which he placed in the grass at the hermit's feet before he left.

Patrul slung his bundle over his shoulder, grabbed his stick, and went on his way. A thief who had been watching the scene followed him with the intention of stealing the silver. Patrul walked alone, with no specific destination, and spent a peaceful night under the stars. Once he was asleep, the thief crept up under cover of darkness. Patrul had laid down his little cloth bag and pot nearby. Finding nothing therein, the thief began searching through the hermit's loose-fitting sheepskin mantle.

Patrul was awakened by the bandit's fumbling. "Why are you rummaging through my clothes?" he cried out. The thief grumbled: "Someone gave you a silver ingot. I want it!"

"Oh dear," the hermit exclaimed. "What a hard life you lead, scurrying about like a madman! You've come all this way for a lump of silver! Poor man! Listen to me now. Retrace your steps and at dawn you'll reach the mound where I was sitting. You'll find the silver there."

The thief was rather skeptical but had spent enough time searching the hermit's things to know that he didn't have the ingot with him. Although he thought it unlikely that he'd find the money where Patrul had sent him, he went back and searched the slopes of the mound. The ingot was there, shining in the grass.

The bandit got to thinking: "That Patrul is no ordinary lama. He's freed himself of all attachment. I've earned myself some very bad karma trying to rob him." Filled with remorse, he went off to find the hermit again. When he finally caught up with him, Patrul berated him: "You again! Always on the run, aren't you? I told you I didn't have the silver. What do you want now?"

The criminal prostrated himself before Patrul to make his confession, his eyes filled with tears. "I haven't come to take anything from you. I found the silver. When I think that I was going to beat you and take everything you have! You are a true wise man. I beg your pardon and wish to become your disciple."

Patrul soothed him. "You don't need to confess to me or beg my pardon. Be generous, invoke the Buddha, and practice his teaching. That will do." Some time later, people found out what had happened and set out to thrash the thief. When Patrul

Rinpoche heard of this, he scolded them sharply. "To mistreat this man is to hurt me. Leave him alone."

Free for Others

What good is freedom if it benefits only oneself? In order to better help others, we must begin by changing ourselves.

Being free also means being able to follow the path of inner transformation. To achieve that, we have to overcome not only external adversity but also our innermost enemies: laziness, lack of focus, and the habits that constantly distract us from or defer spiritual practice.

As we have seen, pleasures, at first attractive, more often than not turn into their opposites. The effort demanded by the spiritual path and by the process of freeing oneself from suffering follows an inverse progression. Sometimes arduous to start with, it gradually becomes easier and inspiring, and little by little imparts a sense of fulfillment that nothing can replace. Its difficulties give way to a profound satisfaction that states of dependency cannot secure. Sukha is a kind of armor, as supple as it is invulnerable. Says one Tibetan sage: "It is easy for a bird to hurt a horse whose back is wounded; it is easy for circumstances to hurt one who is fearful, but they have no power over one who is stable." Such an accomplishment fully deserves the name of freedom.

15

A Sociology of Happiness

People have ready-made answers to many questions about themselves; they know their name, their address, and their party affiliation. But they do not generally know how happy they are, and they must construct an answer to that question, whenever it is raised.

DANIEL KAHNEMAN

One goal of this book is to identify the inner conditions that favor happiness and those that hinder it. But what can we learn from social psychology studies about the factors that influence our quality of life? Psychology and psychiatry in the early twentieth century were mostly concerned with describing and treating psychological disturbances and mental illness. Until recently, however, science had barely looked into our potential for moving from a "normal" state of being to one of optimal well-being and flourishing. Things are now beginning to change as the cognitive sciences and "positive psychology" enjoy a significant surge in interest.

Are we born with varying genetic predispositions to happiness or unhappiness? How do our upbringing and our life experiences favor or undermine our subjective well-being? To what extent is it possible to modify our personality traits and generate a lasting sense of satisfaction? What mental factors contribute to that transformation? Over the past thirty years, all of these questions have been the subject of ample research. Hundreds of thousands of subjects have been studied in some seventy countries and a vast number of results published.[1]

Three main conclusions emerge from such work. First, outward conditions and other general factors — such as wealth, education, social status, hobbies, sex, age, ethnicity, and so on — have circumstantial influence but account altogether for no more than 10 to 15 percent of the variable satisfaction quotient.[2] Second, we seem to have a genetic *predisposition* to being happy or unhappy — about 25 percent of our *potential* for happiness appears to be determined by genes. Yet genes act more like a blueprint that can be applied or ignored depending upon circumstances. Third, we can exert considerable influence on our experience of happiness and unhappiness through the way we live and think, how we perceive life's events, and how we react to them. And fortunately so, because if our capacity for happiness were fixed, it would make no sense to study the phenomenon of happiness or to try to become happier in a lasting way.

These conclusions discredit a host of false ideas about happiness. Writers and philosophers have often ridiculed the idea that happiness is good for the health, that optimists live longer and happier lives, and that one can "cultivate" happiness as a skill. And yet these have gradually now come to be recognized as established facts.

THE GENERAL CONDITIONS OF HAPPINESS

Much research has been devoted to happiness defined as quality of life or, more precisely, as the subjective appreciation of one's own quality of life. The questionnaires used in these studies are simple, if not simplistic, and ask respondents such questions as "Are you very happy, happy, somewhat happy, unhappy, or very unhappy?" The subjects under consideration are then asked to provide information on their social and marital status, their income, their health, the landmark events of their lives, and so on. The correlations are then analyzed statistically. More recent studies are designed to monitor in real time the feelings experienced by people in their daily lives. According to Daniel Kahneman, a psychologist and Nobel laureate, data obtained from such studies provide a more accurate estimate of subjective well-being, because they are less distorted by biased memories and other artifacts.

These general surveys have found that the sense of happiness is higher in countries that ensure their inhabitants' basic resources, greater security, autonomy, and freedom, as well as sufficient educational opportunities and access to information. People are manifestly happier in countries where personal freedoms are guaranteed and democracy secure. This is only to be expected: citizens are happier in a climate of peace. Regardless of economic conditions, those who live under military rule are unhappier.

Happiness rises with social involvement and participation in volunteer organizations, the practice of sports or music, and membership in leisure clubs. It is closely tied to the maintenance and quality of private relationships.

People who are married or cohabiting are, in general, significantly happier than singles, widows and widowers, or the divorced or separated living alone. As for the children of divided parents, they are twice as likely to experience a variety of social, psychological, or academic problems.[3]

Happiness tends to be greater among those who have paying work. Death rate and incidences of illness, depression, suicide, and alcoholism are notably higher among the unemployed.

And yet housewives are no more dissatisfied than professionals. It is also interesting to note that retirement makes life not less satisfying, but rather more so. The elderly see their lives as slightly less pleasant than those of the young, but they enjoy more stable overall satisfaction and feel more positive emotions. Age, it seems, can grant relative wisdom. Happiness tends to be more pronounced among highly energetic people in good physical condition. It does not seem to be linked to climate; contrary to received wisdom, people are no happier in sunny regions than they are in rainy ones, except for the pathological cases of those suffering from depression due to the long winter nights in northern latitudes.

Leisure activities enhance satisfaction, especially among those who do not work (the retired, those of independent means, the unemployed), in part because people are more in voluntary control of what they do. Vacations have a positive effect on well-being, calm, and health. Only 3 percent of people on vacation complain of headaches, as opposed to 21 percent of those working. The same disparity holds true for fatigue and irritability.[4] It should be noted that watching television, as popular as it is, leads to only a minimal increase in well-being. As for those who watch a lot, they are on average less happy. In the United States and in Europe, people spend an average of 3.5 hours a day in front of a television set. That is a whole year of life every seven years!

MONEY DOES NOT BUY HAPPINESS

Obviously, for those who lack the basic means of subsistence and for whom money becomes a question of survival, obtaining more wealth brings a legitimate sense of satisfaction. However — and this might be more surprising to some — it appears clearly that beyond a relatively low threshold of wealth, the level of satisfaction remains unchanged even as income continues to rise. Between 1949 and now, for instance, in the United States, real income has increased more than twofold, while the number of people who declare themselves "very happy" has not only not increased but even decreased slightly.

As Richard Layard, of the London School of Economics, states: "We have more food, more clothes, more cars, bigger houses, more central heating, more foreign holidays, a shorter working week, nice work, and, above all, better health. Yet we are not happier. . . . If we want people to be happier, we really have to know what conditions generate happiness and how to cultivate them."[5]

One of the main sources of people's discontent comes from comparing themselves with others in their family, at their workplace, and among their acquaintances. As Layard explains, "There are many cases where people became objectively better off but felt subjectively worse. One is East Germany, where the living standards of those employed soared after 1990, but their level of happiness fell: with the reunification of Germany, the East Germans began to compare themselves with the West Germans, rather than with the other countries of the former Soviet bloc."[6]

Repeatedly comparing our situation with that of others is a kind of sickness of the mind that brings much unnecessary discontent and frustration. When we have a new source of enjoyment or a new car, we get excited and feel that we are at the top of our game. But we soon get used to it and our excitement subsides; when a new model comes out we become unhappy with the one we have and feel that we can only be satisfied if we get the new one, especially if other people around us have it. We are caught on the "hedonic treadmill" — a concept coined by P. Brinkman and D. T. Campbell.[7] While jogging on a treadmill, we need to keep running simply to remain in the same spot. In this case, we need to keep running toward acquiring more things and new sources of excitement simply to maintain our current level of satisfaction.

This is clearly not an optimal state of mind. To endlessly thirst for more merely in order to remain satisfied, and to grow uneasy when others nearby are faring better than us, has more to do with mental afflictions — envy, covetousness, and jealousy — than with the conditions in which we live. As a Tibetan proverb goes: "To know how to be satisfied is to hold a treasure in the palm of one's hand." Otherwise, once we've got one, we'll want two and begin a cycle of chronic discontent.

An interesting problem psychologists have been dealing with is that of the "happy poor," who are more cheerful and carefree than many rich but stressed people. One study undertaken by Robert Biswas-Diener among the homeless and slum dwellers of Calcutta found that in many spheres — family life, friendship, morality, food, and joyfulness — their satisfaction level was barely lower than that of university students.[8] Conversely, those who live on the streets or in the shelters of San Francisco, and who are generally without social and emotional attachments, claim to be far more unhappy. Sociologists attempt to explain this phenomenon by the fact that many of the Calcutta poor have abandoned the hope of improving their social and financial status and are therefore not anxious on that score. Furthermore, they are far more easily satisfied when they obtain anything, such as food and the like.

This is not merely putting a rosy face on things. When I lived in a poor neighborhood of Delhi, where I was printing Tibetan texts, I knew a lot of rickshaw wallahs, men who pedal all day long, carrying passengers in the backs of their ancient tricycles. On winter nights, they gather in little groups on the street around fires fed with empty crates and cartons. Conversation and laughter are raucous and those who can sing belt out popular songs. Then they go to sleep, curled up on their tricycle seats. They don't lead easy lives — far from it — but I can't help thinking that their good natures and insouciance make them happier than many a victim of stress in a Parisian ad agency or the stock market. I also remember an old Bhutanese peasant. Once when the young abbot of my monastery gave him a gift of a new shirt and one thousand rupees, he looked completely disconcerted and told him that he had never possessed more than three hundred rupees (about seven dollars) at any one time. When my abbot asked him if he had any worries, he thought for a while and then answered:

"Yes, leeches, when I walk through the forest in the rainy season."

"What else?"

"Nothing else."

Diogenes, in his famous barrel, told Alexander: "I am greater than you, my lord, because I have disdained more than you have ever possessed." While the simplicity of a Bhutanese peasant may not have the same weight as the words of a great philosopher, it is still obvious that happiness and satisfaction are not proportional to wealth.

Eighty percent of Americans claim to be happy! But the situation is far from being as encouraging as it looks. Despite the improvement in material conditions, depression is now ten times as prevalent as it was in 1960 and affects an ever younger sector of the population. Forty years ago, the mean age of people succumbing to depression for the first time was twenty-nine; today it's fourteen.[9] Suicide is the cause of 2 percent of deaths worldwide every year, which ranks it above war and murder.[10] In the United States, suicide triggered by bipolar depression, once called manic depression, is the second leading cause of death among teenage girls and the third among teenage boys,[11] and in Sweden, suicide among students has risen 260 percent since 1950.

Between 1950 and 1980, recorded crime rose 300 percent in the United States and 500 percent in the United Kingdom. Although the crime rate has significantly declined since then, it remains much higher than it was fifty years ago, despite the fact that the external conditions of well-being — medical care, buying power, access to education, and leisure time — have improved continuously. How do we explain that?

According to a number of studies reviewed by Richard Layard, this rise may be related to many factors, such as a decreased sense of trust among people, the breaking up of families, the influence of violence being constantly thrust upon television viewers, the fact that people increasingly live alone and that fewer belong to associations organized around culture, sports, politics, philanthropy, and service to the poor and the elderly.[12]

The decrease in trust, for instance, is striking. In 1960, when asked, "Do you think most people can be trusted?" 58 percent of Americans and the same proportion of Britons said yes, while in 1998 that figure had fallen to 30 percent. The vast majority of Americans now think that "these days a person doesn't really know whom he can count on."[13]

Martin Seligman has theorized that "an ethos that builds unwarranted self-esteem, espouses victimology, and encourages rampant individualism has contributed to the epidemic."[14] In his view, exacerbated individualism helps explains the huge increase in the rate of depression in Western societies, partly as a result of the "meaninglessness" that occurs when "there is no attachment to something larger than oneself." Buddhism would add that it is also surely due to the tireless dedication of most of our time to external activities and goals, instead of learning to enjoy the present moment, the company of those we love, the peace of natural environments, and, above all, the flowering of inner peace that gives every second of life a new and different quality.

The excitement and pleasure derived from increasing and intensifying sensory stimuli, from noisy, frenetic, and sensual entertainments, cannot substitute for inner well-being. Excess is meant to shake us out of our apathy, but more often than not it leads only to nervous fatigue coupled with chronic dissatisfaction.

THE HEREDITARY NATURE OF HAPPINESS

Are we born predisposed to happiness or unhappiness? Does genetic inheritance trump other psychological factors, including those linked to the events of early childhood, the environment, and education? Can environment and emotional factors modify the expression of genes? To what extent and for how long is our brain capable of major changes — commonly referred to as brain plasticity? These points have been hotly debated in scientific circles. One possible line of response comes with the study of identical twins who have been separated at birth. They have exactly the same genome but have been raised in conditions that may be extremely divergent. To what extent will they resemble each other psychologically? We can also compare the psychological profile of adopted children to that of their biological parents and then to that of their adoptive parents. Such studies have found that with respect to anger, depression, intelligence, overall satisfaction, alcoholism, neuroses, and many other factors, identical twins separated at birth share more psychological traits than do fraternal twins raised together.

Likewise, psychologically, adopted children far more closely resemble the biological parents who did not raise them than they do the adoptive parents who did. A study of hundreds of such cases led Auke Tellegen and his colleagues to assert that happiness is 45 percent inheritable and that our genes determine approximately 50 percent of the variables among all personality traits considered.[15]

However, other researchers see this as an extreme and dogmatic interpretation. After separation at birth, most of the twins included in these studies tend to be adopted by well-to-do families that have long sought the adoption and take excellent care of the children. The results would probably be very different if some of these children were doted on by their adoptive families while their twin ended up on the streets or in the slums. According to these researchers, the percentage of personality variables that are the product of genes does not exceed 25 percent and represents merely a *potential* whose expression depends on many other factors.

Michael Meaney and his colleagues at Douglas Hospital Research Center in Canada have shown through a series of fascinating experiments[16] that when rats that were genetically disposed to extreme anxiety were entrusted in the first ten days of their lives to overcaring mothers that groomed and licked them constantly and were in physical contact with them as frequently as possible, the genes that regulated the response to stress were blocked (by a process called methylation) and remained unexpressed throughout the rats' lives (unless the rats were subjected to major trauma). Conversely, the offspring of low-caring mothers displayed high amounts of stress. Recent evidence suggests, however, that these latter effects are reversible. If a pup from a low-licking mother is "adopted" by a high-licking mother, it shows normal development. Individual differences in maternal care have been shown to modify not only an offspring's ability to cope with stress later in life, but also its brain and cognitive development. The pups reared by high-licking mothers are not only calmer during stress but show a greater capacity for learning. Meaney and other researchers are now engaged in a major study to examine how this translates to humans. The researchers predict that if the patterns observed in humans are comparable, the children of mothers who are less engaged with their children may be predisposed to problems such as aggressive behavior and attention deficit disorder. This certainly agrees with the Buddhist view that a young child essentially needs affection on a regular basis. It is undeniable that the amount of love and tenderness we receive as little children strongly influences our vision of life. We know that child victims of sexual abuse are at twice the risk as others of suffering from depression as teenagers or adults, and that many criminals were deprived of love and mistreated as children.

In the context of personal transformation, it is also important to point out that among those traits with strong genetic bases, some seem to be barely modifiable (those for weight determination, for instance), while others can be significantly modified by the circumstances of life and mental practice.[17] This is particularly so in the cases of fear, pessimism, and . . . happiness.

PERSONAL CHARACTERISTICS

Happiness does not seem to be linked to intelligence, at least not as measured by IQ tests, or to sex or ethnicity, any more than it is to physical beauty. And yet "emotional intelligence" significantly differentiates happy people from unhappy ones. This concept, coined and described by Peter Salowey and introduced to the general public by Daniel Goleman, is defined as the ability to correctly perceive and take account of other people's feelings. It is also the ability clearly and quickly to identify our own emotions.

According to K. Magnus and his colleagues, happiness goes hand in hand with the capacity to assert oneself with extroversion and empathy — happy people are generally open to the world.[18] They believe that an individual can exert control over herself and her life, while unhappy people tend to believe themselves to be destiny's playthings. It would seem that the more an individual is capable of controlling her environment, the happier she is. It is interesting to note that in everyday life, extroverts experience more positive events than introverts, and neurotics have more negative experiences than stable people. A person may be on a "streak" of bad luck or feel herself to be a magnet for problems, but it is important to keep in mind that it is ultimately our own disposition — extroverted or neurotic, optimistic or pessimistic, self-centered or altruistic — that impels us into the same situation again and again. An open-minded person is more skilled at battling through difficult circumstances, whereas someone who is ill at ease feels increased anxiety that is usually reflected in affective and familial issues and social failure.

A spiritual dimension, whether religious or not, helps us to set goals in life and promotes human values, charity, generosity, and openness — all factors that bring us closer to happiness than to misery. It helps us to spurn the cynical idea that there is no direction to follow, that life is nothing but a self-centered struggle under the battle cry "Every man for himself."

It is easy to imagine a priori how health might have a powerful influence on happiness and how hard it would be to be happy if we were stricken by a serious illness and confined to a hospital. But that turns out not to be the case, and even in such circumstances we soon return to the level of happiness we enjoyed before falling sick. Studies of cancer patients have found that their happiness quotient is barely lower than that of the rest of the population.

HAPPINESS AND LONGEVITY

D. Danner and his colleagues studied the longevity of a group of 178 Catholic nuns born in the early twentieth century.[19] They lived in the same convent and taught at the same school in Milwaukee. Their case is particularly interesting because the outward circumstances of their lives were remarkably similar: the same daily routines, same diet, no tobacco or alcohol, same social and financial status, and, lastly, same access to medical care. These factors eliminated many variables caused by environmental conditions.

The researchers analyzed the autobiographical account that each nun had written before taking her vows. Psychologists who knew nothing about these women assessed the positive and negative sentiments expressed in their writings. Some had repeatedly mentioned that they were "very happy" or felt "great joy" at the thought of entering monastic life and serving others, while others manifested little or no positive emotion. Once the nuns were classified according to the degree of joy and satisfaction expressed in their brief bios, the results were correlated with their longevity.

It turned out that 90 percent of the nuns placed in the "most happy" quarter of the group were still alive at eighty-five, as opposed to 34 percent of those in the "least happy" quarter. An in-depth analysis of their writing allowed the elimination of other factors that might have explained the disparate longevity figures: no link was established between the nuns' longevity and the strength of their faith, the intellectual sophistication of their writing, their hopes for the future, or any other parameter that was considered. In a word, it would seem that happy nuns live longer than unhappy nuns.

Similarly, a two-year study of 2,000 Mexicans over the age of sixty-five living in the United States found that the mortality of those expressing mostly negative emotions was twice as high as that of those of happy disposition who experienced positive emotions.[20] A Finnish survey of 96,000 widowed people showed that their risk of dying doubled in the week following their partner's death.[21] This increased vulnerability has been attributed to the lowering of the immune system's defenses triggered by the grief and depression experienced by the bereaved.

SO WHAT?

How do we explain that there is ultimately so little correlation — 10 to 15 percent — between wealth, health, beauty, and happiness? According to Ed Diener, "It appears that the way people perceive the world is much more important to happiness than objective circumstances."[22] It is also about the goals we set for our own lives.[23] Having a lot of money necessarily plays a role in the happiness of someone who has set personal enrichment as his main objective, but it will have little impact on someone for whom wealth is of secondary importance.

As for the correlations highlighted by social psychology, in most cases it is unknown whether they act as causes or as consequences. We know that friendship goes with happiness, but are we happy because we have a lot of friends or do we have a lot of friends because we're happy? Do extroversion, optimism, and confidence cause happiness or are they manifestations of it? Does happiness promote longevity or do people of great vitality also happen to have happy dispositions? These studies cannot resolve such questions. So what should we make of them?

One may argue that some of these qualities, such as happiness, altruism, and optimism, almost necessarily come in clusters. One cannot experience genuine and lasting happiness while being extremely selfish and pessimistic about everything and everyone, because altruism and a constructive outlook are essential components of authentic happiness.

When the subjects of the above studies were questioned in greater detail on their reasons for claiming to be happy, they cited as major contributing factors their family, friends, a good job, an easy life, good health, the freedom to travel, participation in social life, access to culture, information, and entertainment, and so on. On the other hand, they rarely mentioned an optimal state of mind that they themselves had worked to establish as a skill. It is obvious that even when life's material circumstances provide "all we need" to be happy, we aren't always — far from it. Moreover this "all" has no inherent stability and is bound to fall apart sooner or later, taking happiness with it. Only one or two conditions need to be missing for that to occur. Dependence on such conditions creates anxiety because, consciously or not, we are constantly asking ourselves: "Is this going to hold? For how long?" We begin by wondering with hope and anxiety if we can manage to bring the ideal conditions together, then we become fearful of losing them, and finally we suffer when they vanish. The sense of insecurity is always with us.

Sociological studies tell us very little about the inner conditions of happiness and nothing at all about the ways each individual can develop them. The goal of these studies is limited to highlighting the general conditions that must be improved in order to create "the greatest good for the greatest number." The goal is highly desirable, but the quest for happiness can't be reduced to the arithmetic of material conditions. Such limitations were understood by most researchers. Ruut Veenhoven, for one, asserts that "the determinants of happiness can be sought at two levels: external conditions and internal processes. If we manage to identify the circumstances in which people tend to be happy, we can create similar conditions for everyone. If we come to grips with the internal processes that govern them, we may be able to teach people how to take pleasure in living."[24]

GROSS NATIONAL HAPPINESS

Modern states do not believe that it's their job to make their citizens happy; their concern, rather, is to safeguard security and property.[25]

LUCA AND FRANCESCO CAVALLI-SFORZA

At a World Bank forum held in February 2002 in Kathmandu, Nepal, the representative of Bhutan, a Himalayan Buddhist kingdom the size of Switzerland, asserted that while his country's gross national product was not very high, he was, conversely, more than satisfied with its gross national happiness index. Bhutan's policy of gross national happiness (GNH), viewed with indulgent smiles or private mockery by representatives of the "overdeveloped" countries, was established in the 1980s by King Jigme Singye Wangchuck and ratified by its parliament.

In many industrial nations, economic prosperity is often equated with happiness. However, it is well known that while buying power has risen by 16 percent over the past thirty years in the United States, the percentage of people calling themselves "very happy" has fallen from 36 to 29 percent.[26] We are therefore heading for trouble if we peg our happiness to the

Dow Jones index. Seeking happiness only by improving material conditions is like grinding sand in the hopes of extract-
ing oil.

Unlike GNP, the economic indicator that measures cash
flow through an economy, GNH measures the happiness of the
people as an indicator of development and progress. In order to
improve the quality of life for its people, Bhutan has balanced
cultural and environmental preservation with the development
of industry and tourism. It is the only country in the world
where hunting and fishing are banned throughout the land.
That is in happy contrast to the two million hunters in France.
In addition, 60 percent of the land is required by law to remain
forested.

Bhutan is considered by some to be an undeveloped country, but underdeveloped from whose point of view? There is a
certain amount of poverty, but no destitution or homelessness.
Fewer than a million inhabitants live scattered across a sublime
landscape three hundred miles in breadth. Throughout the
countryside, every family has land, livestock, and a weaving
loom and can meet most of its needs. Education and health care
are free. Maurice Strong, who helped Bhutan to become a
member of the United Nations, used to say: "Bhutan can become like any other country, but no other country can ever return to being like Bhutan."

You may ask dubiously whether these people are genuinely
happy. Sit on a hillside and listen to the sounds of the valley.
You'll hear people singing as they sow seed, as they reap grain, as
they stroll down the road. "Spare me the Pollyanna stories!" you
protest. Pollyanna stories? No, just a reflection of the GNH
index!

16

Happiness in the Lab

There is no large and difficult task that can't be divided into little, easy tasks.

BUDDHIST SAYING

Throughout these pages I have sought to explore the relationships between material conditions and the inner conditions that influence happiness. Without second-guessing the very nature of consciousness[1] — a discussion that would lead us too far astray — it is clear that questions remain about the relationship between happiness and brain functions. We know that many serious mental problems arise from brain pathologies over which the patient seems to have little subjective control and that need to be treated with long-term care. We also know that by stimulating certain zones of the brain, we can instantly elicit depression or feelings of intense pleasure in a subject for the duration of the stimulus. But to what extent can mind training change the brain? How long does it take for those changes to take place and how extensive can they be? Recent discoveries about brain "plasticity" and new research bringing together some of the best cognitive scientists and expert meditators who have trained their minds for years are beginning to shed light on these fascinating questions.

BRAIN PLASTICITY

Twenty years ago almost all neuroscientists believed that the adult brain had very little margin for change and could not generate new neurons. There could only be some limited reinforcement or deactivation of synaptic connections, combined with a slow decline of the brain through aging. It was thought that major changes would wreak havoc in the unbelievably complex brain functions that had been gradually built up in early life. Today ideas have changed considerably and neuroscientists are talking more and more about neuroplasticity — the concept that the brain is continually evolving in response to our experience, through the establishment of new neuronal connections, the strengthening of existing ones, or the creation of new neurons.

In a seminal research project, Fred Gage and his colleagues at the Salk Institute in California studied the response of rats to an "enriched environment." The rodents were transferred from a bland box to a large cage with toys, exercise wheels, tunnels to explore, and plenty of playmates. The results were striking: in just forty-five days, the number of neurons in the hippocampus — a brain structure associated with processing novel experiences and dispatching them for storage in other areas of the brain — grew by 15 percent, even in older rats.[2]

Does this apply to human beings? Peter Ericksson, in Sweden, was able to study the formation of new neurons in cancer patients who, in order to monitor the growth of their tumor, had already been receiving the same drug that had been used to track the making of new neurons in rats. When those elderly patients died, their brains were autopsied and it was found that, just as with the rodents, new neurons had been formed in the hippocampus.[3] It has become clear that neurogenesis in the brain is possible throughout life. As Daniel Goleman writes in *Destructive Emotions,* "Musical training, where a musician practices an instrument every day for years, offers an apt model for neuroplasticity. MRI studies find that in a violinist, for example, the areas of the brain that control finger movements in the hand that does the fingering grow in size. Those who start their training earlier in life and practice longer show bigger changes in the brain."[4] Studies of chess players and Olympic athletes have also found profound changes in the cognitive capacities involved in their pursuit. The question we can now ask is, Can a voluntary inner enrichment, such as the long-term practice of meditation, even when carried out in the neutral environment of a hermitage, induce important and lasting changes in the workings of the brain?

That is precisely what Richard Davidson and his team set out to study in the W. M. Keck Laboratory for Functional Brain Imaging and Behavior at the University of Wisconsin–Madison.

AN EXTRAORDINARY ENCOUNTER

It all began half a world away, in the foothills of the Himalayas, in India, in a small village where the Dalai Lama located his government-in-exile following the Chinese invasion of Tibet.

In the fall of 2000 a small group of some of the leading neuroscientists and psychologists of our time — Francisco Varela, Paul Ekman, Richard Davidson, and others — gathered for five days of dialogue around the Dalai Lama. This was the tenth session in a series of memorable encounters between the Dalai Lama and eminent scientists, organized since 1985 by the Mind and Life Institute at the initiative of the late Francisco Varela, a groundbreaking researcher in the cognitive sciences, and American former businessman Adam Engle.

The topic was "destructive emotions," and I had the daunting task of presenting the Buddhist view in the presence of the Dalai Lama, a test that reminded me of sitting for school exams. Following that remarkable meeting, which has been endearingly recounted by Daniel Goleman in *Destructive Emotions*, several research programs were launched to study individuals who had devoted themselves for twenty years or more to the systematic development of compassion, altruism, and inner peace.

Four years later, in November 2004, the prestigious scientific journal *Proceedings of the National Academy of Sciences* published the first of an ongoing series of papers about what can arguably be described as the first serious study of the impact on the brain of long-term meditation.[5] Meditation states have traditionally been described in terms of the first-person experience, but they now also began to be translated into a scientific language.

To date, twelve experienced meditators in the Tibetan Buddhist tradition (eight Asian and four European, comprising both monks and lay practitioners) have been examined by Richard Davidson and Antoine Lutz, a student of Francisco Varela's who joined the Madison laboratory. These accomplished practitioners, who have completed an estimated ten thousand to forty thousand hours of meditation over fifteen to forty years, were compared, as a control, with twelve age-matched volunteers, who were given meditation instructions and practiced for a week.

MEDITATORS IN THE LAB

I happened to be the first "guinea pig." A protocol was developed whereby the meditator alternated between neutral states of mind and specific states of meditation. Among the various states that were initially tested, four were chosen as the objects of further research: the meditations on "altruistic love and compassion," on "focused attention," on "open presence," and on the "visualization" of mental images.

There are methods in Buddhist practice devoted to cultivating loving-kindness and compassion. Here, the meditators try to generate an all-pervading sense of benevolence, a state in which love and compassion permeate the entire mind. They let pure love and compassion be the only object of their thoughts: intense, deep, and without any limit or exclusion. Although not immediately focusing on particular persons, altruistic love and compassion include a total readiness and unconditional availability to benefit others.

Focused attention, or concentration, requires focusing all one's attention upon one chosen object and calling one's mind back each time it wanders. Ideally this one-pointed concentration should be clear, calm, and stable. It should avoid sinking into dullness or being carried away by mental agitation.

Open presence is a clear, open, vast, and alert state of mind, free from mental constructs. It is not actively focused on anything, yet it is not distracted. The mind simply remains at ease, perfectly present in a state of pure awareness. When thoughts intrude, the meditator does not attempt to interfere with them, but allows the thoughts to vanish naturally.

Visualization consists of reconstituting in the mind's eye a complex mental image, such as the representation of a Buddhist deity. The meditator begins by visualizing as clearly as possible every detail of the face, the clothes, the posture, and so on, inspecting them one by one. Lastly, he visualizes the entire deity and stabilizes that visualization.

These various meditations are among the many spiritual exercises that a practicing Buddhist cultivates over the course of many years, during which they become ever more stable and clear.

In the lab there are two main ways to test the meditators. Electroencephalograms (EEG) allow changes in the brain's electrical activity to be recorded with a very accurate time resolution, while functional magnetic resonance imaging (fMRI) measures blood flow in various areas of the brain and provides an extremely precise localization of cerebral activity.

The meditator alternates thirty-second neutral periods with ninety-second periods in which he generates one of the meditative states. The process is repeated many times for each mental state. In this instance, the instrument measuring the meditators was equipped with 256 sensors. The electrodes detected striking difference between novices and expert meditators. During meditation on compassion, most experienced meditators showed a dramatic increase in the high-frequency brain activity called gamma waves, "of a sort that has never been reported before in the neuroscience literature," says Richard Davidson.[6] It was also found that movement of the waves through the brain was far better coordinated, or synchronized, than in the control group, who showed only a slight increase in gamma wave activity while meditating. This seems to demonstrate that "the brain is capable of being trained and physically modified in ways few people can imagine" and that the meditators are able deliberately to regulate their cerebral activity.[7] By comparison, most inexperienced subjects who are assigned a mental exercise — focusing on an object or an occurrence, visualizing an image, and so on — are generally incapable of limiting their mental activity to that one task.

One of the most interesting findings is that the monks who had spent the most years meditating generated the highest levels of gamma waves. This led Richard Davidson to speculate that "meditation not only changes the workings of the brain in the short term, but also quite possibly produces permanent changes."[8]

"We can't rule out the possibility that there was a preexisting difference in brain function between monks and novices," says Davidson, "but the fact that monks with the most hours of meditation showed the greatest brain changes gives us confidence that the changes are actually produced by mental training."[9] Further supporting this was the fact that the practitioners also had considerably higher gamma activity than the controls while resting in a neutral state, even before they started meditating. As science writer Sharon Begley comments: "That opens up the tantalizing possibility that the brain, like the rest of the body, can be altered intentionally. Just as aerobics sculpt the muscles, so mental training sculpts the gray matter in ways scientists are only beginning to fathom."[10]

A MAP OF JOY AND SADNESS

I mentioned earlier that, properly speaking, there is no center of emotions in the brain. Emotions are complex phenomena that are functions of the interaction of several regions of the brain. There is therefore no point in looking for a "center" of happiness or of unhappiness. Nonetheless, work carried out in the past twenty years, principally by Richard Davidson and his colleagues, has found that when people report feeling joy, altruism, interest, or enthusiasm, and when they manifest high energy and vivacity of spirit, they present significant cerebral activity in the left prefrontal cortex. On the other hand, those who predominantly experience such "negative" emotional states as depression, pessimism, or anxiety and have a tendency to become withdrawn manifest more activity in the right prefrontal cortex.

Moreover, when we compare the activity levels of the left and right prefrontal cortexes of subjects at rest — that is, in a neutral state of mind — we find that the relation between them varies considerably from one person to the next and quite faithfully reflects their temperament. People who are customarily more active on the left side than on the right mostly feel pleasant emotions. Conversely, those whose right prefrontal cortex is more active feel negative emotions more often. Subjects whose left prefrontal cortex is damaged (in an accident or by disease) are especially vulnerable to depression, most likely because the right side is no longer counterbalanced by the left.

These characteristics are relatively stable and manifest from early childhood. One study of nearly four hundred two-and-a-half-year-olds found that those who, upon entering a room with other children, toys, and adults, clung anxiously to their mothers and spoke only reluctantly to strangers presented activity predominantly on the right.[11] However, those who felt secure and went straight off to play and spoke freely and fearlessly had higher activity on the left. The brain clearly bears the signatures of extroversion and introversion, the imprint of a happy or unhappy disposition.

As Goleman comments:

The implications of these findings for our emotional balance are profound: we each have a characteristic ratio of right-to-left activation in the prefrontal areas that offers a barometer of the moods we are likely to feel day to day. That ratio represents what amounts to an emotional set point, the mean around which our daily moods swing. Each of us has the capacity to shift our moods, at least a bit, and to change this ratio. The further to the left the ratio tilts, the better our frame of mind tends to be, and experiences that lift our mood cause such a leftward tilt, at least temporarily. For instance, most people show small positive changes in this ratio when they are asked to recall pleasant memories of events from their past, or when they watch amusing or heartwarming film clips.[12]

What happens in the case of meditators who have cultivated positive states of mind such as empathy and compassion methodically over a long period of time? A few years earlier, Davidson had studied the asymmetry between the right and left prefrontal cortexes of an elderly Tibetan monk who had meditated on compassion several hours a day throughout his life. Davidson had noticed that the predominance of activity on the left was far higher in the monk than in the 175 "ordinary" people tested to that point. This time again, the figures registered by the meditators were outside the distribution curve representing the results of tests on several hundred subjects.

The most astonishing was the spike of so-called gamma activity in the left middle frontal gyrus. Davidson's research had already shown that this part of the brain is a focal point of positive emotions and that fluctuations in its balance are generally modest. But the data drawn from the experiments with the meditators were striking. As they began meditating on compassion, an extraordinary increase of left prefrontal activity was registered. Compassion, the very act of feeling concern for other people's well-being, appears to be one of the positive emotions, like joy and enthusiasm. This corroborates the research of psychologists showing that the most altruistic members of a population are also those who enjoy the highest sense of satisfaction in life.

Using fMRI, Lutz, Davidson, and their colleagues also found that the brain activity of the practitioners meditating on compassion was especially high in the left prefrontal cortex. Activity in the left prefrontal cortex swamped activity in the right prefrontal (site of negative emotions and anxiety), something never before seen from purely mental activity.[13]

Preliminary results obtained by Jonathan Cohen and Brent Field at Princeton University also suggest that trained meditators are able to sustain focused attention upon various tasks over a much longer period of time than untrained controls.

This is all the more remarkable given that the meditators found themselves in a highly unfamiliar environment. They were required to lie flat on their back for prolonged periods of time in the confined environment of the scanner, in which they were not permitted to move their head even a fraction of an inch, lest the data go to waste. This may not seem an ideal situation for meditating, yet Davidson was pleasantly surprised to see the meditators emerge relaxed after this grueling routine in the MRI.

READING FACES

Other remarkable results, described by Goleman in *Destructive Emotions,* were reported by Paul Ekman, one of the world's most eminent emotion scientists, who was then leading the Human Interaction Laboratory on the San Francisco campus of the University of California. Ekman had been among the small group of scientists present at Dharamsala and had observed one of the first meditators to come to the labs, several months earlier. In cooperation with that monk, he had undertaken four studies, in each of which, as he said, "we found things we've never found before." Some discoveries were so novel, Ekman commented, that he was not entirely sure of understanding them himself.

The first experiment drew on a system for measuring the facial expressions used to convey various emotions. The development of this system had been one of the greatest successes of Ekman's career. A series of faces displaying various expressions is shown in very quick succession on a video. It begins with a neutral face, followed by the expression, which remains on-screen for a mere thirtieth of a second. The emotive expression is replaced immediately by the neutral expression, and so on. The test consists of identifying, during that thirtieth of a second, the facial signals one has just seen: anger, fear, disgust, surprise, sadness, or joy.

The ability to recognize such fleeting expressions has been associated with an unusual capacity for empathy and insight. The six microemotions put forward are universal, biologically determined, and expressed facially the same way worldwide.

As Goleman comments: "While there are sometimes large cultural differences in consciously managing the expression of emotions like disgust, these ultrarapid expressions come and go so quickly that they evade even cultural taboos. Microexpressions offer a window on the other person's emotional reality."[14]

Ekman's studies of thousands of subjects had taught him that the most talented at recognizing microexpressions were also the most open to new experiences, the most curious about things in general, and the most reliable and efficient. "So I had expected that many years of meditative experience" — which requires both openness and conscientiousness — "might make them do better on this ability," Ekman explained.

It turned out that two experienced Western meditators whom Ekman had tested had achieved results that were far better than those of five thousand subjects previously tested. "They do better than policemen, lawyers, psychiatrists, customs officials, judges — even Secret Service agents," the group that had proven hitherto to be the most accurate, Ekman noted. He has since developed an interactive CD that teaches this skill to anyone in a few hours. But without this special training, it is only the meditators who display such ability.

THE STARTLE RESPONSE

The startle response, one of the most primitive reflexes in the human body's repertoire of responses, involves a series of very rapid muscular spasms in reaction to a sudden noise or an unexpected and disturbing sight. In all people, the same five facial muscles contract instantaneously, notably around the eyes. The entire thing lasts a mere third of a second.

Like all reflexes, the startle reflex responds to activity in the brain stem, the most primitive part of that organ, and is usually not subject to voluntary control. As far as science is aware, no intentional act can alter the mechanism that controls it.

The intensity of the startle response is known to reflect the predominance of the negative emotions to which someone is subject — fear, anger, sadness, and disgust. The stronger a person's flinch, the more he is inclined to experience negative emotions.

To test the first meditator's startle reflex, Ekman brought him to the Berkeley Psychophysiology Laboratory run by his longtime colleague Robert Levenson. The meditator's body movements, pulse, perspiration, and skin temperature were measured. His facial expressions were filmed to capture his physiological reactions to a sudden noise. The experimenters opted for the maximal threshold of human tolerance — a very powerful detonation, equivalent to a gunshot going off beside the ear.

The subject was told that within a five-minute period he

would hear a loud explosion. He was asked to try to neutralize the inevitable strong reaction, to the extent of making it imperceptible if possible. Some people are better than others at this exercise, but no one is able to suppress it entirely — far from it — even with the most intense effort to restrain the muscular spasms. Among the hundreds of subjects whom Ekman and Levenson had tested, none had ever managed it. Prior research had found that even elite police sharpshooters, who fire guns every day, cannot stop themselves from flinching. But the meditator was able to.

As Ekman explained: "When he tries to repress the startle, it almost disappears. We've never found anyone who can do that. Nor have any other researchers. This is a spectacular accomplishment. We don't have any idea of the anatomy that would allow him to suppress the startle reflex."

During these tests, the meditator had practiced two types of meditation: single-pointed concentration and open presence, both of which had been studied by fMRI in Madison. He found that the best effect was obtained with the open presence meditation. "In that state," he said, "I was not actively trying to control the startle, but the detonation seemed weaker, as if I were hearing it from a distance." Ekman described how, while some changes had been effected in the meditator's physiology, not one muscle in his face had moved. As the subject explained: "In the distracted state, the explosion suddenly brings you back to the present moment and causes you to jump out of suprise. But while in open presence you are *resting in* the present moment and the bang simply occurs and causes only a little disturbance, like a bird crossing the sky."

Although none of the meditator's facial muscles had quivered when he was in the open presence, his physiological parameters (pulse, perspiration, blood pressure) had risen in the way usually associated with the startle reflex. This tells us that the body reacted, registering all the effects of the detonation, but that the bang had no emotional impact on the mind. The meditator's performance suggests remarkable emotional equanimity — precisely the same kind of equanimity that the ancient texts describe as one of the fruits of meditative practice.

WHAT TO MAKE OF IT ALL?

The research, writes Goleman,

> *seeks to map . . . the extent to which the brain can be trained to dwell in a constructive range: contentment instead of craving, calm rather than agitation, compassion in place of hatred. Medicines are the leading modality in the West for addressing disturbing emotions, and for better or for worse, there is no doubt that mood-altering pills have brought solace to millions. But one compelling question the research [with meditators] raises is whether a person, through his or her own efforts, can bring about lasting positive changes in brain function that are even more far-reaching than medication in their impact on emotions.*[15]

As far as the cognitive scientists are concerned, the point of this research is not simply to demonstrate the remarkable abilities of a few isolated meditators, but to make us rethink our assumptions about the potential impact of mental training on the development of constructive emotions. "What we found is that the trained mind, or brain, is physically different from the untrained one. In time, we will be able to understand the potential importance of mind training and increase the likelihood that it will be taken seriously," says Richard Davidson.[16] The important thing is to find out whether that process of mental training is available to anyone with enough determination.

We may wonder how much practice is necessary for the brain to effectuate such changes, especially in an exercise as subtle as meditation. For example, by the time they have reached the competition for admission to national music conservatories, violinists have logged an average of ten thousand hours of practice. Most of the meditators now being studied by Antoine Lutz and Richard Davidson have gone way beyond the equivalent ten thousand hours of meditation. The major portion of their training has been undertaken during intensive retreats, in addition to their years of daily practice.

Ten thousand hours may seem indeed daunting, if not entirely out of reach, to the vast majority of us. Yet there is some comforting news. A study that Richard Davidson published with Jon Kabat-Zinn and others has shown that three months of meditation training with highly active employees of a biotech company in Madison had significantly shifted toward the left the baseline reflecting the differential activities of their right and left prefrontal cortices. The immune system of these apprentice meditators was also boosted and the flu vaccine that they received in the fall, at the end of the training, was 20 percent more effective than in the control group.[17]

What is clearly needed next are more extensive longitudinal studies on the effect of meditation in general and more particularly on the cultivation of loving-kindness and compassion. A few such studies are planned. At the newly created Santa Barbara Institute for Consciousness Studies, B. Alan Wallace will soon lead an eight-month retreat of novice meditators who will meditate eight hours a day and be monitored by scientists from the University of California–Davis. Another research program, "Cultivating Emotional Balance," undertaken at the request of the Dalai Lama and spearheaded by the Mind and Life Institute, was initiated by Paul Ekman and is presently led by Margaret Kemeny at UC–San Francisco. This program is studying the effect of a three-month meditation course on 150 women teachers and has yielded remarkable preliminary results.

If it is possible for meditators to train their minds to make their destructive emotions vanish, certain practical elements of that meditative training could be valuably incorporated into the education of children and help adults to achieve better quality of life. If such meditation techniques are valid and address the deepest mechanisms of the human mind, their value is universal and they don't have to be labeled Buddhist even though they are the fruit of more than twenty centuries of Buddhist contemplatives' investigation of the mind. In essence, the current collaboration between scientists and contemplatives could awaken people's interest to the immense value of mind training. If happiness and emotional balance are skills, we cannot underestimate the power of the transformation of the mind and must give due importance to the profound methods that allow us to become better human beings.

17

HAPPINESS AND ALTRUISM:
DOES HAPPINESS MAKE US KIND OR DOES
BEING KIND MAKE US HAPPY?

The happiest man is he who has no trace of malice in his soul.

PLATO

A man lies on the lawn of the quadrangle of Manchester University, in England, near a well-trod path. He appears to be sick. People pass by. Only a few — 15 percent — stop to see if he needs help. Later the same guinea pig lies on the same lawn, but this time he's wearing the jersey of the Liverpool soccer team, a rival of Manchester's with many fans among the Liverpudlian students. Eighty-five percent of the passersby who are fans of that team stop to see if their pal needs a hand. At the bottom of the path, a group of university researchers questions the passersby, regardless of whether or not they stopped.[1] The study, like many others, confirms the fact that the sense of belonging has considerable bearing on the manifestation of altruism. People are much more inclined to come to the assistance of a friend or of someone with whom they have something in common — ethnicity, nationality, religion, opinion — than to help a stranger to whom they feel no particular connection.

The Buddhist approach is to gradually extend that sense of belonging to all beings. To that end, it is essential to understand at the most fundamental level that all living creatures share our desire to avoid suffering and experience well-being. That understanding cannot remain a mere concept but must be internalized until it has become second nature. Ultimately, when our sense of belonging extends to all living beings, we are intimately touched by their joys and sufferings. This is the most important notion of "universal responsibility" of which the Dalai Lama often speaks.

THE JOYS OF ALTRUISM

What does altruism have to do with happiness? A series of studies conducted on hundreds of students found an undeniable correlation between altruism and happiness, determining that those who believe themselves to be happiest are also the most altruistic.[2] When we are happy, the feeling of self-importance is diminished and we are more open to others. It has been shown, for instance, that people who have experienced a happy event in the past hour are more inclined than others to come to the assistance of strangers.

Acute depression is accompanied by difficulty in feeling and expressing love for others. "Depression is the flaw in love," writes Andrew Solomon in his book *The Noonday Demon: An Atlas of Depression*. More salient yet is the assertion by those who have suffered depression that giving love to others and receiving it is an important aspect of healing. This affirmation agrees with the Buddhist perspective, which holds selfishness to be the main cause of suffering and altruistic love to be the essential ingredient of true happiness. The interdependence of all phenomena in general, and of all people in particular, is such that our own happiness is intimately linked to that of others. As we stressed in the chapter on emotions, the understanding of interdependence is at the core of sukha, and our happiness necessarily depends on that of others.

The work done by Martin Seligman, the pioneer of "positive psychology," shows that the joy of undertaking an act of disinterested kindness provides profound satisfaction. To verify his hypothesis, he asked his students to do two things — to go out and have fun and to participate in a philanthropic activity — and then to write a report for the next class.

The results were striking. The satisfactions triggered by a pleasant activity, such as going out with friends, seeing a movie, or enjoying a banana split, were largely eclipsed by those derived from performing an act of kindness. When the act was spontaneous and drew on humane qualities, the entire day was improved; the subjects noticed that they were better listeners that day, more friendly, and more appreciated by others. "The exercise of kindness is a gratification, in contrast to a pleasure," Seligman concludes[3] — gratifying in the sense of lasting satisfaction and a feeling of harmony with one's inner nature.

We can feel a certain pleasure in attaining our ends to the detriment of others, but such satisfaction is short-lived and superficial; it masks a sense of disquiet that cannot be suppressed for long. Once the excitement has waned, we are forced to acknowledge the presence of a certain discomfort. Benevolence would appear to be far closer to our "true nature" than malice. Living in harmony with that nature sustains the joy of life, while rejecting it leads to chronic dissatisfaction.

ARE WE NATURALLY SELFISH?

While biologists may be suspicious of the notion of "human nature," philosophers have no qualms about offering clear-cut opinions. The seventeenth-century English philosopher Thomas Hobbes, for instance, was convinced that people are fundamentally selfish and that true selflessness is absent in human behavior. Anything resembling altruism is merely selfishness dressed up in fine feelings. Caught one day late in life offering charity to a beggar, he was asked whether he had not just performed a selfless act. He answered: "That man's distress distressed me and in easing him I eased myself." Certainly the concept of original sin, which is peculiar to Christian civilization, and its accompanying sense of guilt are well steeped in such thinking. It has in fact had a considerable influence on Western intellectual thought, and still plays an important role today even with those who do not speak from a religious perspective.

Many evolutionary theorists have long maintained that the genes which prompt selfish behavior have a higher probability of being transmitted to coming generations. Since the carriers of such genes systematically promote their own interests over those of others, the argument goes, they have a greater chance of surviving and reproducing than the altruists. Such stark claims have become more nuanced in recent years, and it is now conceded that cooperative behavior, apparently altruistic, can be useful to the survival and proliferation of the species. For example, Elliott Sober, a philosopher of science, has shown through convincing models that isolated, selfless individuals who come into contact with only selfish and violent individuals will be taken advantage of and tend to disappear quickly.[4] Conversely, when such altruists group together and cooperate with one another, they have a definite evolutionary advantage over the selfish people, who also fight among themselves and therefore may slowly disappear from the population.

TRUE ALTRUISM

Contemporary research in behavioral psychology paints a more optimistic picture. Psychologist Daniel Batson writes: "Over the past fifteen years, other social psychologists and I have conducted more than twenty-five experiments designed to test the nature of the motivation to help evoked by empathy. Results of these experiments support the empathy-altruism hypothesis. None of the egoistic explanations proposed have received more than scattered support."[5] Genuine altruism that is motivated by no other reason than to do good for others is, after all, possible.

In order to bring pure altruism into focus, we have to eliminate various other explanations according to which all selfless behavior is merely selfishness in disguise. The experiments carried out by Batson and his team have found that it is in fact possible to identify several types of altruist. The "false altruists" help because they can't bear their own distress in the face of other people's suffering and are eager to defuse their own emotional tension. They also help because they fear being judged, or out of a desire for praise, or else to avoid feeling guilty. If they have no choice but to intervene, they assist the person in trouble (provided the price to pay isn't too high), but if they can avoid having to watch the painful spectacle of suffering or can slip away without incurring disapproval, they intervene no more frequently than those whose altruism is not developed. "True altruists," on the other hand, offer to help even when they might easily turn away or avoid intervening without being noticed. Research has found that true altruists make up about

15 percent of Western populations, and that their altruism is an enduring trait of their personality.

How can we know whether a so-called altruist isn't acting merely to experience the sense of pride earned by performing a kindness? We must determine whether she would have been just as happy for someone else to do it. For a true altruist, it's the result that counts, not the personal satisfaction of having helped. That is precisely what Batson and his team have demonstrated through their sophisticated studies.[6]

Throughout the real world, instances of genuine altruism abound — think of the many mothers who are sincerely prepared to sacrifice their lives to save their children. This example can be extended even further, since in Buddhism the true altruist learns to consider all beings with the intimacy of a parent.

Dola Jigme Kalsang was a Tibetan sage of the nineteenth century. One day while on pilgrimage to China, he came to the central square of a small town where a crowd had gathered. As he approached, he found that a thief was about to be put to death in a particularly cruel fashion: he was to be made to straddle an iron horse that had been heated to red-hot. Dola Jigme pushed his way through the crowd and proclaimed, "I am the thief!" A great silence fell; the presiding mandarin turned impassively to the newcomer and asked, "Are you ready to assume the consequences of what you have just told us?" Dola Jigme nodded. He died on the horse and the thief was spared. In such an extreme, harrowing case, what could Dola Jigme's motivation have been other than infinite compassion for the condemned? A stranger in that land, he could have gone on his way without anyone's paying him the least attention. He acted out of unconditional benevolence to save the life of a stranger. This is of course the exceptional case of someone who was a renunciant, without a family or anyone depending on him for sustenance or protection, but it tells a lot about the potential for altruism present in the human mind.

A more near-at-hand example is that of Maximilian Kolbe, a Franciscan father imprisoned at Auschwitz who offered to take the place of a family man who, along with nine others, had been selected to die of hunger and thirst in reprisal for another prisoner's escape. Although the word *altruism* itself was only coined in 1830 by Auguste Comte as a counterpart to *egoism,* it is indeed possible to be fundamentally altruistic, that is, more concerned in one's heart with the fate of others than with one's own. Such an attitude may or may not play some part in our disposition from the onset, but it can be enhanced. In fact, as the chapter "Happiness in the Lab" shows, recent research conducted with long-term meditators strongly indicates that altruistic love and compassion are skills that can be extensively trained over the years.

It is interesting to note that according to several studies, people who are best at controlling their emotions behave more selflessly than those who are very emotive.[7] In the face of other people's suffering, the latter are in fact more concerned with managing their own emotions, dominated by fear, anxiety, and distress, than with the suffering of others. Here again inner freedom, which releases us from the shackles of conflictive emotions, is won only by minimizing obsessive self-absorption. A free, vast, and serene mind is far more likely to consider a distressing situation from an altruistic point of view than is a mind relentlessly beset by internal conflicts. Moreover, it is interesting to see how certain people who witness an injustice or an attack are more focused on the wrongdoer and on pursuing, abusing, or manhandling him, than on helping the victim. This is not altruism at all, but anger.

GOLD IS GOLD

If we turn our gaze inward and examine the mind at length, we can recognize that its primal nature is the basic cognitive faculty that "illuminates," in the sense that it sheds the light of awareness on outer phenomena and inner mental events. This faculty underlies all thoughts but is not itself essentially changed by them, as the surface of the mirror is not intrinsically modified by the images reflecting in it. We can also recognize that the negative emotions — anger, for instance — are more marginal and less fundamental than love and affection. They arise mostly in reaction to provocation or some other specific event, and are not permanent states of mind. Even if we are constitutionally cranky and easy to anger, the latter is always triggered by a particular incident. With the exception of pathologies, it is very rare to experience a prolonged state of hatred that is not directed at a specific object. Altruism and compassion, on the other hand, are much more fundamental states that can inhabit our mind as a way of being and endure independently of particular objects or specific stimuli.

Anger can help to overcome obstacles, but it can and must be only episodic. People with a hostile personality, who are always in a state of readiness to become angry, for whom nearly any obstacle, no matter how minor, calls for anger, are highly dysfunctional in society and constantly meet with trouble and sorrow. Conversely, love and affection are far more essential to long-term survival. The newborn would last mere hours without her mother's affection; the disabled elderly would soon die without the care of those around them. We need to receive love in order to know how to give it. After a fit of anger, we often say, "I was out of it," or "I was not myself." But when we spontaneously do some act of disinterested kindness, such as helping a human or an animal to recover its health or freedom, or even to escape death, we have the sense of being in harmony with our true nature. What would it be like to experience that state of mind more often, to feel that the illusory barriers set up by the self have dissolved and that our sense of communion with the other reflects the essential interdependence of all beings?

Destructive mental factors are deviations that gradually distance us from our true nature, to the point that we forget its very existence. And yet nothing is forever and irreparably lost. Even buried in filth, gold remains gold in its essential nature. The destructive emotions are merely veils, superimpositions. Father Pierre Ceyrac, a renowned Jesuit missionary who has cared for thirty thousand children in India over the past sixty years, told me: "Despite everything, I'm struck by the goodness of people, even those who seem to have their hearts and eyes shut. It is other people, all others, who create the fabric of our lives and shape the way we live. Each is a note in the 'great concert' of existence, as the poet Tagore phrased it. No one can resist the call of love. We always end up opening ourselves to it. I truly believe that man is intrinsically good. We must always see the good, the beautiful, in a person, never destroy, always look for someone's greatness without distinction of religion, caste, or belief."

The relationship between having a good heart and happiness is growing ever clearer. They engender and reinforce each other and both reflect oneness with our inner nature. Joy and satisfaction are closely tied to love and affection. As for misery, it goes hand in hand with selfishness and hostility.

Generating and expressing kindness quickly dispels suffering and replaces it with lasting fulfillment. In turn, the gradual actualization of genuine happiness allows kindness to develop as the natural reflection of inner joy.

18

HAPPINESS AND HUMILITY

If you keep your mind humble, pride will vanish like morning mist.

How many times during the day do we feel pain because our pride is hurt? Pride, the exacerbation of self-importance, consists of being infatuated with the few qualities we possess and, often, of imagining ourselves to possess those we lack. It hinders all personal progress, because in order to learn we must first believe that we do not know. In the words of one Tibetan saying: "The water of good qualities does not pool on top of the rock of pride." Conversely: "Humility is like a vessel placed at ground level, ready to receive the rain of qualities."

Humility is a forgotten value in today's world. Our obsession with the image we have to project of ourselves is so strong that we have stopped questioning the validity of appearances and endlessly seek better ways to appear.

What image should we project? Politicians and movie stars have "media advisers" whose job it is to create a favorable image for their client with the general public, sometimes even teaching them how to smile. Newspapers are devoting more and more space to their "people pages," with grabby headlines on "people in the news," their ratings of who's "in" and who's "out." In all of this, what place is there for humility, a value so rare that it might almost be consigned to the museum of obsolete virtues?

The concept of humility is too often associated with self-contempt, a lack of confidence in our abilities, depression linked to a sense of powerlessness, or even to an inferiority complex or a feeling of unworthiness. This represents a significant underestimation of the benefits of humility. Says S. Kirpal Singh: "True humility is freedom from all consciousness of self, which includes freedom from the consciousness of humility. The truly humble man never knows that he is humble."[1] Not feeling that he is the center of the universe, he is open to others and sees himself as part of the web of interdependence.

At the collective level, pride is expressed in the conviction of being superior to others as a nation or a race, of being the guardian of the true values of civilization, and of the need to impose this dominant "model" on "ignorant" peoples by any means available. This attitude often serves as a pretext for "developing" the resources of underdeveloped countries. The conquistadors and their bishops burned the vast Mayan and Aztec libraries of Mexico, of which barely a dozen volumes survive. Chinese textbooks and media continue to describe Tibetans as backward barbarians and the Dalai Lama as a monster. It was pride, above all, that allowed the Chinese to ignore the hundreds of thousands of volumes of philosophy housed in Tibetan monasteries before they demolished six thousand of those centers of learning.

In what way is humility an ingredient of happiness? The arrogant and the narcissistic fuel themselves on illusions that come into continuous conflict with reality. The inevitable disillusionment that follows can generate self-hatred (when we realize that we cannot live up to our own expectations) and a feeling of inner emptiness. Humility avoids such unnecessary distress. Unlike affectation, which needs to be recognized in order to survive, humility naturally abides in inner freedom.

The humble person has nothing to lose and nothing to gain. If she is praised, she feels that it is humility, and not herself, that is being praised. If she is criticized, she feels that bringing her faults to light is a great favor. "Few people are wise enough to prefer useful criticism to treacherous praise," wrote La Rochefoucauld, echoing the Tibetan sages who are pleased to recall that "the best teaching is that which unmasks our hidden faults." Free of hope and fear alike, the humble person remains lighthearted.

Humility as an attitude is also essentially focused on others and their well-being. Studies in social psychology have found that people who overvalue themselves present a higher than average tendency toward aggression.[2] These studies also highlight the relationship between humility and the faculty of forgiveness.[3] People who consider themselves superior judge the faults of others more harshly and consider them to be less forgivable.

Paradoxically, humility promotes strength of character; the humble person makes decisions on the basis of what he believes to be right and sticks by them without concern for his own image or the opinions of others. As the Tibetan saying has it: "Outwardly, he is as gentle as a purring cat; inside, as hard to bend as a yak's neck." This resolve has nothing to do with obstinacy and stubbornness. It arises from the clear perception of a meaningful goal. It is pointless trying to persuade the woodsman with a perfect knowledge of the forest to take the path leading to a cliff.

Humility is a quality invariably found in the sage, who is

compared to a tree whose branches, heavy with fruit, bow to the ground. As for the conceited man, he is more like a bare tree whose branches rear up pridefully. Humility is also reflected in body language that lacks all arrogance and ostentation. In my travels with His Holiness the Dalai Lama, I have seen with my own eyes the immense humility, imbued with kindness, of that universally revered man. He is always attentive to everyone. One day, entering the hall where a banquet was being held in his honor by the European parliament, he noticed the cooks who were watching him through a half-open door. He headed straight for a tour of their kitchen; he emerged shortly thereafter, telling the parliamentary president and fifteen vice presidents: "It smells good!" It was a fine way to break the ice at such a solemn meal.

Westerners are also surprised when they hear great Asian scholars and contemplatives say: "I am nothing, I know nothing." They believe it's a question of false modesty or a cultural tic, when the truth is that these sages simply do not think, "I am wise," or "I am an accomplished meditator." Their humility does not mean they aren't aware of their knowledge and scholarship, but that such learning reveals how much more there is to learn. Once understood, this attitude can be touching and even amusing, as when I was present at a visit paid by two great Tibetan scholars to Dilgo Khyentse Rinpoche in Nepal. The meeting between these remarkable men was full of wit and joyful simplicity. During the conversation, Khyentse Rinpoche asked them to give teachings to the monks of the monastery. One of the scholars answered candidly, "Oh, but I know nothing," and pointing to his colleague, went on, "and *he* doesn't know anything either!" He had taken it for granted that the other scholar would have said the same thing. The latter quickly nodded his head in agreement.

19

OPTIMISM, PESSIMISM, AND NAÏVETÉ

*She loved the rain as much as the sun. Her least thoughts had
the cheery colors of lovely, hearty flowers, pleasing to the eye.*

ALAIN

One morning in the monastery courtyard, I was looking at a tree that held a few red flowers and a dozen sparrows. Everything I saw produced within me a sense of jubilation and of the infinite purity of phenomena. I forced my mind into a downbeat mood and conjured up all sorts of negative feelings. Suddenly the tree looked dusty to me and the flowers sickly; the chirping of the sparrows began to irritate me. I wondered which was the right way to look at things, and came to the conclusion that the first had been the correct way because it generated an open, creative, and liberating attitude and led to greater satisfaction. Such an attitude allows us spontaneously to embrace the universe and beings and to tear away any egocentric divide between the self and the world. On the other hand, when we cling to a negative perception of phenomena, something rings false — we feel "disconnected" from the universe, which comes to seem dull, strange, distant, and sometimes hostile.

The Unsubstantiated Accusations Against Optimism

Psychologists have long believed that mildly depressive people are "realistic" in their outlook. Optimists have a tendency to dwell longer on pleasant incidents than on painful situations and to overestimate their past performance and mastery of things.

This implies that the pessimist tends to go around with his eyes wide open and to assess situations more lucidly than the optimist. "Reality may not always be a barrel of laughs, but you have to see things the way they are," he might say, whereas the optimist is a genial but incurably naive dreamer. "Life will bring him down to earth soon enough," we think. It so happens that this is not true. Further studies have shown that the pessimist's objective, detached, and wary judgment is inadequate. When it's a question of real situations drawn from daily life, the optimist's approach is in fact more realistic and pragmatic than that of the pessimist. If, for example, a cross section of women who drink coffee are shown a report on the increased risk of breast cancer linked to caffeine, or if a cross section of sunbathers are informed that lying out in the sun increases the risk of skin cancer, a week later the optimists have better recall of the reports' details than the pessimists and have taken them more into account in their behavior.[1] Moreover, they concentrate attentively and selectively on the risks that truly concern them, rather than fretting vainly and ineffectually over everything.[2] In this way, they remain more serene than the pessimists and gather their energies for real threats.

If we observe the way in which people perceive the events

of their lives, appreciate the quality of the lived moment, and create their future by overcoming obstacles with an open and creative attitude, we find that the optimists have an undeniable advantage over the pessimists. Many studies show that they do better on exams, in their chosen profession, and in their relationships, live longer and in better health, enjoy a better chance of surviving postoperative shock, and are less prone to depression and suicide.[3] A study was made of more than nine hundred people admitted to an American hospital in 1960. Their degree of optimism and other psychological traits were evaluated in tests and questionnaires. Forty years later, it turns out that the optimists lived 19 percent longer on average than the pessimists — some sixteen years of added life for an octogenarian.[4] Furthermore, Martin Seligman claims that pessimists are up to eight times more likely to become depressed when things go wrong; they do worse at school, sports, and most jobs than their talent would suggest. It was demonstrated that pessimism exacerbates depression and the other difficulties cited, and not the other way around; when such people are taught specifically to overcome pessimism by changing their outlook, they are markedly less subject to depressive relapse. There are definite reasons for this. Indeed psychologists describe pessimism as an "explanatory style" for the world that engenders "learned helplessness."[5]

TWO WAYS OF SEEING THE WORLD

An optimist is somebody who considers his problems to be temporary, controllable, and linked to a specific situation. He will say: "There's no reason to make a fuss about it; these things don't last. I'll figure it out; in any case, I usually do." The pessimist, on the other hand, thinks that his problems will last ("It's not the sort of thing that just goes away"), that they jeopardize everything he does and are out of his control ("What do you expect me to do about it?"). He also imagines that he has some basic inner flaw, and tells people: "Whatever I do, it always turns out the same way" and concludes: "I'm just not cut out to be happy."

The sense of insecurity that afflicts so many people today is closely tied to pessimism. The pessimist is constantly anticipating disaster and falls victim to chronic anxiety and doubt. Morose, irritable, and nervous, he has no confidence in the world or in himself and always expects to be bullied, abandoned, and ignored.

Here's a pessimist's parable. One fine summer's day, a driver got a flat in the middle of the countryside. To add insult to injury, he found that he had no jack. The place was practically deserted. There was one solitary house in sight, halfway up a hill. After a few minutes' hesitation, the traveler decided to go borrow a jack. As he climbed toward the house, he began to think, "What if the owner won't lend me a jack? It would be pretty rotten to leave me in a fix." As he slowly neared the house, he became more and more upset. "I would never do that to a stranger. It would be hateful!" Finally, he knocked on the front door, and when the owner opened up, he shouted: "You can keep your jack, you son of a bitch!"

The optimist, however, trusts that it is possible to achieve her goals and that with patience, resolve, and intelligence, she will ultimately do so. The fact is, more often than not, she does.

In everyday life the pessimist starts out with an attitude of refusal, even where it's totally inappropriate. I remember a Bhutanese official I often had to deal with. Every time I asked him a question, he systematically prefaced his answers with, "No, no, no," regardless of what he was going to say afterward, which gave our conversations a comic tone.

"Do you think we'll be able to leave tomorrow morning?"

"No, no, no. . . . Be ready to leave at nine a.m."

If pessimism and suffering were as immutable as finger-prints or eye color, it would be more sensitive to avoid trum-peting the benefits of happiness and optimism. But if optimism is a way of looking at life and happiness a condition that can be cultivated, one might as well get down to work without further delay. As Alain has written: "How marvelous human society would be if everyone added his own wood to the fire instead of crying over the ashes!"[6]

Even if we are born with a certain predisposition to look for the silver lining, and even if the influence of those who raise us nudges our outlook toward pessimism or optimism, our in-terpretation of the world can shift later on, and considerably, because our minds are flexible.

HOPE

For an optimist, it makes no sense to lose hope. We can *always* do better (instead of being devastated, resigned, or disgusted), limit the damage (instead of letting it all go to pot), find an al-ternative solution (instead of wallowing pitifully in failure), rebuild what has been destroyed (instead of saying, "It's all over!"), take the current situation as a starting point (instead of wasting our time crying over the past and lamenting the pres-ent), start from scratch (instead of ending there), understand that sustained effort will have to be made in the best apparent direction (instead of being paralyzed by indecision and fatal-ism), and use every present moment to advance, appreciate, act, and enjoy inner well-being (instead of wasting our time brood-ing over the past and fearing the future).

There are those who say, like the Australian farmer inter-viewed on the radio during the forest fires of 2001: "I've lost everything, I'll never be able to rebuild my life." And there are people like the navigator Jacques-Yves Le Toumelin, who, as he watched his first ship being torched by the Germans in 1944, paraphrased Rudyard Kipling: "If you can see your life's work destroyed and get straight back to the grindstone, then you will be a man, my son." He immediately built a new boat and circumnavigated the world solo, under sail.

Hope is defined by psychologists as the conviction that one can find the means to attain one's goals and develop the motivation necessary to do so. It is known that hope improves students' test results and athletes' performance, makes illness and agonizing debility more bearable, and makes pain itself (from burns, arthritis, spinal injuries, or blindness, for example) easier to tolerate. It has been demonstrated, for instance, using a method to measure resistance to pain, that people who show a marked tendency to be hopeful are able to tolerate contact with a very cold surface twice as long as those who don't.[7]

RESOLVE

There are many kinds of laziness, but they can all be sorted into three principal types. The first and most obvious boils down to wanting only to eat well, sleep well, and do as little as possible. The second and most paralyzing leads us to abandon the race before we've even crossed the starting line. We tell ourselves: "Oh, that's not for me, that's well beyond my abilities." The third and most pernicious knows what really matters in life but is constantly putting it off to later, while devoting itself to a thousand other things of lesser importance.

The optimist does not give up quickly. Strengthened by the hope of success, she perseveres and succeeds more often than the pessimist, especially in adverse conditions. The pessimist has a tendency to back away from difficulties, sink into resignation, or turn to temporary distractions that will not solve her problems.[8] The pessimist will demonstrate little resolve, for she doubts everything and everyone, foresees the failure of every undertaking (instead of the potential for growth, development, and fruitfulness), and sees every person as a schemer and an egoist. She sees a threat in every new thing and anticipates catastrophe. In a word, when hearing a door creak, the optimist thinks it's opening and the pessimist thinks it's closing.

A few years ago I went to France to discuss ways of undertaking humanitarian projects in Tibet despite the oppressive conditions imposed by the Chinese government. About fifteen minutes into the meeting, someone said, with reference to myself and one of the other participants: "You're talking about the same thing as if it's two different worlds. One of you thinks it'll all end badly, the other thinks everything will turn out fine." The first speaker had said: "To start with, there's little chance that the authorities will put up with you and you'll probably be kicked out right away. And then, how are you going to get permission to build a school? Even if you manage to start building it, you'll get scammed by the contractors, who are in bed with the corrupt local powers. On top of it all, don't forget that you can't force them to teach in Tibetan and classes will end up being held in Chinese." Personally, I found the conversation stifling; my only thought was to get out of there as fast as possible, slip through the net, and get the projects off the ground. Since then, five years ago, in cooperation with an especially enthusiastic friend and the support of generous benefactors, we've built sixteen health centers, eight schools, and twelve bridges. In many cases our local friends asked for permission to build only once the clinic or the school was finished. Thousands of patients and children have been treated and educated in these places. Hesitant at first, the local authorities are thrilled now because they can include these projects in their statistics. From our point of view, the goal we sought — helping those in need — had been accomplished.

Although the optimist may be a little giddy when foreseeing the future, telling himself that it will all work out in the end when that isn't always the case, his attitude is more fruitful since, in the hope of undertaking a hundred projects, followed up by diligent action, the optimist will end up completing fifty. Conversely, in limiting himself to undertake a mere ten, the pessimist might complete five at best and often fewer, since he'll devote little energy to a task he feels to be doomed from the start.

Most of the people I constantly meet in countries where poverty and oppression inspire their assistance are optimists who boldly face up to the extreme disparity between the immensity of the task and the meagerness of their resources. I have a friend, Malcolm McOdell, who has been doing development work in Nepal with his wife for the past thirty years on the basis of the principle of "appreciative inquiry," an extraordinary practical application of optimism.

"Whenever I arrive in a village," he explains, "people's first reaction is to complain about their problems. I tell them: 'Hold on, it's impossible that all you have is problems. Tell me about the assets and good qualities that are particular to your village and to each one of you.' We get together, sometimes in the evening around a campfire. Minds and tongues grow loose and, with a whole new kind of enthusiasm, the villagers make a list of their talents, abilities, and resources. Immediately afterward, I ask them to imagine how they might, all together, put those qualities to work for them. As soon as they've come up with a plan, I ask the final question: 'Who here is prepared, here and now, to take responsibility for such and such aspect of the program?'" Hands shoot up, promises are made, and the work is launched within days. This approach is light-years away from that followed by the problem-listers, who accomplish less, less well and less quickly. McOdell focuses in particular on improving conditions for Nepalese women, some thirty thousand of whom are enjoying the benefits of his initiatives today.

ADAPTABILITY

When difficulties seem insurmountable, optimists react in a more constructive and creative way. They accept the facts with realism, know how to rapidly identify the positive in adversity, draw lessons from it, and come up with an alternative solution or turn to a new project. Pessimists would rather turn away from the problem or adopt escapist strategies — sleep, isolation, drug or alcohol abuse — that diminish their focus on the problem.[9] Instead of confronting them with resolve, they prefer to brood over their misfortunes, nurture illusions, dream up "magic" solutions, and accuse the whole world of being against them. They have a hard time drawing lessons from the past, which often leads to the repetition of their problems. They are more fatalistic ("I told you it wouldn't work. It's always the same, no matter what I do") and are quick to see themselves as "mere pawns in the game of life."

SERENITY

Having foreseen and thoroughly tested every possible avenue, the optimist, even when she has temporarily failed, is free of regret and guilt feelings. She knows how to step back and is always ready to imagine a new solution., without bearing the burden of past failures. That is how she maintains her serenity. Her confidence is as solid as the bow of a ship that cleaves through life's waters, be they calm or stormy.

A friend of mine who lives in Nepal told me how he once

had to take a plane to give an important lecture in the Netherlands the following day. The sponsors had rented a hall, publicized the event in the newspapers, and expected a thousand attendees. At the airport, he learned that the flight had been canceled and that there was no other way to leave Nepal that night. He told me: "I was deeply sorry for the sponsors, but there was really nothing to be done. A deep calm came over my mind. Behind me, I had just said good-bye to my friends in Kathmandu; ahead of me, my destination had just vanished. I felt delightfully buoyant with freedom. On the sidewalk outside the airport, I sat on my bag and joked around with the porters and street kids who happened to be there. To have been sick with worry would have served absolutely no purpose at all. After about half an hour, I stood up and headed off on foot to Kathmandu with my little bag, enjoying the cool of twilight."

I remember a trip I once took to eastern Tibet. Torrential rains, in combination with the almost total deforestation undertaken by the Chinese, had caused devastating floods. Our ATV had a hard time progressing along a potholed road at the bottom of abyssal gorges, alongside a river that had been transformed into a vast, raging torrent. Glowing in the yellowish light of dusk, the stone ramparts seemed to rise to the sky, echoing the roar of the surge. Most of the bridges had been swept away, and the turbulent waters were rapidly eroding the only navigable road remaining. Every so often, a rock would hurtle down the craggy slopes and smash onto the pavement. It was a good test of the passengers' optimism. The differences between them were striking. Some were so worried that they wanted to stop, although there was nowhere to take shelter. Others took it all in with composure and wanted to push on and get through as fast as possible. One of us eventually said to the most anxious: "You love action movies. Well, today's your lucky day — you get to be in one." And we all burst out laughing and took heart.

MEANING

But there is an even deeper dimension to optimism, that of realizing the potential for transformation that is in every human being, regardless of his or her condition. It is that potential, in the end, that gives meaning to human life. The ultimate pessimism is in thinking that life in general is not worth living. The ultimate optimism lies in understanding that every passing moment is a treasure, in joy as in adversity. These are not subtle nuances, but a fundamental difference in the way of seeing things. This divergence of perspective depends on whether or not we have found within ourselves the fulfillment that alone fuels inner peace.

EXERCISE

Experiment with experiencing the same situation through the eyes of optimism and pessimism. Take, for example, an airplane voyage:

Imagine that you are on a long airplane trip en route to a strange city to begin a new job. Suddenly the airplane encounters turbulence. You can see the plane's wings tilting up and down and you visualize the ensuing disaster. Once the turbulence settles down, you realize your seat is too small. You can't find a comfortable position, and your mind is filled with complaints about the state of airplane travel. You are annoyed that the air hostess is taking forever to bring your drink. When you think ahead to your new job, you feel certain that the people you will meet won't like or appreciate you. They will ignore your expertise, keep you away from the most interesting projects, and might even cheat you. You are sure that this trip will be a catastrophe. Why did you ever think you could handle it? You are filled with dread.

Experience the gloomy state of mind such thoughts create.

Then experiment with another way to experience the same situation:

When the plane encounters turbulence, you know that it is part of the journey and vividly feel that every instant that passes by is precious. As the turbulence calms down, you feel grateful and hope that you can use the rest of your life constructively. Although your seat is not particularly comfortable, you find positions that relieve the stiffness of your back and legs. You appreciate how cheerful and helpful the air hostess is even though she is so busy and has to stand up throughout most of the flight. You are excited by the adventures that await you. You imagine that the people there will be interesting and productive and that you will be given many new opportunities. You are convinced that your activities will flourish and that you have the inner resources to overcome any obstacles that may arise.

Experience this buoyant state of mind that is tuned to the positive.

Appreciate the difference between these two states of mind and understand how they came about simply through the workings of your mind although the outer situation remained the same.

20

GOLDEN TIME, LEADEN TIME, WASTED TIME

Those whom summer's heat tortures yearn
*   for the full moon of autumn*
Without even fearing the idea
That a hundred days of their life will then have passed forever.

BUDDHA SHAKYAMUNI

Time often resembles a fine gold powder that we distractedly allow to slip through our fingers without ever realizing it. Put to good use, it is the shuttle we pass through the weft of our days to weave the fabric of a meaningful life. It is therefore essential to the quest for happiness that we be aware that time is our most precious commodity. This does not mean we should get rid of what is meaningful in life but rather of that which causes us to waste our life. As Seneca says: "It is not that we have so little time, but that we waste so much of it."

Life is short. We always lose when we put essential things off. The years or hours remaining to us are like a precious substance that crumbles easily and can be frittered away without noticing. Despite its great value, time has no way of protecting itself, like a child that can be led away by any bystander.

For the active person, golden time is when he can create, build, accomplish, and devote himself to the welfare of others. For the contemplative, time allows him to look clearly into himself to understand his inner world and rediscover the essence of life. It is golden time that, despite the appearance of inactivity, allows him fully to appreciate the present moment and develop the inner qualities that will permit him to better help others. In a hermit's day, every instant is a treasure and time is never wasted. In the silence of his hermitage, he becomes, in the words of Khalil Gibran, "a flute through whose heart the whispering of the hours turns to music."

The idle person talks of "killing time." What a dreadful expression! Time becomes a long, flat, dreary line. This is leaden time; it weighs on the idler like a burden and cripples anyone who cannot tolerate waiting, delay, boredom, solitude, setbacks, or sometimes even life itself. Every passing moment aggravates his sense of imprisonment or dullness. For others, time is nothing more than the countdown to a death they fear or which they may even wish for when they tire of living. To paraphrase Herbert Spencer, the time they are unable to kill ends up killing them.

Experiencing time as painful and insipid, and feeling that we've done nothing at the end of the day, the end of the year, the end of life, reveals how unaware we remain of the potential for development we carry within us.

BEYOND BOREDOM AND LONELINESS

Boredom is the fate of those who rely entirely on distraction, for whom life is one big entertainment and who languish the minute the show stops. Boredom is the affliction of those for whom time has no value.

On the other hand, she who understands the inestimable

value of time uses every break from her daily activities and outward stimuli to sample the delicious clarity of the moment. She has no knowledge of boredom, that drought of the mind.

The same is true of loneliness. Fifteen percent of Americans report experiencing an intense feeling of loneliness once a week. Anyone who cuts himself off from others and the universe, trapped in the bubble of his own ego, feels alone in the middle of a crowd. But those who understand the interdependence of all phenomena are not lonely; the hermit, for example, feels in harmony with the entire universe.

For the distracted man, time is just Muzak droning its notes into the confusion of his mind. This is wasted time. Of such a man Seneca wrote: "He has not lived long — he has existed long. Would you say that a man who had been caught in a fierce storm as soon as he set sail, and, buffeted to and fro by a series of winds raging from all sides, had been driven in a circle around the same course, had had a long journey? It was not a lot of journeying, but a lot of tossing about."[1]

"Distraction" here does not mean the tranquil relaxation of a hike in the woods, but pointless activities and interminable mental chatter that, far from illuminating the mind, mire it in exhausting chaos. This distraction sets the mind to wandering without any respite, misdirects it into side roads and dead ends. Knowing how to use our time to the full does not mean we always have to be in a hurry or obsessed by the clock. Whether we are relaxing or concentrating, resting or intensely active, in all circumstances we must be able to recognize the true value of time.

A Return to Golden Time

Why don't we devote even the briefest of moments once a day to introspection? Are we really satisfied by clever conversation and a little mindless entertainment? Let's look within. There is much to do.

It is worthwhile to spend a moment each day cultivating an altruistic thought and observing the workings of the mind. This investigation will teach us a thousand times more — and far more lastingly — than an hour spent reading the local news or sports results! It's not a question of ignoring the world, but of putting our time to good use. In any case, we don't need to fear going to that extreme, living as we do in an era of ubiquitous distractions, and where access to general information is at the saturation point. We are stuck, rather, in the opposite extreme: zero contemplation. We may devote a few seconds when emotional or professional setbacks make us "put it all in perspective." But how, and for how long? Often enough we're just waiting for the bad moment to "pass" and anxiously looking for some distraction to "take our mind off things." The actors and the sets change, but the show goes on.

Why not sit beside a lake, on top of a hill, or in a quiet room and examine what we are really made of deep inside? Let us first clearly examine what counts most in life for ourselves, then establish priorities among the essential things and other activities that intrude on our time. We can also take advantage of certain phases of active life to commune with ourselves and turn our gaze inward. Tenzin Palmo, an English nun who spent many years in retreat, has written: "People say they have no time for 'meditation.' It's not true! You can meditate walking down the corridor, waiting for the traffic lights to change, at the computer, standing in a queue, in the bathroom, combing your hair. Just be there in the present, without the mental commentary."[2]

Our time is limited; from the day we are born, every second, every step, brings us closer to death. The Tibetan hermit Patrul Rinpoche reminds us poetically that

As your life runs out like the setting sun sinking away,
Death closes in like the lengthening shadows of evening.

Far from making us despair, a lucid awareness of the nature of things inspires us to live each passing day to the full. Unless we examine our lives, we will take it for granted that we have no choice and that it's easier just to do one thing right after the other, as we've always done and always will do. But if we do not abandon futile entertainments and sterile activities, they certainly will not abandon us; they will, in fact, take up more and more space in our lives.

When we keep putting off our spiritual life to tomorrow, we end up copping out every single day. Death draws near with every step we take, every tick and every tock of the clock. It could strike at any moment and we can't do a thing about it. While death is certain, its moment of arrival is unpredictable. As Nagarjuna said seventeen centuries ago:

If this life assailed by many ills
Is yet more fragile than a bubble on the stream,
How wonderful it is to wake from sleep
And having loosed one's breath, to breathe in once again![3]

At the practical level, if we wish to experience our relationship to time more harmoniously, we must cultivate a certain number of qualities. Mindfulness allows us to remain alert to the passage of time and prevents us from being unaware as it flows. The proper motivation is what colors time and gives it value. Diligence allows us to put it to good use. Inner freedom prevents it from being monopolized by disturbing emotions. Every day, every hour, every second, is like an arrow flying toward its target. The right time to start is *now*.

EXERCISE

Appreciate the Value of Time, Savor the Present Moment

Turn your mind inward and appreciate the richness of every single moment that passes by. Instead of being an endless succession of feelings, images, and scattered thoughts, time becomes pure awareness, like a luminous stream of melted gold.

When past thoughts have ceased, and future thoughts have not yet arisen, in the interval is there not a perception of nowness, a pristine, clear, awake, and bare freshness? Remain in it for a while, without grasping at anything, like a small child looking at a vast landscape.

21

ONE WITH THE FLOW OF TIME

*A good life is one that is characterized by complete absorption
in what one does.*

JEANNE NAKAMURA AND MIHALY CSIKSZENTMIHALYI

We all have had the experience of being intensely absorbed
in an activity, an experiment, or a feeling. This is what
psychologist Mihaly Csikszentmihalyi, a leading psychologist
at the Claremont Graduate University, calls flow. In the 1960s,
studying the creative process, Csikszentmihalyi was struck by
the fact that when the creation of a painting was going well, the
artist was completely absorbed in his work and stayed with it
to completion, unaware of being tired, hungry, or uncomfortable. But when the work was done, his interest dropped away
abruptly. He had experienced the state of flow, during which
the fact of being immersed in what we are doing counts for
more than the end result.

Intrigued by this phenomenon, Csikszentmihalyi interviewed numerous artists, mountain climbers, chess players,
surgeons, writers, and manual laborers for whom the sheer en-

joyment of the act was the principal incentive. It is obvious that for a rock climber who has climbed the same rock face dozens of times, being at the top counts for less than the enjoyment of getting there. The same goes for someone cruising around a bay on a sailboat with no particular destination in mind, playing music, or playing a game of solitaire. At such times, one becomes "completely involved in an activity for its own sake. There is a sense of transcending the ego and time. Every action, movement, and thought follows inevitably from the previous one, like playing jazz. Your whole being is involved, and you're using your skills to the utmost."[1] Diane Roffe-Steinrotter, gold medalist at the 1994 Winter Olympics, asserts that she remembers nothing of the downhill event but being immersed in relaxation. "I felt like a waterfall."[2]

William James wrote, "My experience is what I agree to attend to."[3] Entering the state of flow depends closely on the amount of attention given to the lived experience. If we are to enter into flow, the task must monopolize all our attention and present a challenge commensurate with our abilities. If it is too difficult, tension sets in, followed by anxiety; too easy, and we relax and are soon bored. In the experience of flow, a resonance is established between the action, the external environment, and the mind. In most cases this fluidity is felt as an optimal experience with a great sense of satisfaction. It is the inverse not only of boredom and depression, but also of agitation and distraction. It is interesting to note, too, that so long as the state lasts, there is a loss of reflective self-consciousness. All that remains is the alertness of the subject, who becomes one with his action and has ceased observing himself.

To take a personal example, I have often felt that way when interpreting for the Tibetan teachers. The interpreter must first focus all his attention on the discourse, which may last five or ten minutes, then translate it orally, and so on without interruption until the end of a lesson lasting several hours. I have found that the best way to get through it is to immerse myself in a state of mind very similar to what Csikszentmihalyi calls flow. While the teacher is speaking, I leave my mind in a state of complete availability, as free from thought as a blank sheet of paper, attentive yet without tension; then I try to render what I have heard, just as one might pour the contents of a pitcher that has just been filled into another one. One need only remember the starting point and the thread of the teaching; after that, detail follows upon detail, generally without effort. The mind is both focused and relaxed. It is possible in this way to reconstruct a long and complicated teaching quite faithfully. If thoughts or an exterior event should happen to break the flow of the translation, the magic is lost and it can be difficult to get back on track. When this happens, it is not merely a few details that escape me; I go totally blank and nothing at all comes to mind for a moment or two. It's ultimately easier not to take notes, precisely in order to sustain the experience of flow. When all is going well, this fluidity produces a sense of serene joy; self-awareness — that is, a person observing himself — is practically absent; exhaustion is forgotten; and time passes imperceptibly, like the flow of a river that remains undetectable at a distance.

According to Csikszentmihalyi, one can experience flow when undertaking the most mundane tasks, such as ironing or working on a production line. It all depends on how one experiences the passage of time. Conversely, without flow, virtually any activity will be tedious, if not downright unbearable. Csikszentmihalyi has found that some people enter the state of flow more easily than others. Such people generally have "curiosity and interest in life, persistence and low self-centeredness, which results in the ability to be motivated by intrinsic reward."[4]

Taking the state of flow into consideration has improved

working conditions in any number of factories (Volvo automobile, among others); the layout of galleries and objects in museums (such as the Getty Museum in Los Angeles), whereby visitors, naturally attracted by each succeeding exhibit, pass through without growing tired; and most especially in educational institutions — the Key School in Indianapolis, for instance.[5] At this school, children are encouraged to remain absorbed as long as they like, and at their own pace, in a subject that appeals to them, and thus to study in a state of flow. They take more interest in their studies and learn with pleasure.

EXERCISE

Practice "attentive walking"
These are the instructions of the Vietnamese Buddhist master Thich Nhat Hanh:
   "Walking just for the pleasure of walking, freely and firmly, without hurrying. We are present in every step. When we wish to speak, we stop walking and lend all our attention to the person before us, to speaking and to listening. . . . Stop, look around, and see how wonderful life is: the trees, the white clouds, the infinite sky. Listen to the birds, delight in the light breeze. Let us walk as free people and feel our steps growing lighter as we walk. Let us appreciate every step we take."[6]

GIVING FLOW ITS FULL VALUE

The experience of flow encourages us to persist at any given activity and to return to it. It can also, in certain cases, develop into a habit or even a dependency; flow does not only involve constructive and positive activities. The gambler in the grips of the game becomes absorbed by the roulette table or the one-armed bandits to the point where he no longer notices time passing and forgets himself utterly, even though he may be losing his fortune. The same goes for the hunter stalking his prey or the burglar meticulously carrying out his plan.

As satisfying as it may be to cultivate the experience of flow, it is still only a *tool*. If it is to make any long-term improvement in our quality of life, it must be imbued with human qualities, such as altruism and wisdom. The value of flow depends on the motivation coloring the mind. It can be negative in the case of a burglar, neutral for a mundane activity — ironing clothes, say — or positive when we are involved in a rescue operation or meditating on compassion.

Jeanne Nakamura and Csikszentmihalyi write about flow that "its major contribution to the quality of life consists in endowing every momentary experience with value."[7] It can be extremely valuable in helping us to appreciate every moment of existence and putting it to the most constructive use possible. We can thereby avoid wasting our time in morose indifference.

We can also practice increasingly essential and internalized forms of flow. Without the need for external activity, we can learn to rest effortlessly in a state of constant awareness. Contemplating the nature of the mind, for instance, is a deep and fruitful experience combining relaxation and flow. Relaxation in the form of inner calm, flow in the form of a clear and open presence of mind, alert but without tension. Perfect lucidity is one of the principal features that distinguishes this state of mind from ordinary flow. Such pure awareness does not require the subject to observe himself; here, too, there is a quasi-total disappearance of the notion of a "self." This does not hinder direct knowledge of the nature of mind, of the "pure presence" of awareness. The experience is a source of inner peace and openness to the world and others. Finally, the experience of contemplative flow encompasses our entire perception of the universe and its interdependence. You might say that the awakened being remains continuously in a state of serene, vivid, and altruistic flow.

EXERCISE

Enter into the flow of "open presence"

Sit in a comfortable meditation position, eyes gently open, posture straight, and quiet your mind. Then try to make your mind as vast as the sky. Don't focus on anything in particular. Remain relaxed and calm and yet fully aware. Let your mind remain free from mental constructs, yet clear, vivid, and all-pervading. Effortless, yet undistracted. Without trying to actively block sensory perceptions, recollections, and imagination, feel that you are simply uninfluenced by them. Remain at ease. Perceptions cannot alter the basic serene vastness of your mind. Whenever thoughts arise, let them undo themselves as they form, as a drawing made on the surface of the water leaves no trace. Experience the peace you feel for a few moments after the exercise.

22

ETHICS AS THE SCIENCE OF HAPPINESS

It is not possible to live happily if one does not lead a beautiful, righteous, and wise life, or to lead a beautiful, righteous, and wise life if one is not happy.

EPICURUS

What are the criteria that qualify an act as good or bad? Buddhist ethics is not just ways of acting, but a way of being. A human being endowed with loving-kindness, compassion, and wisdom will spontaneously act in an ethical way because he or she is "good at heart." In Buddhism, an act is essentially unethical if its aim is to cause suffering and ethical if it is meant to bring genuine well-being to others. It is the motivation, altruistic or malicious, that qualifies the action as being "good" or "bad," just as a crystal takes the color of the cloth upon which it rests. Ethics also affects our own well-being: making others suffer will bring suffering onto ourselves, either immediately or in the long term, while bringing happiness to others is ultimately the best way to guarantee our own.

Through the interplay of the laws of cause and effect, which Buddhism calls karma — the laws governing the consequences of our actions — ethics are therefore intimately linked to well-being. As Luca and Francesco Cavalli-Sforza write: "Ethics arose as the science of happiness. In order to be happy, is it better to take care of others or to think exclusively of oneself?"[1] Buddhism's ethical precepts are reference points, reminding us to adopt an altruistic and constructive attitude toward others and ourselves. The precepts highlight the consequences of our actions and encourage us to avoid those that provoke suffering.

The monotheistic religions are founded on divine commandments. Certain philosophers have based their thinking on concepts that they believe to be absolute and universal — Good, Evil, Responsibility or Duty. Others adopt a utilitarian point of view that can be summed up as "the greatest good for the greatest number." Contemporary gatherings of philosophers, scientists, politicians, and others who meet to discuss ethical ways of action try to make the best use of rational thinking and available scientific information to solve the dilemmas raised by recent progress in research, such as the manipulation of the environment, genetics, stem cell research, and artificial life support.

In the Buddhist approach to ethics, as the Dalai Lama explains, "a meaningful ethical system divorced of an individual experience of suffering and happiness is hard to imagine."[2] The goal of Buddhist ethics is to free all beings, including oneself, from momentary and long-term suffering and to develop the ability to help others to do so. In order to accomplish this, we must equitably balance our own aspiration for well-being with that of others.

From this perspective, ethics built on abstract concepts has little usefulness. As the neuroscientist and philosopher Francisco Varela has written, a truly virtuous person "does not act out of ethics, but embodies it like any expert embodies his know-how. The wise man *is* ethical, or more explicitly, his actions arise from inclinations that his disposition produces in response to specific situations."³ For this one needs mindfulness, wisdom, and a basic altruistic disposition that is deeply embedded in the mind, yet needs to be cultivated throughout life. This is not about applying rules and principles, but concerns awareness and the development of a compassionate nature. One aspect of compassion is a spontaneous readiness to act for the benefit of others. Altruistic deeds will then naturally flow from such compassion.

It is not a question of defining Good or Evil absolutely, but of remaining alert to the happiness and suffering we cause by our deeds, our words, and our thoughts.

There are two main decisive factors at work here: motivation and the consequences of our acts. Even if we try to predict the results of our actions to the best of our capacities, we have little control over the unfolding of external events. However, we always have the choice to adopt an altruistic motivation and endeavor to help create a positive outcome. We therefore need to check our motivation again and again, as the Dalai Lama explains: "Are we being broad-minded or narrow-minded? Have we taken into account the overall situation or are we considering only specifics? Is our view short-term or long-term? . . . Is our motivation genuinely compassionate? . . . Is our compassion limited just to our families, our friends, and those we identify with closely? . . . We need to think, think, think."⁴

Thus the very core of ethics is our state of mind, not the form our actions take. If we relied solely on a deed's outward manifestation, it would be impossible to distinguish, for instance, between a white lie and a malicious one. If a killer asks you where the person he's chasing is hiding, that is obviously not the moment to tell the truth. The same holds true for an aggressive action. When a mother roughly shoves her child across the street to prevent her from being hit by a car, the act is violent only in appearance; she has saved the child's life. Conversely, if someone approaches you with a big smile and showers you with compliments only to rip you off, his conduct is nonviolent in appearance, but his intentions are actually malevolent.

Clearly, the fundamental question remains: Which criteria determine what means happiness for others and what means suffering? Do we give a bottle to a drunk because it makes him "happy," or do we not give it to him and prevent him from cutting his own life short? Here, the notion of wisdom comes into play alongside altruistic motivation. The main thrust of this book has been to differentiate true well-being from pleasure and other counterfeit forms of happiness. Wisdom is precisely that which allows us to distinguish the thoughts and deeds that contribute to authentic happiness from those that destroy it. Wisdom is based on direct experience, not dogma.

None of this in any way means that there is no need for rules of conduct and laws. These rules are the essential expressions of the accumulated wisdom of the past. They are justified inasmuch as some acts — theft, lying, violence — are almost always harmful. But they are guidelines. It is wisdom that allows us to identify the necessary exception. Theft is generally reprehensible because it is usually motivated by greed and unfairly deprives someone of his or her property, causing pain and suffering. But when, in the course of a famine, compassion motivates us to take food from the overflowing warehouses of a wealthy miser who would not give a morsel of food to those who are starving at his doorstep, the theft is no longer reprehensible. The law remains by and large valid, but compassionate wisdom has sanctioned the exception. As Martin Luther King once said: "Man's inhumanity to man is not only perpetrated by the vitriolic actions of those who are bad. It is also perpetrated by the vitiating inaction of those who are good."

When the suffering caused by a failure to act is greater than that caused by action, action must be undertaken. A failure to act would be to forget the very reason the rule exists, which is to protect people from suffering.

THE OTHER PERSON'S POINT OF VIEW

Compassionate ethics cannot be limited to feeling empathy for the suffering of others, or even to the resolve to do something about it in practical terms. It also implies transcending self-centeredness and gaining the understanding that the barrier dividing self from other is a mental construction. All phenomena, as well as self and others, are deeply interconnected at the level of their most fundamental nature. We therefore must put ourself in the other's shoes and try to imagine what it is like to be at the receiving end of our own behavior.

ONE THOUSAND INNOCENTS OR ONE?

There is a classic dilemma that helps us to better understand Buddhism's pragmatic approach. It is summarized by André Comte-Sponville's question: "If you had to condemn one innocent (or torture one child, as Dostoevsky frames it) to save humankind, should you do it?"[5] No, the philosophers say. "For if justice were to disappear," writes Kant, "human existence on Earth would be of no value."[6] Comte-Sponville goes further:

> *This is where utilitarianism reaches its limit. If justice were merely a contract of convenience . . . a maximization of the collective well-being . . . it would be fair, in order to ensure the well-being of almost everyone, to sacrifice the few without their consent and even if they were perfectly innocent and defenseless. That, however, is just what justice forbids, or should forbid. [John] Rawls,*

*drawing on Kant, is quite right in this respect: justice is
worth more than well-being or efficiency, and is better
than either, and must not be sacrificed to them, even for
the happiness of the greatest number.*[7]

But justice would be sacrificed only if it were decided that
the choice of sacrificing a child to save thousands were acceptable in principle. However, *the question here is not one of accepting it,* but of avoiding as much suffering as possible. Each
of these solutions is as unacceptable as the other. It is not a
question of enshrining the concept of "the happiness of the
greatest number" as dogma; nor is the issue to consider an innocent child as merely the vehicle for saving other people's
lives. But in the face of an unavoidable situation, the issue is to
choose the lesser of two evils in terms of suffering. The choice
has not torn the fabric of justice and it is just as fair to say that
the failure to act would be a tacit condemnation of a thousand
innocents.

It is easy here to fall prey to both abstraction and sentimen-
tality. We fall into dogmatic abstraction when we refuse to
reason on the basis of living experience. It is sentimental to
respond to the death of an innocent child just because we can
imagine it vividly, while viewing the hundreds of inhabitants of
the town as only an abstract entity. We need to turn the question around: "Is it acceptable to sacrifice one thousand innocents to save one?"

While few moral issues are couched in such dramatic terms,
practical ethics must take into account, with insight and compassion, all the ins and outs of a given situation. Such ethics are
an ongoing challenge because they require an impartial and altruistic motivation, as well as the unflagging desire to ease the
suffering of others. They are the hardest to put into practice because they transcend the automatic resort to the letter of the

law and moral codes. Hence, they are also at greatest risk of distortion and manipulation. Indeed, such ethics require a kind of flexibility that is itself a source of danger. If it is co-opted by selfishness and partiality, it can easily be exploited to negative ends that run counter to its initial objectives. Thus the need, for everyone and most especially for those who dispense justice, to develop wisdom and a deep concern for the well-being of others.

"In real life," as Varela has pointed out, "we *always* operate in some kind of immediacy of a given situation. . . . We have a readiness-for-action proper to every specific lived situation."[8] The quality of this readiness depends on the quality of our being and on the altruistic nature of our motivation, not on the righteousness of our abstract moral principles. As the Dalai Lama notes: "Sometimes, we have to act at once. This is why our spiritual development is of such critical importance in ensuring that our actions are ethically sound. The more spontaneous our actions, the more they are likely to reflect our inner disposition in that moment."[9]

THE IDEALIZATION OF GOOD AND EVIL

We may identify two main branches in ethics: one based on abstract principles and one based on lived experience, such as the pragmatic ethics of Buddhism.

Immanuel Kant, for instance, refers to the sense of duty that ultimately and absolutely governs all moral issues. He rejects the idea that one must act for the good of others, moved by altruism fueled by empathy and compassion. For him, such human feelings are not reliable. He appeals rather for adherence to universal and impartial moral principles. For him, good is a duty that must lead to the happiness of humankind as a whole, although happiness cannot be a goal in itself: "But it does not follow that this distinction between the principle of happiness and that of morality is an *opposition* between them, and pure practical reason does not require that we should *renounce* all claim to happiness, but only that the moment duty is in question we should take *no account* of happiness."[10]

Duty is constrained by the necessity of being universal and disregards specific cases. This ignores the very nature of human experience. As Francisco Varela explains: "The proper units of knowledge are primarily *concrete,* embodied, incorporated, lived; knowledge is about situatedness and context; the uniqueness of knowledge, its historicity and context, is not a 'noise' concealing an abstract configuration in its true essence."[11]

These various notions of an absolute Good generally come back to a belief in the existence of a transcendent entity (God, Ideas, Ideal Good) that exists by itself, independent of the world of transitory phenomena. As we've seen, Buddhism's vision is altogether different. Evil is not a demonic power external to ourselves, and good is not an absolute principle independent of us. Everything occurs in our minds. Love and compassion are reflections of the true nature of all living beings — what we have called basic goodness. Evil is a deviation from this basic goodness which can be remedied.

UTILITARIAN ETHICS

According to Jeremy Bentham, an English philosopher of the eighteenth and nineteenth centuries and a founder of moral utilitarianism, "the greatest happiness of the greatest number is the foundation of morals and legislation."[12] Buddhism agrees with this much more human approach. However, commendable and altruistic though its goals are, utilitarianism bases its analyses on a rather fuzzy assessment of the nature of happiness, lumping together superficial pleasures and deep-felt happiness. Buddhism draws on personal change — inner transformation — to enrich the ethical mind with wisdom, allowing it to adopt a more altruistic motivation and to put to use an enhanced clarity in order to fine-tune its judgment. Again, the major shortcoming of the utilitarian system, in the long run, is the risk of confusing pleasure with genuine happiness, or more accurately, of reducing the latter to the former.

CONDEMNATION, PUNISHMENT, AND REHABILITATION

Ethics can also be considered as a "medical" discipline, wherein a series of symptoms allows us to foresee and prevent the discomforts caused by the negative emotions and to cure those affected. From that point of view, the incarceration of a criminal might be considered more as hospitalization than as an irreversible sentence. He must be imprisoned in order to prevent him from doing harm and so long as he remains a danger to society. But rather than believing that a criminal cannot have a true change of heart, Buddhism says that a person's goodness remains intact deep within even when it is horribly marred at the surface. This is not about naively ignoring the extent to which that good nature can be buried beneath hatred, greed, and cruelty; rather it is about understanding that the mere fact of its existence always allows for its potential reemergence.

Nor should punishment ever be a form of vengeance, the most extreme of which is the death penalty. Revenge is a deviation from justice, since its main intent is not to protect the innocent but to hurt the guilty and to "clean" society from the offensive "enemy." This is cowboy justice, not enlightened living. In such instances any act whose primary motivation is to inflict suffering or to kill, as in the death penalty, cannot be considered ethical.

The Limits of Utilitarianism

Utilitarianism advocates the maximization of the overall sum of pleasures available to any given community. However, because it has no meaningful criteria for assessing happiness, it may become arbitrary, even absurd. Applied blindly, this maximization principle can in fact lead to the sacrifice of certain members of society. Aristotle, for instance, was in favor of slavery — if there were no slavery, all the intellectuals would have to go to work and abandon their lofty and dignified activities! That was a utilitarian deviation before its time. Such specious reasoning is inconceivable in Buddhism, which asks us continually to put ourselves in the other person's place. In so doing, no sensible person could deem the condition of slavery to be satisfactory.

One of the most important critiques of utilitarianism was formulated by the contemporary American philosopher John Rawls. He rejected the doctrine of collective happiness as ultimate justification for our acts and proposed in its stead respect for the inviolability of individual rights, along with the principle of equal freedom and equitable cooperation.

According to Rawls, an action cannot be *good* if it is not first *just*. From the Buddhist point of view, these two concepts are intrinsically linked. An action deemed just under a dogmatic ethic can be bad in reality. Such is the case with Kant's pathetic refusal to accept a lie that could save a human life. According to him, any lie, for whatever reason, is an injustice toward all humanity, for in arrogating the right to lie one would destroy the credibility of all speech in general. It would be hard to stray further from justice.

In asserting the priority of the just over the good, Rawls is idealizing the just and depreciating the good by presupposing man to be fundamentally selfish and unable to function without first calculating his own best interests.

> *Since each desires to protect his interests, his conception of the good, no one has a reason to acquiesce in an enduring loss for himself in order to bring about a greater net balance of satisfaction. In the absence of strong and lasting benevolent impulses, a rational man would not accept a basic structure merely because it maximized the algebraic sum of advantages irrespective of its permanent effects on his own basic rights and interests.*[13]

We may have to accept the fact that exacerbated individualism, born of a powerful attraction to the self, is ubiquitous in contemporary societies. But is this the most inspiring source from which to derive the ethical principles that will regulate our behavior? The philosopher Charles Taylor wisely remarked: "Much contemporary moral philosophy . . . has focused on what is right to do rather than on what is good to be, on defining the content of obligation rather than the nature of good life; and it has no conceptual place left for a notion of the good as the object of our love and allegiance or as the privileged focus of attention and will."[14]

As Varela comments:

> *In traditional communities, there are models of ethical expertise who can be singled out as even more expert than the common run (the "wise ones"). In our modern society, however, such role models for ethical expertise (unlike, say, role models for athletic expertise) are more difficult to identify. This is one of the important reasons why modern ethical thinking has such a nihilistic flavor.*[15]

One may be an excellent pianist, mathematician, gardener, or scientist and still be cranky and jealous, but in the West one can be considered a great moralist and yet not live by one's moral principles. We must simply recall here the Buddhist requirement that a person and his or her teachings be compatible. Ethics is not like any ordinary science. It must arise from the deepest understanding of human qualities, and such understanding comes only when one undertakes the journey of discovery personally. An ethic that is built exclusively on intellectual ideas and that is not buttressed at every point by virtue, genuine wisdom, and compassion has no solid foundation.

ETHICS AND NEUROSCIENCE

When we face an ethical dilemma, a compassionate utilitarian approach requires a lucid analysis of the situation and a genuinely altruistic motivation. For this we must overcome the powerful emotional conflicts that arise when the decision entails a painful sacrifice or a personal loss. Recent neuroscience research indicates that brain regions associated with reasoning and cognitive control are involved in resolving moral dilemmas in which utilitarian values require difficult emotional decisions such as we saw above in the sacrifce of an innocent child.

Philosopher and neuroscientist Joshua Greene's research has revealed that considering such decisions elicits greater activity in regions of the brain associated with cognitive control.[16] These areas are in competition with areas of the brain associated with emotional responses. He has speculated that the social and emotional responses that we have inherited from our primate ancestors underlie the absolute prohibitions that are central to dogmatic views such as that of Immanuel Kant, according to which certain moral lines ought not to be crossed regardless of the greater good that might otherwise be achieved. In contrast, the impartial evaluation that defines altruistic utilitarianism is made possible by structures of the frontal lobes of the brain that evolved more recently and support high-level cognitive control.

As Greene remarks: "Should this account prove correct, it will have the ironic implication that the Kantian 'rationalist' approach to moral philosophy is, psychologically speaking, grounded not in principles of pure practical reason, but in a set of emotional responses that are subsequently rationalized." This would confirm that an altruistic ethical choice, which considers in depth the best way of minimizing others' suffering, should not be obscured by emotional distress and personal biases. Such a utilitarian choice does not result from a cold-blooded calculation, but from genuine compassion reinforced by wisdom.

ETHICS IN CRISIS?

History attests to the fact that utopian ideals and dogmas claiming to know Good from Evil have led through the centuries to intolerance, religious persecution, and totalitarian regimes. The proponents of such ideals have echoed their tired formula in many variations on the theme: "In the name of the Absolute Good, we shall make you a happy person. Should you refuse, however, we must regretfully do away with you."

Unable to adhere to absolute laws, alienated from divine commandments, dismayed by the thought that humankind is fundamentally evil, and confined to a fluctuating ethic based on the opposing theories of myriad philosophers and moralists, modern man is at a loss. Writes Han de Wit: "This fiasco has given birth to moral defeatism at the very heart of modern Western culture."[17]

For its part, the ethic of genuine altruism, informed by the discoveries of neuroscience, prefers to navigate the ceaseless current of ever-changing phenomena driven by the wind of benevolence. It is only by the constant cultivation of wisdom and compassion that we can really become the guardians and inheritors of happiness.

23

HAPPINESS IN THE PRESENCE OF DEATH

Remember that there are two kinds of lunatics: those who don't know that they must die, and those who have forgotten that they're alive.

PATRICK DECLERK

Death seems to be so distant, yet it is always so near. Distant because we always imagine it at some time yet to come; near because it can strike at any moment. While our death is certain, its hour is unpredictable. When it comes, no eloquence can persuade it to wait, no power can stop it, no wealth buy it off, no beauty seduce it.

KEEPING DEATH IN MIND TO ENRICH OUR LIFE

How do we face death without turning our back on life? How can we think about it without despair or dread? Etty Hillesum wrote: "We cannot live fully by excluding death from life, but by welcoming death into our lives, we grow and enrich our lives."[1] The way we think about death has a considerable impact on our quality of life. Some people are terrified of it, others prefer to ignore it, yet others contemplate it so as to better appreciate every passing moment and to recognize what is worth living for. Accepting death as a part of life serves as a spur to diligence and saves us from wasting our time on vain distractions. While we are all equal in having to meet death, each of us prepares for it in his own way. The twelfth-century Tibetan sage Gampopa wrote: "At the start, we should fear death like a stag trying to escape from a trap. At midway, we should have nothing to regret, like a peasant who has carefully tended to his field. At the end, we should be happy, like someone who has accomplished a great task."

It is better to learn how to profit from the fear of death than to ignore it. We do not need to live haunted by death, but we must remain aware of the fragility of existence. This understanding will help us appreciate fully the time we have left to live. Death often strikes without warning. We may be in good health, enjoying a fine meal with our friends, and yet be living out our final moments. We leave behind our friends, our interrupted conversation, our half-eaten meal, our unfinished plans.

Nothing to regret? Can anyone who has made the most of human life's extraordinary potential have anything to regret? The farmer who has labored, sown, and reaped his harvest, in good weather and in bad, has nothing to regret; he has done his best. We may blame ourselves only for what we have neglected to do. Someone who has used every second of her life to become a better person and to contribute to others' happiness can die in peace.

"I WILL BE NOTHING, ALL WILL BE NOTHING."

Is death like a flame being extinguished, a drop of water being absorbed into parched soil? If so, as Epicurus asserted, it has no bearing on happiness: "So death, the most frightening of bad things, is nothing to us; since when we exist, death is not yet present, and when death is present, then we do not exist."[2] But what if death is just a transition and our consciousness will continue to experience countless states of existence? We will need to face this important passage not by focusing on our fear of the suffering of the moment, but by adopting an altruistic, peaceful attitude, free of grasping at possessions and loved ones.

In any case, it is surely preferable to spend our final months or moments in serenity than in anxiety. What good does it do to be tormented by the thought of leaving our loved ones and possessions behind and obsessing over the decay of our body? As Sogyal Rinpoche explains: "Death represents the ultimate and inevitable destruction of that to which we are most attached: ourselves. Clearly, therefore, the teachings on non-ego and the nature of the mind can be of enormous help."[3] As death draws near, then, it is best to adopt a serene, selfless, and detached attitude. In that way death need be neither a mental torment nor a physical ordeal.

We should not wait until the last minute to ready ourselves, because that is hardly the right time to consider embarking on a spiritual journey. "Are you not ashamed," wrote Seneca, "to reserve for yourself only the remnant of life, and to set apart for wisdom only that time which cannot be devoted to any business? How late it is to begin to live just when we must cease to live!"[4] We must get started now, while we are healthy in body and mind.

OTHER PEOPLE'S DEATHS

How can we deal with the death of another person? While the death of a loved one sometimes feels like an irreparable trauma, there is another way to think of it, because a "good death" is not necessarily tragic. In the West nowadays, people are only too ready to avert their eyes from death. It is disguised, covered up, sanitized. Since there is no material way to avert it, we prefer to remove death altogether from our consciousness. When it does come along, it is all the more shocking, because we are unprepared for it. Meanwhile life has been slipping away day after day, and if we have not learned to find meaning in its every passing moment, all it has meant to us is wasted time.

In ancien régime Europe, the entire family gathered around the dying member, the priests administered the sacrament, and last words were heard. Still today — in Tibet, for example — people tend most often to die among their family and friends. This also allows children to see that death is a natural part of life. If a spiritual master is at the bedside, death comes serenely and the loved ones are comforted. If in addition the dying person is an experienced practitioner, nobody has any worries for him. Often people returning from a cremation will say, "It went really well." A U.S. ambassador to Nepal, following the cremation of a friend — an American Buddhist nun who had died in Kathmandu — told me that he had never been to such an uplifting funeral.

The Wise Man's Death

The wise man enjoys a very special kind of freedom: prepared for death, he appreciates every moment of life's bounty. He lives each day as if it were his only one. That day naturally becomes the most precious of his existence. When he looks at the sunset, he wonders: "Will I see the sun rise again tomorrow morning?" He knows that he has no time to lose, that time is precious, and that it is foolish to waste it in idleness. When death finally comes for him, he dies tranquilly, without sadness or regret, without attachment to what he is leaving behind. He leaves this life as the eagle soars into the blue. The hermit Milarepa sang this song:

Fearing death, I went to the mountains,
Over and over I meditated on death's unpredictable coming,
And took the stronghold of deathless unchanging nature.
Now I have gone beyond all fear of dying.

24

A PATH

We must be the change we wish to see in the world.

MAHATMA GANDHI

We sometimes have to feel like explorers, burning with the desire to do what's worth doing and to live life in such a way that we have no regrets when it comes time for us to die. Let us learn freedom. The key point of spiritual practice is to gain control over our mind. It is said: "The goal of asceticism is to achieve mastery of the mind. Without that, what good is asceticism?" "Asceticism" means "exercise," in this case the training of the mind.

Our aim in taking the spiritual path is to transform ourselves with a view to helping others free themselves from suffering. This may at first make us aware of our present powerlessness to do so. Then comes the desire to improve ourselves so as to overcome that obstacle.

Once we have embarked on the spiritual path and begun practicing it resolutely, the important moment comes several months or several years later when we realize that nothing is as it was and, in particular, that we have become incapable of knowingly harming others. And that pride, envy, and mental confusion are no longer the uncontested masters of our minds. We need to ask ourselves if our spiritual practice makes us better people and contributes to the happiness of others. It is important to ask that question over and over again and to focus lucidly upon it. What have we achieved? Stagnation, regression, or progress? Once inner well-being is firmly grounded within us, it becomes easier to gradually extend its radiance to all those around us and to our social activity.

There is no one method that will allow us to progress unhindered toward liberation from suffering. The diversity of ways reflects the diversity of people. Every one of us starts from the point at which we find ourself, with our own temperament, our own intellectual architecture, our own beliefs. Every one of us can find a congenial method for working on our thought processes and gradually freeing ourself from the yoke of harmful emotions.

Some may wonder whether it is a luxury to seek to dispel their own inner pain in order to attain inner freedom when so many others are suffering from famine, extreme poverty, war, and countless other disasters. Why don't we simply try to relieve their suffering immediately? If that were possible, scientists too would give up their research just to work on emergency cases. Likewise, what would be the point of spending five years building a hospital? Electrical and plumbing work doesn't cure anybody. Why not just head for the street, set up some tents, and begin treating the sick straightaway? What would be the need for studying, learning, and becoming expert in any given field? The same holds true for the path to inner transformation — it can never be arbitrary. The knowledge, love, and compassion of the sage don't just appear out of nowhere, like a flower blooming in the clear blue sky. As Aristotle said, "It would not be fitting to leave the greatest and noblest of all things to chance."

LISTENING, THINKING, MEDITATING

Like any apprenticeship, the practice of the spiritual path has several stages. We must first be taught and then assimilate the teaching. A child is not born with innate knowledge. We must then take care to ensure that the knowledge does not become like a beautiful book that is rarely opened. Deep consideration must be given to its meaning. The Buddha told his followers: "Do not accept my teachings out of mere respect for me. Examine them and put them to the test as the goldsmith examines gold by cutting, heating, and hammering."

Mere intellectual understanding is not enough. It is not by leaving the doctor's prescription by the bedside or learning it by heart that we are cured. We must integrate what we have learned so that our understanding becomes intimately bound up with our mind's flow. Then it ceases to be theory and becomes self-transformation. Indeed, as we've seen, that is the meaning of the word *meditation:* familiarization with a new way of being. We can familiarize ourselves with all sorts of positive qualities in this way — kindness, patience, tolerance — and continue to develop them through meditation.

Throughout this exercise, practiced at first in brief but regular sessions, we seek within ourselves a particular quality that we then allow to permeate our entire being until it becomes second nature. We can also meditate to acquire inner calm by stabilizing the mind through concentration on an object: a flower, a feeling, an idea, a representation of the Buddha. The mind is unstable at first, but we learn to tame it, just as we would return a butterfly to the flower of concentration every time it flutters away. The goal is not to turn our mind into a dutiful but bored student, but to make it flexible, stable, strong, lucid, vigilant — in short, to make it a better tool for inner transformation instead of abandoning it to its fate as a spoiled child resistant to all learning.

Finally, we can meditate in a nonconceptual way on the very nature of the mind by looking directly at consciousness itself as an open presence, a pure awareness that always lies behind the screen of thoughts, or by contemplating the very nature of the thoughts that cross our mind.

There are many other ways of meditating, but as varied as they are, they all share the common function of being part of the process of inner transformation. Meditation differs from mere intellectual reflection in that it involves a constantly recurrent experience of the same introspective analysis, the same effort to change, or the same contemplation. It is not about experiencing some sudden flash of understanding, but about coming to a new perception of reality and of the nature of mind, about nurturing new qualities until they become integral parts of our being. Meditation is a skill that requires resolve, sincerity, and patience far more than it does intellectual panache.

Meditation is followed up with action, that is, by being applied in everyday life. Of what use is a "great session" of meditation if it doesn't translate into improvement of our whole being, which can then place itself at the service of others? Once the seeds of patience, inner strength, serenity, love, and compassion have come to maturity, it is to others that we must offer their fruit.

LIKE A WOUNDED STAG

But we need time and the right conditions to reach that maturity. It is often helpful, in order to stabilize and develop a meditative practice and inner transformation, to seek out the quiet solitude of a secluded place. That is what a wounded stag would do, hiding in the forest until his injuries heal. Here the wounds are those of ignorance, animosity, envy. In the whirl-wind of daily life, we often feel so hurt and drained that we are too weak even to do the exercises that would give us strength.

Withdrawing into solitude does not mean losing interest in what happens to other people. Quite the contrary, putting some distance between ourselves and the world's activity gives us a new perspective on things, broader and more serene, and helps us to better understand the dynamic of happiness and suffering. By finding our own inner peace, we learn how to share it with others.

These times of solitude are useful only to the extent that the understanding and strength we gain from them are able to hold up against life's storms. And that has to be verified not only in adversity, when we are vulnerable to dejection, but also in success, which can often move us to arrogance and compla-cency. This is no easy thing; our habits and inclinations are tenacious. They are like rolls of paper that we try to flatten but that spring back and curl up the moment we let go. It requires patience. It should come as no surprise that a hermit can spend years discovering the true nature of his mind.

And yet he is not cut off from society, since he taps into the most ancient source of human behavior. He doesn't dedicate his life to contemplation because he has nothing better to do or because he's been rejected by society; he dedicates himself to elucidating the mechanisms of happiness and suffering with the idea that it will be of benefit not only to himself, but also and above all to others.

In our modern societies, it would hardly be reasonable to expect many men and women to devote months or years to the life of contemplation. On the other hand, anyone can set aside a few minutes a day, and occasionally a day or two, to sit and look clearly into his own mind and into his perception of the world around him. This is as essential as sleep to one who is exhausted or as fresh air to one who has long breathed the polluted air of the city.

WHERE THE PATH LEADS

Everybody (or almost everybody) is interested in happiness. But who is interested in enlightenment? The very word seems exotic, vague, and distant. And yet ultimate well-being comes from fully eliminating delusion and mental toxins, and thus suffering. Enlightenment is what Buddhism calls the state of ultimate freedom that comes with a perfect knowledge of the nature of mind and of the world of phenomena. The traveler has awakened from the sleep of ignorance, and the distortions of the psyche have given way to a correct vision of reality. The divide between subject and object has vanished in the understanding of the interdependence of all phenomena. A state of non-duality has been achieved, above and beyond the fabrications of the intellect and invulnerable to afflictive thoughts. The sage has come to see that the individual self and the appearances of the world of phenomena have no intrinsic reality. He understands that all beings have the power to free themselves from ignorance and unhappiness, but that they don't know it. How could he fail to feel infinite and spontaneous compassion for all those who, spellbound by ignorance, wander lost in the trials of samsara?

While such a state may seem very far removed from our daily concerns, it is certainly not beyond reach. The real problem is that it is so close we can't see it, just as the eye doesn't see its own lashes. An echo of this Buddhist concept is heard in Ludwig Wittgenstein: "The aspects of things that are most important for us are hidden because of their simplicity and familiarity."[1] Enlightenment is genuinely within reach insofar as we all carry within us the potential of our true nature. Unlike Rainer Maria Rilke, who wrote that "we will all die unfinished," Buddhism says that we are all born complete, since each being holds within him a treasure that needs only to be actualized. But that doesn't happen by itself. Milk is the source of butter, but it won't make any if we simply leave it to its own devices; we have to churn it. The qualities of enlightenment are revealed through transformation at the far end of the spiritual path.

The fact is, each stage is a step toward fulfillment and profound satisfaction. The spiritual journey is like traveling from one valley to another — beyond each pass lies a landscape more magnificent than the one behind it.

BEYOND HAPPINESS AND SUFFERING

From the point of view of absolute truth, neither happiness nor suffering has any real existence. They belong to the relative truth perceived by the mind that remains in the grip of confusion. She who understands the true nature of things is like a navigator landing on an island made entirely of pure gold; even if she looks for ordinary pebbles, she won't find any.

The Tibetan hermit and wandering bard Shabkar sang of enlightenment and compassion:

> *Relaxed, at ease in that very state of freedom,*
> *I arrive at the immense sky-realm*
> *That is an unconditioned absolute state.*
> *When it is left to itself, as a vast sky*
> *Utterly transparent and serene,*
> *The poisonous, painful bindings that are mental constructs*
> *Loosen by themselves.*

When I remain in this state
Which is like a transparent, empty sky,
I experience joy beyond words, thought, or expression.

Looking on with the eyes of a wisdom
That is more immense than the all-encompassing sky,
The phenomena of samsara and nirvana
Become delightful spectacles.
Within that brilliant continuum,
There is no need for effort,
Everything occurs by itself,
Completely at ease, very naturally:
Complete contentment!

Compassion toward sentient beings
Once my mothers, surges up from deep within me —
These aren't just empty words:
Now I'll work to benefit others![2]

A FINAL TESTIMONY

I can honestly say that I am a happy man, just as I can say that I know how to read or that I'm in good health. If I had been continuously happy ever since falling into a magic potion when I was little, that statement would be of little interest. But it hasn't always been so. As a child and teenager, I studied the best I could, loved nature, played music, skied, sailed, watched birds, and learned photography. I loved my family and my friends. But it never occurred to me to declare myself *happy*. Happiness wasn't a part of my vocabulary. I was aware of a potential I seemed to feel within me, like a hidden treasure, and sensed it in others. But the nature of that potential was hazy and I had no idea how to actualize it. The sense of flourishing I now feel at every moment of my existence was constructed over time and in conditions conducive to understanding the causes of happiness and suffering.

The good fortune of meeting with remarkable people who were both wise and compassionate was decisive in my case, because the power of example speaks more forcefully than any other communication. They showed me what it is possible to accomplish and proved to me that one can *become* enduringly free and happy, providing one knows how to go about it. When I am among friends, I share their lives joyfully. When I am alone, in my retreat or elsewhere, every passing moment is a delight. When I undertake a project in active life, I rejoice if it is successful; and if it doesn't work out, I see no reason to fret over it, having tried to do my best. I have been lucky enough so far to have had enough to eat and a roof over my head. I consider my possessions to be tools, and there is not one I consider to be indispensable. Without a laptop I might stop writing, and without a camera I might stop sharing pictures, but it would in no way impair the quality of every moment of my life. For me the essential thing was to have encountered my spiritual masters and received their teachings. That has given me more than enough to meditate on to the end of my days!

My deepest wish is that the ideas gathered in this book may serve as tiny lights along the path of temporary and ultimate happiness of all beings.

> *As long as space endures,*
> *And as long as sentient beings exist,*
> *May I, too, remain*
> *To dispel the misery of the world.*
>
> SHANTIDEVA

Notes

Epigraph

Luca and Francesco Cavalli-Sforza, *La Science du bonheur* (Paris: Odile Jacob, 1998).

Introduction

1. Matthieu Ricard, *Animal Migrations* (New York: Hill and Wang, and London: Constable, 1970).
2. Jean-François Revel and Matthieu Ricard, *The Monk and the Philosopher: A Father and Son Discuss the Meaning of Life* (New York: Schocken, 2000).
3. Paul Ekman, Richard J. Davidson, Matthieu Ricard, and B. Alan Wallace, "Buddhist and Psychological Perspectives on Emotions and Well-Being," *Current Directions in Psychological Science* 14:2 (April 2005), 59–63.

Chapter 1: Talking About Happiness

Epigraph: Jean-Jacques Rousseau, *Emile ou l'éducation*, 1762.
1. Henri Bergson, "Les Deux sources de la morale et de la religion," in *Remarques finales* (Paris: PUF, 1997).
2. Ruut Veenhoven, "Advances in Understanding Happiness," Erasmus University Rotterdam and University of Utrecht, Netherlands,

translated from "Progrès dans la compréhension du bonheur," *Revue Québécoise de Psychologie* 18 (1997).

3. André Burguière, *Le Nouvel observateur,* special issue "Le Bonheur," 1988.

4. Robert Misrahi, *Le Bonheur, essai sur la joie* (Paris: Optiques, Hatier, 1994).

5. André Comte-Sponville, *Le Bonheur, désespérément* (Nantes: Editions Pleins Feux, 2000).

6. Katherine Mansfield, *Bliss and Other Stories* (North Stratford, N.H.: Ayer, 1977).

7. Etty Hillesum, *Etty: A Diary 1941–43,* trans. Arnold J. Pomerans (London: J. Cape, 1983).

8. Rabindranath Tagore, *Stray Birds* (New York: Macmillan, 1916).

9. Hillesum, op. cit.

10. Georges Bernanos, *Journal d'un curé de campagne* (Paris: Plon, 1951).

Chapter 2: Is Happiness the Purpose of Life?

Epigraph: Epicurus, "Lettre à Ménécée," in *Lettres et maximes,* trans. M. Conche (Paris: Epiméthée, PUF, 1995).

1. Chögyam Trungpa, *Cutting Through Spiritual Materialism,* John Baker and Marvin Casper, eds. (Boston: Shambhala, 1973).

2. Dominique Noguez, *Les Plaisirs de la vie* (Paris: Payot et Rivages, 2000).

3. Immanuel Kant, *Critique de la raison pure,* trans. Tremesaygues et Pacaud (Paris: PUF, 1971).

4. Immanuel Kant, *Critique de la raison pratique,* trans. François Picavet (Paris: PUF, 1971).

5. Romain Rolland, *Jean-Christophe,* vol. VIII (Paris: Albin Michel, 1952).

Chapter 3: A Two-Way Mirror

1. Dalai Lama, public talk given at Coimbra, Portugal, Nov. 26, 2001. Translated from Tibetan by M. Ricard.

2. Marcus Aurelius, *Pensées,* vol. 19 (Paris: Société d'Editions, 1953).

3. B. Alan Wallace, *Buddhism with an Attitude: The Tibetan Seven-Point Mind Training* (Ithaca, N.Y.: Snow Lion, 2003).

4. Richard Layard, *Happiness: Lessons from a New Science* (London: Allen Lane, Penguin Books, 2005).

5. Pascal Bruckner, *L'Euphorie perpétuelle* (Paris: Grasset, 2000).

6. Alain, *Propos sur le bonheur* (Paris: Gallimard, 1998).

CHAPTER 4: FALSE FRIENDS

Epigraph: Dilgo Khyentse, *The Hundred Verses of Advice of Padampa Sangye* (Boston: Shambhala, 2004).

1. Christophe André, *Vivre heureux: psychologie du bonheur* (Paris: Odile Jacob, 2003).

2. Paul Ekman, *Emotions Revealed* (New York: Times Press, 2003).

3. P. Brickman, D. Coates, and R. Janoff-Bulman, "Lottery Winners and Accident Victims: Is Happiness Relative?" *Journal of Personality and Social Psychology* 36 (1978), 917–27.

4. Michael Argyle, "Causes and Correlates of Happiness," in D. Kahneman, E. Diener, and N. Schwarz, eds., *Well-Being: The Foundations of Hedonic Psychology* (New York: Russell Sage Foundation, 2003).

5. Jean-Paul Sartre, *La Nausée* (Paris: Gallimard, 1954).

6. G. C. Whiteneck et al., "Rocky Mountain Spinal Cord Injury System," *Report to the National Institute of Handicapped Research*, 1985: 29–33.

CHAPTER 5: IS HAPPINESS POSSIBLE?

1. Misrahi, op. cit.

2. D. G. Myers, *The American Paradox* (New Haven: Yale University Press, 2000).

3. Arthur Schopenhauer, *The World as Will and Representation,* trans. E.F.J. Payne (New York: Dover, 1969).

4. Sigmund Freud, *Malaise dans la civilisation,* trans. Odier (Paris: PUF, 1971).

5. Martin Seligman, *Authentic Happiness* (New York: Free Press, 2002).

6. Dalai Lama and Howard Cutler, *The Art of Happiness: A Handbook for Living* (Rockland, Mass.: Compass, 1998).

7. Wallace, op. cit.

8. Comte-Sponville, op. cit.

9. Cavalli-Sforza, op. cit.

CHAPTER 6: THE ALCHEMY OF SUFFERING

1. M.D.S. Ainsworth, "Infant-Mother Attachment," *American Psychologist* 34 (1979), 932–37. P. R. Shaver and C. L. Clark, "Forms of Adult Romantic Attachment and Their Cognitive and Emotional Underpinnings. In G. Noam and K. Fischer, eds., *Development and Vulnerability in Close Relationships* (Hillsdale, N.J.: Erlbaum, 1996). P. R. Shaver and M. Mikulincer, "Attachment Theory and Research: Core Concepts, Basic Principles, Conceptual Bridges." In A. Kruglanski and E. T. Higgins, eds., *Social Psychology: Handbook of Basic Principles,* 2nd ed. (New York: Guilford, 2005).

2. M. Mikulincer and P. R. Shaver, "Attachment Security, Compassion, and Altruism," *Current Directions in Psychological Science* 14 (2005), 34–38.

3. G. Corneau, *La Guérison du coeur: nos souffrances ont-elles un sens?* (Paris: Laffont, 2001).

4. E. Fernandez and D. C. Turk, "The Utility of Cognitive Coping Strategies for Altering Pain Perception: A Meta-analysis," *Pain* 38 (1989), 123–35.

5. Lisa K. Mannix, Rohit S. Chadurkar, Lisa A. Rubicki, Diane L. Tusek, Glen D. Solomon: "Effect of Guided Imagery on Quality of Life for Patients with Chronic Tension-Type Headache," *Headache* 39 (1999), 326–34.

6. Tenzin Choedrak with Giles Van Grasdorff, *The Rainbow Palace* (London: Bantam, 2000).

7. Ani Pachen and A. Donnelly, *Sorrow Mountain: The Journey of a Tibetan Warrior Nun* (New York: Kodansha America, 2000).

CHAPTER 7: THE VEILS OF THE EGO

Epigraph: Chandrakirti, *Madhyamakalankara.* Chandrakirti (seventh century) was one of the great Indian commentators on the teachings of the Buddha and of Nagarjuna.

1. Han de Wit, *De Lotus en de roos: Boeddhisme in dialoog met psychologie, godsdienst en ethiek* (Kampen: Kok Agora, 1998).

2. Private correspondence.

3. Aaron Beck, *Prisoners of Hate: The Cognitive Basis of Anger, Hostility, and Violence* (New York: HarperCollins, 1999).

4. D. Galin, "The Concepts of 'Self,' 'Person,' and 'I,' in Western Psychology and in Buddhism," in B. Alan Wallace, ed., *Buddhism and Science: Breaking New Ground* (New York: Columbia University Press, 2003).

5. Charles Scott Sherrington, *The Integrative Action of the Nervous System* (New Haven: Yale University Press, 1948).

CHAPTER 8: WHEN OUR THOUGHTS BECOME OUR WORST ENEMIES

Epigraph: Alain, op. cit.

1. Andrew Solomon, *The Noonday Demon: An Atlas of Depression* (New York: Scribner, 2001).

2. Ibid.

3. Dilgo Khyentse, *The Heart Treasure of the Enlightened Ones* (Boston: Shambhala, 1993).

4. Nicolas Boileau, *Épitre V. à Guilleragues* (Paris: Gallimard, 1995).

CHAPTER 9: THE RIVER OF EMOTION

1. See R. J. Davidson and W. Irwin, "The Functional Neuroanatomy of Emotion and Affective Style," *Trends in Cognitive Science* 3 (1999), 11–21; R. J. Davidson, "Cognitive Neuroscience Needs Affective Neuroscience (and Vice Versa)," *Cognition and Emotion* 42 (2000), 89–92; A. R. Damasio, *Descartes' Error* (New York: Avon, 1994); and E. T. Rolls, *The Brain and Emotion* (New York: Oxford University Press, 1999).

2. See Nico H. Fridja, "Emotions and Hedonic Experience," in Kahneman, Diener, and Schwarz, eds., *Well-Being,* 204.

3. Ekman, Davidson, Ricard, and Wallace, op. cit.

4. Ibid.

5. L. Cosmides and J. Tooby, "Evolutionary Psychology and the Emotions," in M. L. Lewis and J. Haviland-Jones, eds., *Handbook of Emotions,* 2nd ed. (New York, Guilford, 2000). P. Ekman and W. V. Friesen, "The Repertoire of Nonverbal Behavior: Categories, Origins, Usage, and Coding," *Semiotica* 1 (1969), 49–98. C. Izard, *The Face of Emotion* (New York: Appleton-Century-Crofts, 1971).

6. See especially H. S. Friedman, *Hostility, Coping, and Health* (Washington, D.C.: American Psychological Association, 1992) and J. Vahtera, M. Kivimaki, A. Uutela, and J. Pentti, "Hostility and Ill Health: Role of Psychosocial Resources in Two Contexts of Working Life,"

Journal of Psychosomatic Research 48 (2000), 89–98. It should be noted, however, that in the West hostility and violence are thought of not as emotions per se, but rather as character or personality traits.

7. W. Barefoot et al., "The Health Consequences of Hostility," in Chesney et al., eds., *Anger and Hostility in Cardiovascular and Behavioral Disorders* (New York: McGraw-Hill, 1985).

8. R. J. Davidson, D. C. Jackson, and N. H. Kalin, "Emotion, Plasticity, Context, and Regulation: Perspectives from Affective Neuroscience," *Psychological Bulletin* 126 (2000), 890–906; also Ekman, op. cit.

9. Solomon, op. cit.

10. Ekman, Davidson, Ricard, and Wallace, op. cit.

11. D. Myers, "Happiness," in *Psychology,* 6th ed. (New York: Worth, 2001).

12. Barbara Fredrickson, "Positive Emotions," in C. R. Snyder and Shane J. Lopez, eds., *Handbook of Positive Psychology* (New York: Oxford University Press, 2002).

13. William James, *The Principles of Psychology* (Cambridge, Mass.: Harvard University Press, 1890/1981).

CHAPTER 10: DISTURBING EMOTIONS

1. Dolf Zillmann, "Mental Control of Angry Aggression," in D. Wegner and P. Pennebaker, *Handbook of Mental Control* (Englewood Cliffs, N.J.: Prentice Hall, 1993).

2. J. E. Hokanson et al., "The Effect of Status, Type of Frustration, and Aggression on Vascular Process," *Journal of Abnormal and Social Psychology* 65 (1962), 232–37.

3. C. Daniel Batson, Nadia Ahmad, David A. Lishner, and Jo-Ann Tsang, "Empathy and Altruism," in *Handbook of Positive Psychology* 35 (2002), 485–97.

4. Alain, op. cit.

5. Dalai Lama, *Ancient Wisdom, Modern World: Ethics for the Next Millennium* (London: Little, Brown, 1999).

6. Dilgo Khyentse, *Heart Treasure.*

7. Ekman, *Emotions Revealed.*

8. Alain, op. cit.

9. Ekman, Davidson, Ricard, and Wallace, op. cit.

CHAPTER 11: DESIRE

1. Schopenhauer, op. cit.
   2. Christian Boiron, *La Source du bonheur* (Paris: Albin Michel, 2000).
   3. Alain, op. cit.
   4. K. C. Berridge, "Pleasure, Pain, Desire, and Dread: Hidden Core Processes of Emotion," in Kahneman, Diener, and Schwarz, eds., *Well-Being*.

CHAPTER 12: HATRED

1. Beck, op.cit.
   2. Dalai Lama and M. Ricard, *365 Dalai Lama: Daily Advice from the Heart* (London: Thorsons Element, 2003).
   3. Hillesum, op. cit.
   4. Paul Lebeau, *Etty Hillesum, un itinéraire spirituel* (Paris: Albin Michel, 2001).

CHAPTER 13: ENVY

1. Swami Prajnanpad, *Lettres à ses disciples,* vol. 3, *La Vérité du bonheur* (Paris: L'Originel, 1990).

CHAPTER 14: THE GREAT LEAP TO FREEDOM

1. A. Comte-Sponville, *Petit traité des grandes vertus* (Paris: PUF, 1995).

CHAPTER 15: A SOCIOLOGY OF HAPPINESS

Epigraph: Daniel Kahneman, "Objective Happiness," in Kahneman, Diener, and Schwarz, eds., *Well-Being*.

1. Ruut Veenhoven, for example, has inventoried and compared no fewer than 2,475 scientific publications on happiness, in *Bibliography of Happiness.* RISBO, *Studies in Social and Cultural Transformation,* Erasmus University, Rotterdam, Netherlands, 1993.
   2. F. M. Andrews et al., *Social Indicators of Well-being* (New York: Plenum, 1976), and E. Diener, "Subjective Well-being," *Psychological Bulletin* 96 (1984), 542–75.

3. D. A. Dawson, *Family Structure and Children's Health: United States, 1988*. Department of Health and Human Services publication 91-1506. *Vital and Health Statistics*, series 10, no. 178 (Washington, D.C.: National Center for Health Studies, 1991).

4. M. Argyle, "Causes and Correlates of Happiness."

5. Layard, op. cit.

6. Ibid.

7. P. Brickman and D. T. Campbell, "Hedonic Relativism and Planning the Good Society," in M. H. Appley, ed., *Adaptation-Level Theory: A Symposium* (New York: Academic Press, 1971).

8. R. Biswas-Diener and E. Diener, "Making the Best of a Bad Situation: Satisfaction in the Slums of Calcutta," in *Social Indicators Research*, 2002.

9. Martin Seligman, *The Optimistic Child* (New York: Houghton Mifflin, 1996).

10. WHO, "World Health Report, 1999."

11. From the website of NIMH (National Institute of Mental Health), *Suicide Facts for 1996*.

12. Layard, op. cit.

13. Gallup poll of 1994.

14. Seligman, *Authentic Happiness*.

15. A. Tellegen et al., "Personal Similarity in Twins Reared Apart and Together," *Journal of Personality and Social Psychology* 54 (1998), 1030–39.

16. D. Francis, J. Diorio, D. Liu, and M. J. Meaney, "Nongenomic Transmission Across Generations of Maternal Behavior and Stress Responses in the Rat," *Science* 286 (1999), 1155–58.

17. Martin Seligman, *What You Can Change and What You Can't* (New York: Knopf, 1994).

18. K. Magnus et al., "Extraversion and Neuroticism as Predictors of Objective Life Events: A Longitudinal Analysis," *Journal of Personality and Social Behavior* 65 (1993), 1046–53.

19. D. Danner et al., "Positive Emotions in Early Life and Longevity: Findings from the Nun Study," *Journal of Personality and Social Psychology* 80 (2001), 804–13.

20. G. Ostir et al., "Emotional Well-being Predicts Subsequent Functional Independence and Survival," *Journal of the American Geriatrics Society* 98 (2000), 473–78.

21. J. Kaprio, M. Koskenvo, and H. Rita, "Mortality After Bereavement: A Prospective Study of 95,647 Widowed Persons," *American Journal of Public Health* 77 (1987).

22. E. Diener, "Subjective Well-being," in *Psychological Bulletin* 96 (1984), 542–75.

23. E. Diener et al., "Resources, Personal Strivings, and Subjective Well-being: A Nomothetic and Idiographic Approach," *Journal of Personality and Social Psychology* 68 (1994), 926–35.

24. Veenhoven, "Advances in Understanding Happiness."

25. Cavalli-Sforza, op. cit.

26. D. Leonhardt, "If Richer Isn't Happier, What Is?" *New York Times,* May 19, 2001, B9–11.

CHAPTER 16: HAPPINESS IN THE LAB

1. For a discussion of this topic see B. Alan Wallace, *The Taboo of Subjectivity: Toward a New Science of Consciousness.* New York: Oxford University Press, 2000, as well as Matthieu Ricard and Trinh Xuan Thuan, *The Quantum and the Lotus* (New York: Crown, 2002).

2. G. Kemperman, H. G. Kuhn, and F. Gage, "More Hippocampal Neurons in Adult Mice Living in an Enriched Environment," *Nature* 386 (April 3, 1997), 493–95. For a general review, see Gerd Kemperman and Fred Gage, "New Nerve Cells for the Adult Brain," *Scientific American,* May 1999.

3. P. S. Ericksson et al., "Neurogenesis in the Adult Human Hippocampus," *Nature Medicine* 4:11 (Nov. 1998), 1313–17.

4. Daniel Goleman, *Destructive Emotions: How Can We Overcome Them?* (New York: Bantam, 2003).

5. A. Lutz, L. L. Greischar, N. B. Rawlings, M. Ricard, and R. J. Davidson, "Long-Term Meditators Self-Induce High-Amplitude Gamma Synchrony During Mental Practic," *PNAS* 101:46 (Nov. 16, 2004).

6. Davidson interviewed by Sharon Begley in "Scans of Monks' Brains Show Meditation Alters Structure, Functioning," *Wall Street Journal,* Nov. 5, 2004, B1.

7. Davidson interviewed by Mark Kaufman in "Meditation Gives Brain a Charge, Study Finds," *Washington Post,* Jan. 3, 2005, A5.

8. Ibid.

9. Begley, op. cit.

10. Ibid.

11. R. J. Davidson and M. Rickman, "Behavioral Inhibition and the Emotional Circuitry of the Brain: Stability and Plasticity During the Early Childhood Years," in L. A. Schmidt and J. Schulkin, eds., *Extreme*

Fear and Shyness: Origins and Outcomes (New York: Oxford University Press, 1999).

12. Goleman, *Destructive Emotions.*

13. Lutz et al., op. cit.

14. Goleman, *Destructive Emotions.*

15. Ibid.

16. Kaufman, op. cit.

17. R. J. Davidson, J. Kabat-Zinn, et al., "Alterations in Brain and Immune Function Produced by Mindfulness Meditation," *Psychosomatic Medicine* 65 (2003), 564–70.

CHAPTER 17: HAPPINESS AND ALTRUISM

1. Reported in *Science in Action,* BBC World Service, 2001.

2. E. Diener and M.E.P. Seligman, "Very Happy People," *Psychological Science* 13 (2002), 81–84.

3. Seligman, *Authentic Happiness.*

4. E. Sober, "Kindness and Cruelty in Evolution," in *Visions of Compassion,* Richard J. Davidson and Anne Harrington, eds. (New York: Oxford University Press, 2002).

5. C. Daniel Batson, "Why Act for the Public Good? Four Answers," *Personality and Social Psychology Bulletin* 20 (1994), 603–10.

6. C. Daniel Batson, Janine L. Dyck, et al., "Five Studies Testing Two New Egoistic Alternatives to the Empathy-Altruism Hypothesis," *Journal of Personality and Social Psychology* 55:1 (1988), 52–57.

7. Nancy Eisenberg, "Empathy-Related Emotional Responses, Altruism, and Their Socialization," in Davidson and Harrington, *Visions of Compassion.*

CHAPTER 18: HAPPINESS AND HUMILITY

Epigraph: Dilgo Khyentse, *Heart Treasure.*

1. S. Kirpal Singh, 1968, unpublished article.

2. M. Perez, K. D. Vohs, T. E. Joiner, "Discrepancies Between Self- and Other-Esteem as Correlates of Aggression," *Journal of Social and Clinical Psychology* 24:5 (Aug. 2005), 607–20.

3. J. J. Exline and R. F. Baumeister, Case Western Reserve University, 2000. Unpublished data cited in J. P. Tangney, "Humility," in Snyder and Lopez, eds., *Handbook of Positive Psychology.*

CHAPTER 19: OPTIMISM, PESSIMISM, AND NAÏVETÉ

Epigraph: Alain, op. cit.

1. L. G. Aspinwall et al., "Understanding How Optimism Works: An Examination of Optimistics' Adaptative Moderation of Belief and Behavior," in *Optimism and Pessimism: Implications for Theory, Research, and Practice* (Washington, D.C.: American Psychological Association, 2001).

2. L. G. Aspinwall et al., "Distinguishing Optimism from Denial: Optimistic Beliefs Predict Attention to Health Threat," *Personality and Social Psychology Bulletin* 22 (1996), 993–1003.

3. Seligman, *Authentic Happiness*.

4. T. Maruta et al., "Optimists vs. Pessimists: Survival Rate Among Medical Patients over a 30-Year Period," *Mayo Clinic Proceedings* 75 (2000), 140–43.

5. M. Seligman, *Learned Optimism: How to Change Your Mind and Your Life* (New York: Free Press, 1998).

6. Alain, op. cit.

7. C. R. Snyder et al., "Hope Theory," in Snyder and Lopez, eds., *Handbook of Positive Psychology*. Curry et al., "The Role of Hope in Student-Athlete Academic and Sport Achievement," *Journal of Personality and Social Psychology* 73 (1997), 1257–67.

8. Charles S. Carver and Michael F. Sheier, "Optimism," in Snyder and Lopez, eds., *Handbook of Positive Psychology*.

9. C. S. Carver et al., "Assessing Coping Strategies: A Theoretically Based Approach," *Journal of Personality and Social Psychology* 56 (1989), 267–83. Also K. R. Fontaine et al., "Optimism, Perceived Control over Stress, and Coping," *European Journal of Personality* 7 (1993), 267–81.

CHAPTER 20: GOLDEN TIME, LEADEN TIME, WASTED TIME

1. Seneca, *On the Brevity of Life*.

2. Vicki Mackenzie, *Cave in the Snow: A Western Woman's Quest for Enlightenment* (London: Bloomsbury, 1998).

3. Nagarjuna, *Suhrlleka,* translated from Tibetan by Matthieu Ricard.

CHAPTER 21: ONE WITH THE FLOW OF TIME

Epigraph: J. Nakamura and M. Csikszentmihalyi, "The Concept of Flow," in Snyder and Lopez, eds., *Handbook of Positive Psychology.*
1. M. Csikszentmihalyi, "Go with the Flow," in *Wired* magazine, Sept. 1996.
2. "Like a Waterfall," *Newsweek,* Feb. 28, 1994. Cited by Daniel Goleman, *Emotional Intelligence* (New York: Bantam, 1995).
3. William James, op. cit.
4. Csikszentmihalyi, "Go with the Flow."
5. S. Whalen, "Challenging Play and the Cultivation of Talent. Lessons from the Key School's Flow Activities Room," in N. Colangelo and S. Astouline, eds., *Talent Development III* (Scottsdale, Ariz.: Gifted Psychology Press, 1999).
6. From a guide to practices and activities written by the monks of Plum Village, France.
7. Nakamura and Csikszentmihalyi, op. cit.

CHAPTER 22: ETHICS AS THE SCIENCE OF HAPPINESS

Epigraph: Epicurus, *Maximes capitales.*
1. Cavalli-Sforza, op. cit.
2. Dalai Lama, *Ancient Wisdom, Modern World.*
3. Francisco J. Varela, *Ethical Know-how: Action, Wisdom, and Cognition* (Stanford, Calif.: Stanford University Press, 1999).
4. Dalai Lama, *Ancient Wisdom, Modern World.*
5. Comte-Sponville, *Petit traité.*
6. Immanuel Kant, *The Philosophy of Law: An Exposition of the Fundamental Principles of Jurisprudence as the Science of Right.*
7. Comte-Sponville, *Petit traité.*
8. Varela, op. cit.
9. Dalai Lama, *Ancient Wisdom, Modern World.*
10. Immanuel Kant, *Critique of Practical Reason.*
11. Varela, op. cit.
12. Jeremy Bentham, *The Principles of Morals and Legislation* (New York: Prometheus, 1988).
13. John Rawls, *A Theory of Justice* (Cambridge, Mass.: Belknap Press, 2005).

14. Charles Taylor, *Sources of the Self: The Making of Modern Identity* (Cambridge, Mass.: Harvard University Press, 1989).

15. Varela, op. cit.

16. J. Greene et al., "The Neural Basis of Cognitive Conflict and Control in Moral Judgment," *Neuron* 44 (2004), 389–400.

17. De Wit, op. cit.

CHAPTER 23: HAPPINESS IN THE PRESENCE OF DEATH

Epigraph: Patrick Declerk, "Exhortations à moi-même," in "La Sagesse d'aujourdhui," *Le Nouvel observateur,* special issue, April–May 2002.

1. Hillesum, op. cit.

2. Epicurus, "Lettre à Ménécée," in *Lettres et maximes.*

3. Sogyal Rinpoche, *The Tibetan Book of Living and Dying* (San Francisco: HarperSanFrancisco, 1992).

4. Seneca, op. cit.

CHAPTER 24: A PATH

1. Ludwig Wittgenstein, *On Certainty* (Über Gewissheit) (New York: Harper and Row, 1969).

2. Matthieu Ricard et al., trans., *The Life of Shabkar* (Ithaca, N.Y.: Snow Lion, 2001).

COPYRIGHT ACKNOWLEDGMENTS

About the Author

Matthieu Ricard is a Buddhist monk who had a promising career in cellular genetics before leaving France to study Buddhism in the Himalayas thirty-five years ago. He is a bestselling author, translator, and photographer and an active participant in current scientific research on the effects of meditation on the brain. He lives and works on humanitarian projects in Tibet and Nepal.

ABOUT THE TRANSLATOR

Jesse Browner is a novelist and translator living in New York City. He has translated works by Jean Cocteau, Rainer Maria Rilke, Paul Éluard, and others.